Mastering the Ethical Dimens

D0121092

To my mother, Joan Florene Franck

Mastering the Ethical Dimension of Organizations

A Self-Reflective Guide to Developing Ethical Astuteness

Donna Ladkin

Professor of Leadership and Ethics, Plymouth Graduate School of Management, Plymouth University, UK

Edward Elgar
PUBLISHING

Cheltenham, UK • Northampton, MA, USA

Published by
Edward Elgar Publishing Limited
The Lypiatts
15 Lansdown Road
Cheltenham
Glos GL50 2JA
UK

Edward Elgar Publishing, Inc.
William Pratt House
9 Dewey Court
Northampton
Massachusetts 01060
USA

A catalogue record for this book
is available from the British Library

Library of Congress Control Number: 2014950968

ISBN 978 1 78195 408 9   (cased)
ISBN 978 1 78195 409 6   (paperback)
ISBN 978 1 78195 410 2   (eBook)

Typeset by Servis Filmsetting Ltd, Stockport, Cheshire
Printed and bound in Great Britain by T.J. International Ltd, Padstow

Contents in brief

Full contents

LEVEL IV   ETHICS IN THE ORGANIZATION AND BEYOND

Acknowledgements

This book is based on an MBA elective I taught at Cranfield School of Management in the UK over two academic years (2010–12). It is to those who joined that highly experimental adventure in developing ethical astuteness in business school students that I must give greatest thanks. In particular I must say 'thank you' to Ruth Bender, Paul Hughes, Andy Logan, Leo Murray and Claus Springborg for contributing their teaching expertise to the course. Special recognition goes to my 'MEDO Readers', Evgenyia Asimova, Anna Baggoley, Henry Chow, Ignacio del Castillo, Claudia Garcia, Vatsan Govindarajan, Mark Grenfell-Shaw, Ilan Pragaspathy, Vijaya Ravindran, Steve Roberts, and David Rodriguez who faithfully read chapters and provided me with invaluable comments and constructive feedback.

Two academic colleagues, Wendelin Küpers and Rajiv Maher, each expert in his own field of philosophy and corporate responsibility respectively, read extended sections of the text and offered new insights and apt corrections. For their thoughtfulness and care I am grateful. Thanks go to Nazia Hussain for providing me with timely information about the Arabic practice of *wasta*. Additionally, much appreciation goes to Francine O'Sullivan at Edward Elgar Publishing who believed in and encouraged this project from its inception. Aisha Bushby, Dee Compson and Jane Bayliss, also of Edward Elgar are to be thanked for their faithful shepherding of the text from manuscript to publication.

As is apparent within the Parsifal tale that makes its way into the book, no journey of this nature is accomplished without the support of creatures, highwaymen and both good and bad witches. My band of legendary helpers includes Beatriz Acevedo, Patricia Gaya, Charlotte Johnson, Chellie Spiller and my flat-coated retriever, Zelda. I'll leave it to the five of you to allocate roles!

Finally, my heartfelt appreciation goes to two people without whom this journey would not have come to completion. Thank you to Alison Cain – friend, colleague and copy-editor whose attention to detail and care for this project has enriched the text, as well as my life, in more ways than I can say. Finally, to Robin, my partner in love and life, I offer a huge debt of gratitude.

Daily you show me how the 'ethics of care' works in practice. I hope something of what you have taught me shines through these pages.

DML
Kingsbridge, Devon,
June 2014

1

Groundings

Welcome . . .

. . . to a developmental journey designed to build your capacity to handle ethical dilemmas in organizations with greater mastery. If you've picked up this book, it probably means you already have an interest in how you might fulfil your role as an organizational manager or leader in a way that aligns with your values or principles. That's a great starting point for developing ethical astuteness. However, it's not enough. Case after case demonstrates that individuals can find themselves accused of acting unethically without intending to do 'wrong'. How does that happen? How can managers who hold good values and principles, who would never intend to cheat, steal or lie, find themselves inadvertently cheating, stealing or lying? This book suggests that along with holding sound values and principles, those who want to navigate the murky waters of organizational life ethically need to develop a range of practical skills – paying attention, asking good questions, attending to timing, building networks of wise 'others' with whom they can confer – in order to do so.

This book is based on the assumption that rather than relying on formal codes of practice or ethical frameworks, the most potent tool managers have in navigating difficult ethical territories is themselves – their bodies, hearts and minds. By bringing the combined intelligence of these three aspects together, you have the best chance of both spotting ethical dilemmas before they are full-blown ethical problems, and engaging with them effectively before they become ethical catastrophes.

You will have gathered that this text aims to be different from many other 'business ethics textbooks' in that it places you, the practising organizational leader or manager, squarely at its centre. The book aims to help you gain the skills of perception, self-reflexivity, inquiry and discernment, which will enable you to better align your ethical principles with those of the groups and organizations in which you work and play. To do this, the text offers a number of concepts and frameworks to increase your store of knowledge. More importantly, it introduces activities to try out, either on your own or with others, in order to practise the habits that are fundamental to building ethical astuteness.

How does it work?

Each of the nine remaining chapters is organized into one of four 'mastery levels'. The first, 'Foundational Practices', introduces the building blocks on which everything else in the book is grounded. Chapter 2 focuses on honing the most fundamental skill: 'paying attention'. Paying attention, although it sounds very simple, is a complex art. It includes the ability to pay attention to what you are paying attention to, as well as paying attention to what you are *not* paying attention to. You will be introduced to two key concepts: your 'inner arc of awareness', and your 'outer arc of awareness'. The first invites you to notice the ongoing chatter that most of us have playing through our minds most of the time and to become aware of its habits. The second invites you to notice those things in the external world that routinely snag your attention. Of course, there is a constant interplay between inner and outer arcs of awareness. Generally speaking, we notice things in our outer world that can be prompted by our inner concerns. (This is why, for instance, you may have noticed many more funeral homes in your vicinity once someone close to you dies.)

Along with gaining insight into your habitual patterns of perception, the second foundational practice is that of 'inquiry'. The power of asking good questions (Chapter 3) is often overlooked in the haste to find answers to tough organizational dilemmas. However, asking good questions – those that open up a situation to reveal previously unnoticed new connections and ramifications – is critical to developing ethical mastery. Interestingly, through developing the skill of asking good questions you will also become more aware of your inner and outer arcs of awareness. In this way, the journey towards ethical mastery builds on itself, with each step forming the foundation for the next practice. These two capacities: 'paying attention' and 'inquiring' lay the groundwork for all that follows.

The next level of mastery 'Perceptual Practices' focuses on helping you to develop moral perception (Chapter 4) and moral imagination (Chapter 5). Aristotle, whose ideas inform much of this book, believed that being able to act ethically was based on the capacity to 'perceive correctly'. Mastery level II offers activities ranging from keeping a photo-diary to visiting a local art gallery to assist you in developing your own perceptual capacities. The aim of these practices is to help you start to notice aspects of situations you would never have noticed before. It's important to offer a word of caution at this point – in these early stages of developing enhanced perceptual capacity it is likely that you will feel more, rather than less, confused about how to handle ethical dilemmas. That is one reason why it is so important to undertake the course with others who will be feeling similarly disoriented. Greater clarity is the intended, eventual outcome!

The third level of mastery concerns action. Paradoxically, it begins with the suggestion that you should put off acting for as long as possible. However, this is 'not acting' in a particular way, characterized by the term 'negative capability' (Chapter 6). It addresses issues of anxiety and in particular the question of how to contain your anxiety while you are trying to figure out the 'best' way forward. How do you stand in a place of uncertainty without 'irritably grasping for an answer', as John Keats, who is credited with the concept of negative capability, suggests? It poses questions about what needs to be in place before you are able to move forward into 'right action'. Finally, this mastery level works towards action through the method offered by Aristotle of 'moving towards the mean' which is elaborated in Chapter 7.

The final level of mastery invites you to extend your ethical astuteness into larger organizational, inter-organizational (Chapter 8) and intercultural contexts (Chapter 9). How can you develop communities of ethical practice within your own organization? Together, how can you anticipate the unintended consequences of decisions by imagining their impacts rippling throughout organizations and into the external environment? In this section, issues of political engagement are addressed and the possibility of acting both ethically and politically offered. Spreading the net of ethical concerns further, this section examines the habits required to engage in cross-cultural ethical issues with greater awareness and wisdom. The final chapter, Chapter 10, presents touchstone ideas for you to take with you as you continue your journey towards ethical mastery. By the time you have finished the book, the hope is that you will have developed habits of perceptual awareness, inquiry and critical reflexivity, which will enable you to deal more effectively with the range of contexts you will face in your life as a manager or leader working in organizations.

A few more thoughts about underpinning assumptions

As will be explained later in this chapter, the ideas offered here are primarily informed by two approaches to ethics. The first is based in 'virtue' ethics. Initially articulated by Aristotle in his *Nicomachean Ethics* (Aristotle, 2009), and later brought to contemporary awareness by Alistair MacIntyre in his book *After Virtue* (1985), this approach suggests that acting ethically is primarily based on developing a 'virtuous' character. A person of good virtue will, by his or her nature, be able to recognize and follow the 'ethical path' according to this framework. The second underpinning approach is that of 'relational ethics', an ethical stance grounded in feminist ethics and most notably associated with the work of Carol Gilligan (Gilligan, 1982). From this orientation, acting ethically is always a process of balancing one's own needs, wants, desires and aspirations against those of the other. Also evident in the ethical understanding of many of the indigenous peoples of North America, rather than being based on any set of rules, this perspective recognizes 'ethics' as an orientation of respect toward those with whom we are in relation (Cheney and Weston, 1999). Both virtue and relational ethics will be described in greater depth later in this chapter.

Along with these informing frameworks, another important assumption central to the text is the need for re-examining taken-for-granted values and beliefs. The starting point for developing ethical mastery is in identifying your current values and considering whether or not they are 'out of date'. Much of what we believe to be 'good', 'true' or 'right' is based on beliefs carried with us from childhood, or unquestioningly adopted from the norms of society in which we live. Seldom do we consciously re-examine those views unless a situation arises where we are forced to confront them. I'll offer a story from my own experience to illustrate this point:

> A number of years ago I decided to embark on a Master's degree in environmental philosophy. I had studied philosophy as an undergraduate but was delighted to discover a new strain of thinking within philosophical discourse, that of 'environmental ethics'. I had always had a strong commitment to issues of ecological well-being and was keen to learn more about how philosophers approached this territory.
>
> I began the programme with very strongly held views about what was 'right' and what was 'wrong' in terms of how humans interact with other creatures and the broader environment. For instance, three of my most firmly held beliefs were that it was wrong to eat other animals (I had been a practising vegetarian for many years), that fox hunting was wrong (at the time that I did the course, there was an ongoing strident debate about the ethics of fox hunting in the UK) and that nuclear energy was 'bad' and should be avoided at all costs.
>
> By the end of the degree, I had come to think very differently about these issues. I actually began to see that my choice of being vegetarian was largely possible due to the food miles incurred by transporting the beans and nuts I ate in favour of locally bred lamb or chicken. I did a project on the ethics of fox hunting and actually changed my mind completely about seeing fox hunting as a 'moral wrong'.

I came to believe that in the broader picture, fox hunting served a particular role within the communities in which it was practised, which could not be declared so unequivocally 'wrong' As for the foxes, I began to see that being hunted was certainly not 'fun' for them, but it was probably more akin to their natural way of being and dying in the world than by other means such as traps or poison. Certainly I would not join the hunt myself, but I held a much more neutral stance about others doing so. I still held on to my views about nuclear energy, but I came to see that issue slightly differently too as I was swayed by the persuasive arguments of James Lovelock (2009) on the matter. In short, each of these ethical standpoints that I had clung to unquestionably shifted as I reconsidered them. When I changed the perspective from which I had been viewing them, different aspects of each became apparent. In particular, reconsideration caused me to notice the wider context informing each, rather than remaining narrowly focused on my own perspective. Taking others' perspectives into account prompted me to shift my own views.

Similarly, this book partly aims to help you reconsider your long-held values and beliefs and consciously re-examine them. Day-to-day life rarely offers such an opportunity. In doing so, you may decide to stick with those beliefs. However, you may also reconsider your positions and how they affect your actions. Such a process of re-examination can foster a more inquiring attitude towards not only long-held beliefs but to the way you operate in the world more generally.

Other important assumptions that inform this book include the following:

- Ethics are an intrinsic and inherent part of organizational life.
- The more senior you are in an organization, the more significant part of your role will be taken up with dealing with ethical dilemmas.
- Even people who want to act ethically can find themselves in difficulty and not know what to do when they face ethically ambiguous situations.
- Dealing well with ethical situations isn't just a matter of having good intent or staying true to certain 'values'. Even people who adhere to good values can find themselves acting in ways that they may consider unethical in retrospect, or that others may judge as unethical in the moment. Furthermore, even 'good' values can compete with one another in particular contexts.
- The good news is: through practice you can develop skills that will enable you both to recognize the ethical aspects of organizational situations, and to respond to them with greater discernment and wisdom.

The text is primarily written for students on undergraduate or Master's-level degree courses in business or leadership. However, it will also be of help to anyone within an organization who takes ethics seriously and wants practical help in dealing with the often murky waters of ethical decision making and action.

Travelling companions

Depending on the length of the journey you are about to take, carrying a few supplies with you is generally a good idea. This journey is no different. The most basic travelling companions you will find useful include the following:

- A *notebook* dedicated to catching your reflections and thoughts while you travel. This is intended to be a safe, private place to note your responses to the activities offered throughout the book, thoughts that occur to you even when you are not consciously engaged with the book, and a reference point for holding ideas and images that you can reflect upon during and after the 'formal' journey.
- A *camera* that you can capture striking images with along the way. A camera is also a great tool for noticing what you are noticing and tracking how your perceptions change.
- A *sense of openness*: you will enjoy the journey much more if you approach it with a sense of openness and curiosity, both about yourself and about the world around you. Be prepared to shift your understandings, perceptions and beliefs.
- A *friend (or two)*: although it is perfectly possible to undertake this as a solo expedition, you will probably experience significant benefits from travelling with another person. Often we come to know our own thinking better by sharing it with someone else. Additionally, other people can identify our 'blind spots' and contradictions in a way we never can. If you are doing this as part of a business ethics course within a university setting, you may well undertake it in 'learning groups'. If you are reading it as a solo explorer, I encourage you to find at least one other person with whom you can discuss your reflections.

A key process: reflecting

In addition to these travelling companions, another important aspect of this journey and the way you can engage in it for optimal benefit relates to the process of 'action and reflection' introduced as part of each activity. 'Action learning' is the watchword for a type of experiential learning process in which you take deliberate action of one type or another, reflect on it, and then modify your behaviour the next time a similar situation arises in order to create an outcome more aligned with your purpose and goals. Popularized by the work of management development scholars such as Reg Revans (2011) and Donald Schon (1984), reflecting on action and then being able to modify it is a key feature of being able to learn the rough and tumble of everyday managerial life.

In the remainder of this chapter, some of the theoretical and philosophical frameworks that underpin approaches to ethical behaviour are introduced in order to provide you with more general foundational knowledge. Before diving into that more theoretical territory, it's crucial to reflect on where you are now as you begin. Spend ten minutes or so jotting down your responses to the questions in Box 1.1 in your notebook:

 BOX 1.1

REFLECT ON WHERE YOU ARE NOW

 QUESTIONS TO CONSIDER

1 As you start this journey towards ethical mastery, what are your hopes for yourself?
2 Is there a particular situation you are already involved in that you would like to apply the learning you will gain here to? If so what is it?
3 What are the value-based positions that you hold unquestioningly at the moment?

Now that you've noted down your own responses to these questions, let's look at some of the approaches to ethics that are most commonly part of the business ethics courses. You might like to pay attention to where you believe your own approach to ethics is located.

Key definitions and theoretical starting points

Values, ethics and morals

Before moving on it is important to be clear about the meaning given to three key terms used throughout the book: values, ethics and morals. I am not claiming to offer definitive versions of each; their exact meanings are still debated among philosophers and ethics scholars. However, it is helpful for you to have an understanding of how I am using these terms, and to notice how those definitions align with your own.

Values

Throughout the book the term 'values' will be used to mean those central beliefs an individual holds concerning how they should or should not behave. Drawing from the work of the American social psychologist Milton Rokeach, they are seen as 'abstract ideals, positive or negative, not tied to any specific attitude, object or situation, representing a person's beliefs about ideal modes of conduct and terminal goals' (Rokeach, 1968, p. 124). The important aspect of the definition to note is that values are held internally by the individual, and may or may not influence their observable behaviours.

Morals and ethics

There is a good deal of debate concerning the distinction between these two terms. For some, morality is connected with a cultural understanding of what correct behaviour is, and 'ethics' involves 'applying moral precepts to concrete problems' (Wines and Napier, 1992, p. 833). Others equate morals with values held by individuals, with ethics being the formalized codes of conduct accepted by professions, organizations or indeed cultures (Rest, 1986). This book does not adhere to a strict distinction between the two terms. Generally speaking the text refers to 'ethics' rather than 'morals' as it fits within the larger field of business 'ethics'. However, occasionally the word 'moral' crops up, for instance in relation to the concept of 'moral imagination'. This is done in order to represent the words most regularly used in the broader literature. Both 'morals' and 'ethics' are seen to be centrally concerned with the regulation of social interaction. Most importantly for their meaning throughout the book, they refer to ideal or aspirational ways of acting and behaving towards one another.[1]

The essential distinction then is between values, which are internally held ideals, and morals or ethics, which are the way in which those values are embodied in day-to-day interactions with others as we deal with practical situations together. As suggested above, a person's values will inform how they engage ethically (in fact, a core value might be that it is *desirable to engage* at an ethical level). Merely holding 'good' values, however, does not always result in ethical engagement. This point will be illustrated in greater detail later in the book.

There are three frameworks that are often used as the foundations for any approach to business ethics: deontological approaches, utilitarian approaches and virtue-based approaches. Each will briefly be described below, including information about its origins and the way it has been applied within organizational contexts.

Deontological frameworks: it's the principle that counts!

'Deontological' approaches to ethics offer 'principles' upon which ethical decisions and actions can be decided. These are notions, such as, 'Thou shalt not kill', or 'It is never right to steal from another person'. The root of the word, '*deont*', is from the Greek, meaning 'it is right'. Deontological approaches are primarily concerned with identifying the principles that can be applied to ethical dilemmas and acting accordingly.

One of the key Western philosophers associated with deontological frameworks is Immanuel Kant (1724–1804). It is helpful to place Kant within his own historical frame in order to better understand the approach he developed. Kant is most widely known as an Enlightenment philosopher, committed to rationality as the highest capacity human beings could achieve. It is important to understand that this commitment to rationality did not arise from 'nowhere'. Prior to rationality's claim on a human way of knowing, Western cultures relied heavily on the Church as the ultimate arbiter of truth and knowledge. Faith in an all-powerful God was more important than reliance on human cognition.

Immanuel Kant's works are far-ranging in their aspiration to bring rationality to all aspects of living, including aesthetics (see his *Critique of Judgement*) and most importantly for our purposes, ethics. His book *The Fundamental Principles of the Metaphysics of Ethics* (Kant [1785] 1938) asserts the possibility of an absolute moral law, as contained within his idea of the 'categorical imperative'. The 'categorical imperative' states, 'Act only on that maxim which will enable you at the same time to will that it be a universal law' (ibid., p. 38). In other words, according to Kant, one should only act in a way that would be acceptable for all human beings to act given identical circumstances.

As an example, let's consider, as Kant does, whether or not suicide is 'ethical' from this perspective. Would it be correct to say that committing suicide would be universally acceptable? What if, as Kant speculates, killing oneself would represent an act of self-love because going on to continue to live a life that causes pain 'threatens more evil than it promises comfort' (ibid., p. 39)? Kant argues that such a view contradicts the very purpose of life itself, which is to promote, rather than curtail, life. Given that suicide is thus contradictory to the very purpose of life itself, it cannot be held as a universal law and is consequently not ethical, according to the categorical imperative.

Through this simplistic example, both the strengths and the weaknesses of deontological approaches become apparent. You can see that deontological approaches are based on broad generalities. They do not consider specific cases and particular circumstances. For instance, they would not address the situation of a very elderly person who has a debilitating disease, is in pain every day and whose life has become sheer misery. In such a specific instance, one might consider enabling this individual to end his or her own life as an act of compassion or mercy, rather than as something horrendous. However, from a deontological framework for making ethical decisions, even in these circumstances suicide would be considered wrong.

Another idea that is central to Kant's ethical philosophy is the principle that human beings should never be used as a means to achieve certain ends. Kant writes:

> Now I say: Man and every rational being anywhere exists as end in itself, not merely as means for the arbitrary use by this or that will; but in all his actions, whether they are directed upon himself or upon other rational beings, he must always be looked upon as an end. (Ibid., pp. 45–6)

In other words, Kant emphasizes the importance of human beings never being used as 'means' to achieve an end. Human beings, and any being that has rationality, should always be considered an 'end' in itself. This principle of Kant's philosophy suggests that the idea often used as justification for business activity that 'the end justifies the means' is not correct if human beings are involved. To explore how a deontological approach works in practice the next activity in Box 1.2 asks you to compare where you stand on certain issues with the way others in your group stand.

 BOX 1.2

GROUP ACTIVITY: DEONTOLOGICAL APPROACHES IN ACTION

Issues that often reveal a deontological standpoint include:

- capital punishment;
- abortion;
- social benefits;
- tax avoidance.

Choose one of the issues above or perhaps another one that is more pertinent to your own context. Invite people to stand on one side of the room or the other, depending on ➡

whether they are 'for' the topic, or 'against' it. Those who do not have a clear view can be invited to stand in the middle of the room. Give each side ten minutes to develop their 'case' for the view that they take. Then, allow each side to present its case. Those in the middle of the room are invited to join the group that convinces them, if that happens, or they can remain in the middle of the room. Ask yourself the following:

 QUESTIONS TO CONSIDER

1 How does it feel to be with others who share your position?
2 How does it feel to put together an argument for your position?
3 What were your arguments actually based on?
4 How did it feel to listen to the other side?
5 What did you notice about yourself as you listened to the other side – was there any possibility that your opinion would be changed?

To take this exercise a step further, after the arguments have been aired, invite people to swap sides and, once again, reform their arguments. This time the task is to argue from the opposing position. Ask yourself the following:

 QUESTIONS TO CONSIDER

1 How does it feel to argue for the opposite view?
2 How well had you listened to the arguments previously and did you find yourself using them?
3 What happens when you have to argue from a position other than the one you believe?

Pay particular attention to the different ways in which you respond to each aspect of this exercise.

How are deontological approaches used within organizations?

Most 'codes of conduct' that form the basis of formal business ethics are based on a deontological approach to ethics. Such codes offer rules for those within organizations to follow and transgressing those rules is seen to constitute unethical behaviour. But there can be problems with codes of practice. For instance, some authors have shown that adherence to codes of practice can add to the possibility of 'moral myopia', a situation where individuals miss the bigger ethical issues in their adherence to codes of conduct that indicate it is all right to do certain things.[2]

This illustrates one of the problems with deontological approaches: they provide general principles that exist outside of context. As will be discussed in Chapter 9 which considers cross-cultural ethics, general rules may not always provide clear guidance about what the 'right' thing to do is in specific situations. For instance, many US- and UK-based multinational corporations prohibit the acceptance of gifts from those with whom they are dealing with in business. However, in many African and Asian cultures, the giving of gifts is part of how relationships are developed, and not to accept a gift can cause great offence. Although the general rule is in place to prohibit the unethical practice of bribery, in certain contexts not accepting gifts can be considered rude and can harm relationships.

Furthermore, in our daily lives, and in organizational life in particular, context plays a significant role in both our reading and interpretation of what even constitutes an 'ethical dilemma'. Because principles are often couched in such general terms, it is possible to believe you are adhering to one, while still being judged as acting unethically from the perspective of others.

Considering the greater good: utilitarian approaches

Utilitarian approaches are based on the belief that 'what is good' is that which brings the most happiness or least amount of pain to the greatest number of people. Philosophers associated with this approach include the British-born Jeremy Bentham (1748–1832) and John Stewart Mill (1806–73). Utilitarian approaches suggest that ethical action should be determined by the consequences of a particular action. As Mill writes: 'All action is for the sake of some end; and rules of action, it seems natural to suppose, must take their whole character and colour from the end to which they are subservient' (Mill [1863] 2002, p. 2).

Mill suggests that the best ethical decisions are those that generate more benefits than disadvantages and those that produce the greatest amount of happiness to the greatest number of people. Also referred to as the 'greatest happiness principle', this view holds that: 'actions are right in proportion as they tend to promote happiness, wrong as they tend to produce the reverse of happiness' (ibid., p. 5).

There is, of course, significant debate about what actually constitutes 'happiness', 'pleasure' and 'pain'. Critics of utilitarian approaches debate the extent to which pleasure and pain are equally experienced by all human beings, therefore suggesting that an accurate 'measure' of these experiences is impossible to assess. For instance, is it correct to assume that 'one unit of pain' equates to 'one unit of happiness', even if it were possible to measure 'pain' and 'happiness' in units? Nonetheless, the general maxim that actions that cause many people pain should be avoided and those that cause many people happiness should be encouraged, has an intuitive 'rightness' about it.

Utilitarian approaches within organizations

Utilitarianism is often the approach that decision-makers within organizations invoke when they weigh the pros and cons of alternative actions. For instance, a company may decide to lay off a certain number of workers in an effort to avoid bankruptcy. This action is often informed by the notion that it is better to create relatively less unhappiness by firing a small number of people, rather than to foster a great deal of unhappiness if the firm fails and everyone loses their jobs.

Although there is a sort of 'face validity' to utilitarian approaches, actually implementing them can be problematic. For instance, in the example of a firm laying off employees, it is impossible to know with any precision the amount of unhappiness caused by making some people redundant as opposed to the happiness of those left in the firm. From a purely quantitative perspective, it is often difficult to calculate the exact numbers of people affected by such decisions. What if many more people are dependent on those who are made redundant than on those who remain in employment?

Additionally, as J.S. Mill himself points out, different people experience such an event differently. Some of those who are fired may actually be relieved to be out of work and may very happily find other jobs to do. Those remaining in the organization might suffer from 'survivors' syndrome' and find themselves under increasing pressure as they are compelled to take on more work in the wake of losing their colleagues. Different people experience 'pain' in different ways. How is it possible to equate the pain of an individual who has been with the company from their youth to that of individuals who have only recently joined and may have relatively few social ties there? These sorts of questions often arise when organizations try to use utilitarianism in making decisions.

Perhaps you can get a better understanding of the issues involved by trying out a utilitarian approach yourself, as shown in Box 1.3.

BOX 1.3

GROUP ACTIVITY: APPLYING UTILITARIANISM

You are the senior team of an organization that has run into difficult times. In order to save the firm, you have decided to let staff go (i.e., fire them). Using a utilitarian approach, together come up with a plan for how you will do this. It is important in this exercise that you come up with a solution that represents all of your ideas. The important aspect here is the discussion, not the actual answer you decide upon:

? QUESTIONS TO CONSIDER

1 How do you take into account the range of views you might have about how to do this in your final decision?
2 What are the main points of discussion?
3 In the end, how do you make the decision about how to make the required cuts?
4 What kinds of emotional reactions arise in you from doing this activity?
5 What do you learn from doing this activity?

It's character that matters: an introduction to virtue ethics

Another approach to ethics in organizations that is receiving increasing support within organizational contexts is that of 'virtue ethics'. Although many people know about virtue ethics because of Alistair MacIntyre's book, *After Virtue*, this ethical perspective has its roots in Greek philosophy and the work of Aristotle. The nub of this approach is that in order to act ethically, one must develop a 'virtuous' character. As an individual of virtue, one is able to determine the most appropriate response to ethical issues.

Developing an ethical character comprises a number of different capabilities that can only be developed over years and in the company of 'wise others'. As previously mentioned, this book itself is informed by a 'virtue ethics' approach and, aligned with that, offers you different exercises and activities to practise in order to build your 'virtuous' muscle. In this way it is very different from the two previous approaches that situate ethical astuteness with the ability to reason. Here, ethical mastery is a whole-person event that requires you to engage in a particular manner with the entire domain of inter-personal and social relations.

First, for instance, virtue ethics require that you are able to 'perceive correctly' in Aristotle's terms. Unless the ethical component of a situation is recognized, it will be impossible to recognize the ethical choices on offer. As one of my MBA students commented as he embarked on this course, 'I never thought in my job as a manager I was facing ethical decisions every day. I just thought I was getting my job done'. It was during the course that he realized that almost every decision he made had an ethical component. This becomes more marked the higher you sit in organizational hierarchies, because, generally speaking, the higher you are in an organizational hierarchy, the more people will be affected by your decisions.

Once you have perceived that there is an ethical issue at hand, the next question concerns how you might resolve it. Aristotle provides guidance on this point by suggesting that one's actions should always tend towards 'the mean'. That is, in his view ethical action is often grounded in the 'middle way' – the point between two extremes. To give an example offered by Aristotle himself, in order to find what is courageous in a certain situation, the mid-point between cowardice and recklessness needs to be identified. Finding that mid-point and behaving in alignment with it is the path most likely to be virtuous. However, Aristotle recognizes that discovering 'the mean' is not easily done. Sometimes the 'mean' can only be found by watching wise others and noticing how they navigate towards it.

This notion leads to the third key aspect of virtue ethics, the idea that developing a virtuous character is not something that can be done in isolation. Aristotle noted that even in the relatively less complex arrangements of Greek society, arriving at virtuous ways forward was not easy. Crucially, wise others from the larger community need to be involved. This communal involvement in fostering virtue is captured in the term *'phronesis'*. This very important concept will be explored in greater depth in the final chapter of this book.

For now, it is important to note that community plays a key role in any rendition of virtue ethics. It is through the larger community that individuals learn a range of perspectives about a situation, learn from role models (see the activity in Box 1.4) and most importantly, challenge their own intentions and assumptions. Aristotle was alert to the many ways human beings have of convincing themselves of their own good intentions. Engagement with a community of others who will provide the necessary mirror to blind spots is an essential means by which those intents can be exposed and reconsidered.

BOX 1.4

INDIVIDUAL ACTIVITY: EXPLORING VIRTUE

Identify a person in your life who you consider to be 'wise' or of a 'virtuous' character. For this activity, it is important that you identify someone who you can actually go and speak with (so unfortunately Martin Luther King or Gandhi won't work). Why do you consider them to be wise or virtuous? What have you seen them do that makes you believe this about them? How do you imagine they have gone about developing this character? Jot your reflections about this down in your notebook.

Now, arrange to have a conversation with them to discover what they think about 'ethics' and how they have developed their own 'ethical' way of being in the world. You might frame your talk with them by telling them about this course you are taking and explaining 'virtue ethics' to them in your own words. You might pose them questions such as the following:

1 What do you do when you face an ethical dilemma?
2 Who have been the role models in your own life for ethical action?
3 When you find yourself in a situation where you don't know what the 'right' thing to do is, what do you do?
4 What advice would you give someone who aspires to act ethically within organizations?

After the conversation, reflect on what the person you talked with said. What surprised you about what they said? Are there things that this person does to deal with ethical situations that you had not thought of before? What did you learn by doing this activity? Note your thoughts down in your journal.

Virtue ethics applied to organizations

Because the focus of virtue ethics lies with individual character, it may be more difficult to understand how this framework can be useful within organizational arenas. However, the business ethicist James Whetstone suggests that applying either deontological or consequentialist approaches like utilitarianism without the aid of 'virtue' is highly problematic. He suggests that it is the idea of 'what is virtuous' and 'what is not virtuous' that acts as a guiding principle for applying other frameworks correctly, writing: 'Realistically, a truly virtuous manager is an unrealizable ideal. But nevertheless this ideal represents a set of virtuous character dispositions toward which a real, and necessarily imperfect, manager can strive' (Whetstone, 2001, p. 107).

He goes on to propose that within an increasingly globalized business environment, 'virtue' ethics may well prove much more applicable than either deontological or utilitarian approaches because of the need for sensitivity that is core to virtuous behaviour. Certainly, recent emphasis within manager and leadership development on personal development hearkens back to an appreciation of the importance of developing individual excellence – a notion akin to virtue.

These three approaches to ethics are commonly used within business ethics textbooks and courses. Much of the thinking within this book is informed by a fourth approach, 'relational ethics', which is introduced next.

Relational approaches to ethics

Closely aligned with notions of an 'ethics of care' (Gilligan, 1982; Noddings, 1984) relational ethics are grounded in the belief that the starting point for ethical engagement is the desire to act with respect, compassion and empathy towards others. The American feminist writer Grace Clement (1996) highlights three key aspects of 'care ethics':

- Context is seen to be important in understanding what is correct in a certain situation.
- Human beings are seen to be fundamentally interconnected.
- Relationality is central.

Much of my own understanding of relational ethics is grounded in Native American approaches to ethics, as articulated in the writings of the American environmental philosophers Jim Cheney, Charles Weston and J. Baird Callicott. In looking to their understanding of ethics, which draws primarily from the Ojibwa tradition, a number of aspects are distinctive from the previous European-based frameworks. First, from this perspective, ethical regard is not just extended to other human beings but is also due to animals and plants as well as other aspects of nature. (This is not just true of Native American indigenous traditions but is a common feature of other indigenous traditions as well.) The idea that moral regard is due to creatures and entities beyond humans poses an important question about the scope of moral consideration that should be considered within any ethical deliberation.

Another important aspect of the Ojibwa ethical approach is that it is based in a process of 'coming into right relations' (Cheney and Weston, 1999). In this way, acting ethically is essentially a relational dynamic. At its heart is the question of how one's own wishes, needs and desires can be balanced in relation to another's wishes, needs and desires. Importantly, this suggests that acting ethically does not require me to denigrate or disregard my own wishes, needs and desires. I am due moral consideration, too. However, I must balance that consideration against what others are also due. Sometimes it is clear who those others are; I can see them, they are my immediate family or friends. At other times, they may be human beings on the other side of the planet who I do not know, who are very different from me but whose lives are materially affected by the choices I make in my life.

A third way in which Ojibwa understanding of ethics differs from that of European-based ethical frameworks is that in the Ojibwa tradition there is actually no word that directly translates to the English word 'ethics'. Jim Cheney and Charles Weston write about how the Ojibwa people they worked with were dismayed by the need for a term such as 'ethics'. As they explain, the entire orientation of the Ojibwa people towards others and the world around them is one characterized by deep respect. Cheney and Weston capture this approach in the term: 'an epistemological orientation of respect', and write about it as the general 'etiquette' that should be extended to all creatures (ibid.). This suggests a fundamentally different assumption about how one is to 'be' in the world in relation to others. Furthermore, this approach places ethical regard at the centre of all relationships. I think it is very difficult to actually fully comprehend the implications of such a position. It is certainly radically different from an understanding of ethics as 'decision-making' as is so often the case within Western ethical approaches. This book tries to incorporate something of this understanding through its emphasis on relational practices.

The relational approach reveals some of the complications and complexities of ethical engagement. First, how far does one's sphere of moral consideration extend? How might it even be possible to take into account the way in which my actions may be materially affecting another? One realization is clear from both of these questions; it is impossible to know a 'true' answer to either of them. Extending moral consideration is, after all, a matter of discernment rather than something that can be determined in any objective way. This is exemplified by the very fact that 'who' or 'what' is worthy of ethical regard has changed (and continues to change) over history. It is easy to feel confused as the scope of 'ethics' extends. As one of the MBA students complained, 'I feel completely overwhelmed now – how do I actually do anything if I have to think of all of the people any action I take will affect?'

That is indeed a challenge! Certainly the aim of the book is not to catapult those who read it into paralysis. However, perhaps a little bit of paralysis is necessary in the beginning stages of perceiving ethics everywhere. The sense of being 'overwhelmed' might encourage you to step back, take a deep breath and comprehend that there is indeed a different way of thinking about ethics.

Before taking the next steps on this journey of ethical mastery, there is one last term I'd like to spend a bit of time explaining. Although it has already been mentioned, the meaning of 'moral consideration' is worth elaborating in more detail.

Moral consideration

Moral consideration refers to making a judgement that a person (or creature, or entity) is worthy of ethical regard (Callicott, 1996). As already indicated, ideas about who is worthy of such consideration have changed through time and are context dependent. During Aristotle's time, only land-owning men were considered to be agents who needed to be considered from an ethical perspective. Women and slaves existed in the same category as chattel and therefore were not due the same rights as they are in present Greek society. Similarly, in more recent history, African slaves in America were not thought to be worthy of the same sort of moral consideration as European-born Americans. We consider this view abhorrent these days, but in that context it was relatively unquestioned.

Today's more current dilemmas about ethical consideration concern animals and the rights of the Earth itself. For instance, the American philosopher Peter Singer maintains that animals are due ethical consideration. His book *Animal Liberation* (Singer, 1995) argues that animals should be granted equal moral consideration to human beings, and suggests that the idea that humans deserve superior consideration is a form of 'speciesism'. Advocacy groups such as the British-based People for the Ethical Treatment of Animals (PETA) take the view that animals should be treated as creatures worthy of ethical regard. Many indigenous peoples assume that the Earth should be valued and considered as if it is due moral consideration. Today, these views may seem rather strange. However, it is interesting to speculate about how people in the future may regard our relationships with other animals and the Earth. They may think us similarly 'barbaric' to those who did not extend ethical regard to women and African slaves.

Finally, a word about mastery

This book has been very purposefully entitled, *Mastering the Ethical Dimension of Organizations*. It sets out a course of action for developing 'mastery', that is, the 'comprehensive knowledge or skill within a subject or occupation' (Taylor, 2011).

There is a growing body of writing about the nature of 'mastery' itself. For instance, in his book, *Outliers*, Malcolm Gladwell indicates that 'phenomenal achievers' such as Mozart or Tiger Woods will have spent the equivalent of 10 000 hours – or roughly ten years – practising their area of expertize (Gladwell, 2009). Furthermore, he reminds us that practising needs to be done 'mindfully'. It is not good enough just to throw a basketball at a hoop for 10 000 hours – the aspiring basketball star needs to attend to what he or she is doing as they toss the ball at the hoop and assess what it is that 'works' and adjust their movements accordingly. This kind of attentive practice is thus critical to the accomplishment of mastery.

I don't expect readers to accompany the text with 10 000 hours of practice! However, the book is underpinned by the notion that, similarly, ethical astuteness is only achieved through actual, embodied practice. Becoming a 'master' of ethical territory, that is, being able to recognize the ethical aspect of situations, being able to imagine the consequences of actions on others, asking pertinent questions that shed light on the most ethically salient aspect of a situation and acting wisely, requires practising certain behaviours and developing them into habits.

The next two chapters introduce you to practices that form the bedrock of good ethical habits. Like brushing your teeth after meals or saying 'thank you' after someone has done you a favour, when done regularly they can become second nature. As such they can enhance the skill with which you engage your own moral compass as you navigate your way through the tricky territories of organizational life.

NOTES

1 Generally in most texts concerning ethics 'the other' is assumed to be another 'human'. I would like to offer the possibility that ethical consideration could extend to other non-humans, such as animals, but also seemingly inanimate others, such as the Earth, as well.

2 Cohan (2002) similarly writes an interesting piece about Enron, attributing many of the difficulties there with what he calls 'information myopia'. For an interesting article about the role 'sanctioning systems' themselves can have on people not noticing the ethical component of situations, see Tenbrunsel and Messick (1999).

Level I

Foundational practices

2

Paying attention

Let's begin with:

A story from the Zen tradition

There was once a man who dreamed of attaining spiritual enlightenment. He studied the wise books and meditated and prayed. When he felt he had learned as much as was possible from these sources, he decided to go on a pilgrimage to meet a Wise Sage living on top of a mountain (Wise Sages, after all, always live on top of mountains!) in order to discover what more he should do.

He approached the Sage's hut with trepidation. He prostrated himself before the old man sitting at its entrance. 'Master', he said, 'every day I meditate. Every day I give alms to the poor and pray for their salvation. Every day I try to do good works. What more is it that I can do to achieve enlightenment?'

The Wise Sage looked at the seeker for a moment and took in his desperation. He slowly replied, 'Pay attention'.

The seeker was not impressed. He had after all expected to be directed to a mystic text, or be told to pray a certain prayer. 'I don't understand', he implored, 'what should I pay attention to?'

The Wise Sage thought about the question for a few minutes. Then he slowly responded, 'Pay attention'.

After having endured all of the discomfort of walking to the very top of the steep mountain to seek the Sage's advice, the pilgrim was not happy with this advice and became angry. 'I have walked many miles to see you. And this is the advice you give me? Certainly you can offer me something more?'

The Sage smiled slightly, stood up, and as he turned into his hut, he spoke these sole two words to the man again, 'Pay attention'.

Most of us working in organizations are not necessarily wishing for spiritual enlightenment (although, of course, some of us may be). However, the Sage's words are just as pertinent to those seeking ethical mastery as to those seeking more spiritual aspirations. As the Wise Sage advised the seeker, the most important step in that journey may seem absurdly simple – it is merely to 'pay attention'.

Using the word 'merely' to describe this activity belies its difficulty. Paying attention is a very challenging thing to do. As mentioned in the first chapter, at any one moment we are being bombarded by sense data pertaining to everything from the temperature of the room to our state of hunger to whether or not we are interested or bored. For most people, the mind is a creature akin to a 'monkey' or 'elephant' that wanders off of its own accord and seldom dwells in the present moment. Given all of this, the seeker in the story above poses the first important question that reveals something of the complexity of paying attention; that is, deciding what to pay attention *to*.

One of the difficulties with deciding what to pay attention to is that generally we don't actively decide what to pay attention to; we just pay attention to what we habitually pay attention to. It can require a conscious act to pay attention to the world differently and to notice aspects of it we habitually neglect. We may deal with issues such as 'financial problems' or 'interpersonal issues' without recognizing their ethical aspects. Certain words and phrases: 'return on investment', 'risk', 'competitor', take us into certain ways of perceiving situations. Such shortcuts are both helpful when we are in time-pressured environments, but they can also stop us from seeing the layers of implications involved.

Perception is such an important aspect of ethical mastery that it will be revisited in the next level of mastery, which focuses on developing moral perception and moral imagination. However, this chapter begins at the most basic level of all, that of becoming aware of your own habitual patterns of attention. It does so by drawing a distinction between 'inner' and 'outer' arcs of awareness.[1] Although this distinction is being made, in fact it is rather arbitrary, as the two interrelate and contribute to one another on an ongoing basis. In fact, if we did not have an outer arc of awareness to attend to, our inner arc would be rather impoverished. These ways of attending need one another. However, for the purposes of unravelling how attention works, we'll start by working with the 'outer arc' of awareness before examining the 'inner arc' of awareness more closely.

Noticing your 'outer arc of awareness'

Your 'outer arc of awareness' comprises all the external aspects of the world to which you routinely attend. For instance, you will have developed habits concerning your 'range of your attention'; that is, the extent to which you habitually notice more proximal or more distant aspects of the outer world. You will have developed temporal habits of awareness – do you constantly look ahead to the future or are you a person who spends more time reminiscing about the past? How much peripheral vision do you use? What is the habitual quality of your outer perception – do you tend to regard the outer world with razor-sharp discernment or do you tend to approach the world through a softer focus?

All of these different ways of attending result in habitual ways of picking up sensations and, therefore, knowledge about the world. In this section of the chapter, you will be invited both to notice your habitual outer arc of awareness and to experiment with different ways of paying attention to the outer landscape.

Let's start, in Box 2.1, by trying an activity aimed at helping you to identify the kinds of things that habitually snag your outer attention.

 BOX 2.1

PAIR ACTIVITY: OBSERVING A BUSY PLACE

It is essential that you undertake this activity with another person.

Together you need to agree on a place where you can both go at the same time to just sit and observe for 20 minutes. It should be a relatively busy place where there will be a range of activity – for instance, a train or bus station, the intersection of road junction, a café or fast-food outlet. It should be a place where you can sit for 20 minutes unobtrusively – that is, no one should notice or be anxious about what you are doing.

You will need some paper and a writing implement – or you may take your computer – basically you need a means to be able to watch and record what you are noticing.

Meet your partner at the designated place. Find a place to sit relatively close together – that is, one of you should NOT be on one side of a busy space and the other at the other side – you need to be able to have a similar range of vision.

Have some form of timer with you. Set it for 20 minutes.

Now that you are there, with your friend, your timer and your writing device, the activity is to just jot down what you see. For 20 minutes, write down what you notice.

Ready, Set, GO!

When the timer rings, you may want to move to a different, more comfortable place. If you are comfortable where you are, do stay there.

Now compare lists of what you noticed. As you do so, ask yourselves the following questions: ➡

QUESTIONS TO CONSIDER

1 What kinds of things have I noticed that are different from the kinds of things my companion noticed?
2 What kinds of things have we both noticed?
3 Is there a 'theme' to the kinds of things we have each noticed (i.e., has one of you noticed more about the people in the place, their relationships, how they are dressed, what they are doing or instead has one of you paid more attention to the surroundings themselves, their state of cleanliness, the way they are structured)?
4 What surprises you about your partner's list?
5 What does the comparison tell each of you about the kinds of things you notice – do you see a connection with the kinds of things you attend to in your life more generally?
6 What have you learned from doing this activity?

Write down your responses to these questions, as well as any other reactions you have had to doing this exercise, in your journal.

Although this activity is done out of the context of your ordinary life, hopefully it has shed light on two things. First, in any situation there are a multitude of things to perceive and you can never perceive them all at once. Second, you will tend to make a habit of focusing on certain kinds of things and by focusing on those you will inevitably lose sight of other things. In this way, your habitual outer arc of awareness can become more apparent by doing an activity like this.

What does noticing your outer arc of awareness have to do with developing ethical mastery? The key link between your outer arc of awareness and ethical mastery concerns the habitual scope of moral consideration you extend. You will recall from Chapter 1 that moral consideration involves identifying others who are due ethical regard. In exercising ethical astuteness, you first need to recognize the existence of others who are 'worthy' of being thought of from a moral perspective. The habitual scope of your outer arc of awareness will play a significant role in determining who and what you perceive as being due that kind of regard.

If your outer arc of awareness is trained largely on those people and places most proximate to you, you are likely to view only those people as worthy of ethical regard. Those outside of your outer arc of awareness will not be noticed in the first place – so it will be impossible to extend ethical regard to them. This has important implications when thinking of the ethical component of an issue such as climate change, for instance. Those of us in high-lying areas may not focus our outer arc of awareness on people in low-lying areas who will experience flooding due to climate change. They are out of sight and it can be challenging to link my petrol-guzzling vehicle with the distress of flood victims in far off countries. In his film, *An Inconvenient Truth*, Al Gore draws attention to this link by framing climate change as an 'ethical issue', rather than a purely environmental or economic one.

The limits of one's outer arc of awareness can be implicated in a phenomenon dubbed 'moral myopia', when the moral component of a situation is not noticed. In their research into how advertising agents related to ethical issues inherent in their campaigns, Drumwright and Murphy (2004) encountered 'myopic' responses ranging from 'short-sightedness to near blindness'. In particular, their study showed that although the advertising executives they interviewed could be more aware of the moral implications of their collegial relations, their inability to see the unintended consequences of their work on wider societal levels was almost universal. Interestingly, the variable that most influenced executives' ability to see moral issues was the culture of the organizations they worked in. How the organization you work in affects your ability to perceive well from an ethical perspective will be explored later in this chapter and in much more depth in Chapter 8.

Factors that influence the 'outer arc of awareness'

Drumwright and Murphy's advertising executives demonstrate how organizational culture can foster the propensity to see and talk about ethical issues or not. Even before such social forces come into play, the way in which we think of ourselves – that is, our 'identity commitments' – plays a critical role in shaping our outer arc of awareness. The next section develops this idea further.

Issues of identity

Who we consider ourselves to be plays a central role in what we pay attention to in our outer world. For instance, as an American-born woman of mixed ethnic heritage living in the UK, I find myself quick to notice American accents and skin colouring that suggest someone may come from a similar background. Because of my experiences during the Civil Rights movement in the United States, I tend to 'prick up my ears' when I hear anything that sounds like it is indicative of discrimination or unfairness due to race or gender. When I enter a room full of people, I am quick to notice the ethnic diversity (or not!) within the space, as well as the proportion of other females present. All of these aspects of my own identity alert me to how race, gender and cultural relations are played out within the different contexts I operate in. My experience suggests that such issues are not as salient for white, male colleagues who regularly enter rooms where the majority of people share their gender and race affiliations.

It is important to note here that in stating these identity commitments I am in no way claiming any ethical 'superiority' to those white males!! Indeed, they will be alert to contextual issues that I will not be sensitive to, due to their own identity commitments. The important point is to recognize the role identity plays in determining both what is noticed and what is *not* noticed about the different contexts within which we work and play. Our own identity is a fundamental sifting mechanism by which perceptual data is focused on or discarded. Given its importance, it might be useful to do a quick 'identity inventory' now (Box 2.2).

 BOX 2.2

INDIVIDUAL ACTIVITY: IDENTITY INVENTORY

Quickly respond to each of the prompts below. You may like to record your responses in your notebook:

- What is your gender identity?
- What is your age?
- What is your sexual orientation?
- Are you a parent?
- How do you identify yourself in terms of family relations (i.e., eldest daughter, younger son, father, middle child, only child etc.)?
- In what country were you born?
- What country do you consider home?
- Do you have a particular disability?
- Do you have a particular health-related issue?
- What do you consider your ethnic heritage?
- How would you describe yourself from a socioeconomic perspective?
- Would you attach yourself to any particular religious doctrine?
- What is your level of education?
- What is your profession or occupation?
- What language(s) do you speak?
- What sports club do you support?
- Are you part of any sports club?
- What do you do in your spare time?

➡

←

Now consider which answers carry the most weight in terms of the way in which you think of yourself. Can you identify any of the above identity commitments that colour what you attend to in the external world? What do you habitually NOT pay attention to because of these identity commitments (i.e., do you not pay attention to those with disabilities because you are an able-bodied sportsperson, for example)?

Another important way in which we form our own identity is in relation to how we think of 'the other'. In fact, some theorists argue that it is not possible to construct a sense of our own identity without 'the other' to compare ourselves to. How 'the other' is constituted, however, plays an important role in how we think of them from an ethical perspective. The next section explores this idea in more detail.

Who constitutes 'we'? Who is 'the other'?

If acting ethically is constituted as the way in which the rights, desires and aspirations of others are balanced against our own, then it is vital to determine 'who the other *is*'. Generally speaking, people who are closer to us through kinship bonds or other aspects of psychological identification are easier to include in our circle of moral consideration. Our understanding of who constitutes 'us' as opposed to 'the other' is subject to a myriad of influences. In today's society the media play a significant role in influencing how 'the other' is constituted. Newspapers, magazines, television, Facebook, Twitter are all forms of communication through which we shape views about ourselves and about other people. The way in which 'difference' and 'similarity' are emphasized through these channels often works at a subliminal level – under the surface of our conscious awareness. The following activity in Box 2.3 is designed to help you identify how that influence works at a more conscious level.

BOX 2.3

ACTIVITY: NOTICING HOW 'THE OTHER' IS CHARACTERIZED

This activity can be undertaken either on your own, with another person or in a group. Choose at least three newspapers or news-based websites that are recognized for their differences in political orientation. For instance, in the UK you may choose *The Guardian*, *The Times* and the *Daily Express*. In the USA you may look at the *New York Times*, *The Herald Tribune* and the *Financial Times*.

Browse through each of the newspapers, noting its 'tone'. Can you ascertain the particular 'agenda' that underpins its writing? This may be particularly clear within its editorial section. Now consider each of these questions:

? QUESTIONS TO CONSIDER

1 Given what you are reading, who do you believe the paper considers to be its primary readership? What political party would you expect its readers to support?
2 How does the newspaper make clear who it considers to be the 'we' who it assumes will be going along with its stance?
3 Who is 'the other'? How does the newspaper characterize them?
4 If you were to accept what the newspaper is putting forward in an uncritical manner, what are some of the things you would believe?
5 How might these beliefs influence your actions?

Now either write about what you have learned by doing this exercise in your journal or discuss what you have discovered with your buddy or discussion group. In particular, you may reflect on the question: 'What have you noticed by doing this activity that you have not noticed before?'

If indeed, this activity has enabled you to notice something you have not noticed before, your outer arc of awareness has been expanded. Just accessing a source that you usually ignore (for instance, reading a different newspaper) will automatically expand the range of what you notice (provided you don't automatically dismiss anything that differs from your habitual viewpoint!).

This exercise aims to demonstrate the way in which media sources try to influence both who is viewed as 'the other' and how they are characterized. There is a second influence on our outer arc of awareness that is also important to notice here: the very way in which those groups we are part of direct our attention. In businesses, this is often towards particular 'targets', measured in terms of profitability or return on investment. In addition to the formal messages organizations declare about their priorities, they also emit more subtle directives about what is important. For instance, if an organization proclaims its number one priority is 'customer care' but the majority of time in meetings is spent discussing finances, employees understand the actual organizational priority to be finance, rather than customer care. This may have the knock-on effect of encouraging staff to attend more to the cost of providing care to their customers, than to the actual quality of the care extended.

This directive about what is important can be communicated overtly or more subtly. On the overt extreme is the story told to me by one of my MBA students who had joined a consulting firm dedicated to providing 'learning solutions' to its clients:

> Keen to enact the firm's commitment to customer satisfaction, the young consultant set out to provide learning events that would eventually be delivered by the client organization itself. He found himself being taken aside by a more senior consultant who asked what he thought he was doing. When the young consultant explained his aim of empowering the client to eventually provide their own learning resource, the more senior consultant laughed. 'That's not what we are about', he explained. 'We don't want to sell them permanent solutions – we just want to sell solutions that will generate more work for us'.

Moral intensity

As well as being influenced by the communication we receive about 'who we are', 'who is the other' and 'what is important around here', an additional aspect that informs our outer arc of awareness from an ethical perspective is 'moral intensity'. Moral intensity refers to how 'close to home' an experience is experienced as being (May and Pauli, 2002; Watley and May, 2004). In other words, it speaks of the degree to which we can truly empathize with the moral outcomes of an action. Moral intensity is normally heightened when an issue affects us or those nearest to us. If our comfort and security is threatened by the development of a nuclear power station in our own neighbourhood, we are much more likely to note the ethical consequences of this act than if the power station is built in a remote and sparsely populated wilderness area.

Moral intensity tends to increase in relation to specific individuals rather than to abstract groups of others. For instance, in campaigns to raise money after flooding or other natural disasters, aid agencies often highlight the plight of particular families or unique victims. Our heartstrings seem more readily tugged at by the plights of individuals suffering rather than by faceless groups presented as statistics.

The power of raising the moral intensity of a situation to influence the way in which business people think about the consequences of their decisions has been demonstrated empirically. For instance, in their study of how executives from Walmart began to engage with their suppliers in a more ethical way, John McVea and R. Edward Freeman (2005) describe the effect of bringing actual photos of child sweatshop workers into the stakeholder mapping process. Confronted by the actual faces of the children who were working inhumane hours, executives set higher standards for their suppliers.

Busy-ness, assumed purpose and other social effects

The previous sections have identified three basic factors that affect the span of our outer arc of awareness – our habits, our identity and what we perceive to be the 'moral intensity' of a situation. There are other features worth highlighting here that affect how broadly we scan the outer world:

- *Being busy and stressed.* There is nothing that quite reduces the span of our outer arc of awareness as much as the experiences of being overly-busy and stressed. Being overly busy often encourages the tendency to act on whatever seems most critical at a given moment, rather than to scan a broader landscape for what else might be important.
- *What we believe our purpose is in a given situation.* There are a number of studies that indicate that when human beings are given a certain purpose, they tend to focus on that purpose and this can result in not noticing things that are not connected with that purpose. Take the case of commuters on their way to work in Washington DC, who did not attend to the virtuosic violin playing of Joshua Bell in a Metro station.[2] The most chilling example I have seen of people being so obsessed by the goal of 'getting their job right' that they ignore the larger implications of what they are doing, is a series of letters between gas chamber manufacturers and the Nazi government. The manufacturers seemed to do their utmost to get every detail of the building of the chambers absolutely 'right' without questioning the moral implications of the purpose the chambers would be put to.
- *Compassion fatigue.* It seems that human beings only have a certain capacity for recognizing the pain of others. Aid agencies note how difficult it can be to raise funds for disaster victims when there have been a number of disasters already.
- *Hopelessness.* When people feel they cannot adequately help, they often just stop looking.
- *The belief that there are other people around who will help.* Known as the 'bystander effect' (Darley and Latane, 1968), a number of studies have

indicated that if a person believes they are the only person around when someone falls ill or needs help, they will indeed help. However, if they believe there are others around who can help (and are perhaps better equipped to do so), people can be reluctant to lend a hand. The outer arc of awareness is in this way influenced by beliefs about the proximity of others.

Generally, ethical mastery is developed by activating a broader, rather than narrower, outer arc of awareness. Doing so gives you a better chance of noticing the ethical component of a situation in the first place. The following activities in Box 2.4 aim to help extend your outer arc of awareness.

 BOX 2.4

ACTIVITIES FOR EXPANDING YOUR OUTER ARC OF AWARENESS

The following activities are offered as starting points for expanding your outer arc of awareness. You might like to practise one a week for the remainder of the course. Alternatively you may like to choose a few and repeat them for a number of weeks. Whichever you do, keep track of both what you do and your experiences within your journal:

- When you encounter a situation that you are not sure of, think of a metaphor that is in some way analogous to the situation. For instance, what kind of 'weather', is the situation like? What is the 'smell' of the situation? If the characters involved were Greek gods and goddesses, which ones would they be? What insights do you gain by thinking of the situation in a metaphorical way?
- When you find yourself in a perplexing situation, begin asking questions about the history that has brought you to this point. What was the genesis of the problem? Who has been involved at what points and what are their agendas? Where might this issue go in the future?
- Follow a current newspaper story from the perspective of two different newspapers.
- Explore a website for a special interest group that supports an agenda that is very different from your own. For instance, if you are a supporter of gun control, follow a website dedicated to the right to bear arms.
- Pick up a magazine from an area that is very different from anything you have explored before. For instance, you might look at *Popular Mechanics* if you are from the humanities or you could look at *Scientific American* if you don't usually look at that magazine.
- Read a copy of *National Geographic* from cover to cover.
- Go to a theatrical performance or dance performance or a concert that you would not normally attend.
- Listen to a radio station that you don't usually listen to.
- Follow a blog that you don't usually read.

➡

What do you learn by doing these activities about your own habitual outer arc of awareness? What do you find yourself noticing now that you have undertaken these activities? Write your observations in your journal.

You may have noticed a sense of resistance to trying out an activity aimed at extending your outer arc of awareness. A voice inside may have suggested that spending precious minutes exploring areas you don't usually pay attention to is a waste of time. This resistance might be connected to the second aspect of paying attention explored in this chapter: your 'inner arc of awareness'.

Exploring your 'inner arc of awareness'

Rather than explaining what your 'inner arc of awareness' is, the next activity in Box 2.5 aims to provoke a first-hand experience of it.

 BOX 2.5

INDIVIDUAL ACTIVITY: EXPERIENCING YOUR INNER ARC OF AWARENESS

Ideally you should read all of the instructions for the next exercise through and then do it from memory. It's not difficult to remember the steps involved, and I will summarize them with trigger words at the end of the longer explanation.

It is important to start this process in a relaxed state. In order to feel and notice your inner arc of awareness, it is helpful for you to feel that you don't have to respond to anything in particular. The first step in achieving this state is to relax the muscles in your body. If there is a great deal of muscle tension in the body, feelings and indications of your inner arc of awareness can be blocked, which is why it is important to start this process as relaxed as possible. In fact, if the place you are in allows you to lie down, that would be perfect! Otherwise, just sitting comfortably in a chair will work.

Start by just noticing your breath. Don't change it; just notice how it is at the moment. You could notice where it seems to originate in your body. What part of the chest moves as you breathe in and out? How slow or fast is it? Just notice its rhythm and underlying quality; is it relaxed and fluid, is it jagged and uneven, is it shallow or is it deep? Just notice. One of the most important capabilities in developing moral perception is the ability to delay making a judgement. We can begin to learn to delay making decisions and judgements just by noticing the self and how easy it is to come to harsh conclusions about the self.

➡

←

The next step is to purposefully and intentionally deepen your breathing. Start by focussing on the out breath. On the next out breath, just let yourself breathe out a bit longer than usual. This may involve bringing a gentle pressure into the diaphragm area so you get the feeling of air at the very bottom of the lungs moving upwards. Doing this should not be forced or cause a sense of unease; it is just a slight extension of the out breath. You will find that when you next inhale, your lungs naturally now take in more air than they did in the earlier breath. Once again, do not force this intake of breath but just allow your lungs to easily expand a bit more than they usually would.

Now notice the way in which your breath moves in and out of the body and gently deepen your breath by repeating the above pattern. Simply allow more air to move out of the body at the bottom of the exhalation and notice how this automatically opens the lungs to take in more air when you inhale. You may become aware of how this easy rhythm of breath moving in and out of the body vitalizes your body and refreshes your thinking process. Just allowing yourself to bring awareness to your breath can bring you a sense of perspective and clarity.

While in this state of attention, you might also notice any thoughts or emotions that arise for you. It can be difficult to focus solely on the breath. Generally, we are accustomed to our minds flitting from one concern to another, but by just focusing on the breath, our thoughts can become more apparent to us. Rather than trying to get rid of each thought or feeling that arises, it is important to be able to notice them. THIS PROCESS IS NOT ABOUT 'EMPTYING THE MIND' as in the case of many meditation practices. In fact, in some ways you are trying to do just the opposite –to 'NOTICE' rather than try to 'empty'.

If you have now read this through, it is time to actually practise. These key words might act as trigger points for moving from one part of the exercise to the next. Ideally you would spend about a minute in each phase of the activity, so that the entire process takes five–six minutes.

Relax
Breathe NORMALLY
Breathe OUT
Breathe IN
Breathe OUT and IN
Notice THOUGHTS

The stream of thoughts you will encounter as you pay attention is indicative of your inner arc of awareness. It is the ongoing narrative of your mind. When you bring your attentional awareness to this stream of thought, you are discovering what it is your mind pays attention to. Like the outer arc of awareness, our inner monologue has habitual patterns. After spending a bit of time tuning into your own inner stream of thought, reflect on the following questions:

➡

QUESTIONS TO CONSIDER

1 Does your mind habitually wander more into the past or the future?
2 What characterizes the 'content' of your inner monologue? For instance, does it dwell on work issues, family issues, things you wish you had done differently, events you are looking forward to?
3 Does your inner monologue follow a linear line of thought or is it more random in the topics it lands on?
4 Would you say your inner monologue is more critical or more supportive of you?
5 Would you characterize your inner monologue as more critical or more supportive of others?

It is important that you do not *judge* your answers to these questions but rather that you merely notice them. Write down your reflections in your journal.

The first step on the path to ethical mastery requires attending to our habitual patterns of noticing and thinking. When I first began using this technique, whenever I began to focus on my breath, I would find my mind almost immediately jumping to make lists of things I needed to do. I began to realize how making those lists inevitably made me feel stressed and pressured. Through slowing my mind down, I inadvertently became more aware of all of the things I needed to do and, in fact, rather than calming down, I often felt even more stressed!

I also began to see how this was a pattern related more generally to other aspects of my life. It seemed that whenever I had a moment of peace and quiet for myself, I would fill it with ideas of things I wanted to do or needed to do or should do. It often meant that by the end of the day I would be mentally exhausted from creating this never-ending list of activities.

By focusing on this tendency, I realized I could also make choices about letting this thinking pattern go. Instead of letting these ideas roll around and around in my head, I learned to write them down. As well as writing them down, I allocated a specific time to attend to them. By doing this they no longer spiralled round in my head like a constant source of nagging.

This drastically altered how I experienced each day. Rather than constantly feeling overwhelmed and unable to cope, I found myself feeling more 'in charge' of how I spent my time. I certainly would not claim total mastery of this tendency, and when I have much to do I still fall into the 'whirling task list mode'. Increasingly, however, I am at least able to *notice* that

I have succumbed to this habit and, with enough willpower, I can alter it.

What does all of this have to do with acting ethically? In order to perceive well, it is best not to be stressed and overly concerned about the self. Ethical engagement – the ability to think about others as well as the self, requires a kind of openness and spaciousness of thinking and feeling. It is very difficult to put yourself in another's shoes if you are feeling very unhappy and uncomfortable in your own! A first step in providing yourself with a good platform for ethical engagement is to be comfortable and unstressed yourself. Noticing your habitual inner arc of awareness can help you to identify the unhelpful patterns of inner thoughts that 'wind you up' and make you less available to the present moment and its ethical implications.

Noticing your inner arc of awareness is also important because it can give some indication of the internal architecture of the way in which your thoughts are organized. This internal architecture consists of 'schemas' – those internal frames for recognizing and organizing what we perceive. Schemas play a critical role in our ability to perceive 'correctly' from a moral point of view, so it is worth spending some time examining them in more depth.

Schemas: the inner architecture of perception

Because we are constantly being bombarded by sensory data, we develop 'coordinate point systems' or 'frameworks' for instantaneously deciding which data need attention and which can be discarded. Without such frameworks life would be too complicated as we would constantly have to make conscious decisions about what to pay attention to. These frameworks can be referred to as 'schemas'. Schemas act as perceptual coordinate systems that organize sense data as they occur; they are the 'structures through which awareness is organized' (Bartunek, 1984, p. 355). We see something that looks like a man in a brown coat and think, 'Ah, that's Uncle Fred', or we notice a bright splash of red amidst the green of a hedgerow and think, 'Ahh, it's a strawberry!'

Schemas enable us to organize our perceptual field efficiently. In this way they are extremely helpful to us. The problem is, sometimes by providing such shortcuts they stop us from noticing when a new piece of sensory data differs from those it 'looks like' and should be considered differently. For instance, we may encounter something awry in the way finances of our company are being organized and we label it 'an accounting irregularity' without enquiring further to discover if there is an ethical implication for the irregularity. We may engage schemas that separate 'economic realities' from 'ethical concerns' and consequently prevent us from noticing the ethical components of economic situations.

Schemas are not just individually determined; they are also influenced by the people and groups with whom we engage. Certain bits of sense data are seen to be more important in some communities than in others and we tend to adopt the schemas of the groups we belong to. For example, the ethics scholar Dennis Gioia has written extensively about the role schemas played in the decision that Ford made to continue selling its 'Pinto' sports car, even after it was known that the design of the car made it extremely dangerous in rear-end collisions (Gioia, 1992). The critical point here is that the *data* that such accidents would occur were unquestionable. Ford executives knew that passengers would die because of the car's design. It was the schema that was used to make sense of this knowledge that played a critical role in Ford's decision to continue manufacturing the car. Gioia explains how at the time profitability was the overriding schema through which decisions were made in the Company. Because the cars would still be profitable even after paying for lawsuits Ford might have to fight because of the car's design, it continued to manufacture it.

As the Ford example demonstrates, schemas play an important role in the identification of ethical issues. This is because most issues encountered in organizations don't appear helpfully packaged as 'ethical issues'. As a number of the students on the ethics course I teach explained during the early part of the course, 'Although I'd worked in business for a long time, I never thought I'd ever dealt with an ethical issue. I just thought I had decisions to make'. Issues in organizations are generally framed through the lens of 'finances', 'marketing possibilities' or 'logistics challenges'. Data are often considered through the schema of 'return on investment' or 'business performance'. Very rarely are organizational issues considered through the lens of 'moral virtue'. In fact, it is often left to those outside the organization to point out the ethical consequences of an organization's actions.

What is the connection between 'inner arcs of awareness' and 'schemas'?

It is extremely difficult to identify your own schema because rather than being a discrete 'thought' it is a framework for sifting through and ordering thoughts in relation to one another. Earlier in this chapter I mentioned my own propensity to mull over and plan the many things I feel I need to accomplish in a day. This might suggest that rather than 'how can I enjoy the present moment?' one of the schemas that organizes my world concerns task accomplishment. Because my 'task achievement' schema is so prioritized, I can find myself finding phone calls from friends or exchanges with neighbours as irritating disruptions, rather than times to enjoy. A similar sort of link is revealed by grumpy administrators in universities, for instance, who mumble, 'We could get so much more done here if it weren't for the students'. When a student in need of assistance approaches such an administrator, they can be perceived as an 'inconvenience', rather than the person who the administrator is actually hired to help.

There is an important link between the frameworks that organize what you pay attention to and your ability to spot the ethical aspect of a situation. Without a schema to alert you to ethical concerns, you are unlikely to notice when ethical issues arise. Your 'inner arc of awareness' will not have a ready-made sensor for such data. The next part of the chapter delves a bit more deeply into how you might go about recognizing your schemas and noticing the impact they have on your general level of ethical awareness.

Identifying your schemas

Noticing the schemas you hold is crucially important for developing ethical mastery. However, as mentioned previously, schemas are extremely difficult to identify. Additionally, we are very seldom prompted to examine our underlying schemas – we just 'know how we feel about things'. Inquiring into the schema that is influencing one's viewpoint can demonstrate the limits of any particular position. If, as in the case of the Ford motorcar company, the underlying organizational schema makes profitability its highest priority, profitability will be the frame through which all other decisions are sifted. This happens not because individuals within the organization are bad or unethical, but because this is the way the organization's 'priority of perception' is organized.

Schemas can become more apparent by consciously attending to the kinds of things you habitually attend to. When you undertook the activity to recognize your inner arc of awareness in Box 2.5, was there a theme recognizable in your stream of consciousness? Given an unfocused mind, what was the content of your thoughts? You might like to glance back at the notes you made after doing that activity. Can you recognize underlying 'pathways of thought'? For instance, can you identify a preoccupation with either relationships or with the tasks you need to do? Was your inner attention focused on actions you wish you had done better or on plans for the future? Can you identify any patterns in your thought process? What do these patterns indicate about your schemas?

Another useful method for recognizing your own schemas is through dialogue (and in particular, disagreement) with others. In discussion with others listen for the clues that indicate the way your argument is organized. How does it differ from the way in which the person you are speaking with organizes their argument? Notice here: I'm not actually suggesting you identify the specifics of their argument but rather the underlying principles that inform their argument.

Think back to the activity in Box 1.2, Chapter 1 where you were invited to debate your views about capital punishment, abortion and tax avoidance. If you held the view that 'capital punishment is wrong', for instance, then your organizing schemas might have something to do with ideas that the taking of another human life is always wrong. Alternatively, that view could emerge from a schema about the imperfections of any system and the possibility of such a system wrongly convicting and executing an innocent person. You may believe in ideas of rehabilitation, which would suggest that after a certain time in prison, people can change and it is unfair to kill them today for acts they would never commit in the future. Each of these is a different informing schema, which leads to the same belief about the injustice of capital punishment. The activity in Box 2.6 summarizes this section.

 BOX 2.6

INDIVIDUAL ACTIVITY: IDENTIFYING YOUR SCHEMAS

It may be helpful at this point to spend some time trying to identify some of the schemas that hold a central place in how your inner perceptions are organized. It has two steps:

Step 1: As suggested in the previous section review the observations you made about your inner arc of awareness. Can you identify the different preoccupations apparent in your thoughts? Do any themes emerge as you examine your list? If you had the opportunity to compare your stream of thoughts with those of others, do you recall ways in which they differed? Have a go at suggesting two of the organizing schemas that are revealed through this exercise. Write down in your notebook what you think they might be.

Step 2: Refer back to the notes you took after the debate/discussion about capital punishment, abortion and tax avoidance in Box 1.2, Chapter 1. Can you identify the 'informing principle' that underpinned your argument? Does it relate in any way to the schema(s) you identified in Step 1?

What has doing this activity told you about your schemas? How might you test this understanding in the upcoming weeks? Note your reflections down in your journal.

Bringing inner and outer arcs of awareness together

As mentioned earlier in this chapter, inner and outer arcs of awareness are intertwined in ways that make separating them as done in this chapter rather nonsensical. We notice things in our outer world because our inner world is constructed of schemas that have been developed through paying attention in certain ways. If we have trained as a musician, for instance, we will probably be much more alert to the music in the spaces we inhabit, whereas if we have loved motor cars all of our life we will notice the new model Mercedes Benz that has just passed us on the road in a way that one who has not developed 'motor car schemas' will not.

Having said this, human beings are creative, innovative creatures and part of our adaptive capacity enables us both to extend our schemas and notice things about the world in ways we have not noticed them before. At first, extending our inner and outer arcs of awareness takes conscious effort. It is the aim of the book to provide you with practical ways of both becoming more conscious of your own habitual arcs of awareness and extending them in accessible ways. Becoming more aware of how they work in your own life and the limitations they place on your ability to read a situation from an ethical perspective is foundational to increasing your level of moral perception – the topic of the next mastery level.

Before turning to moral perception, however, there is another foundational practice to be introduced: that of asking good questions. The work you have done so far provides an important base for developing your skills of inquiry, because noticing when something is not quite 'right' in your inner or outer attentional landscape provides the perfect starting point for generating powerful questions.

NOTES

1 I owe my appreciation of the concepts of inner and outer arcs of awareness to the work of the British leadership and organization studies scholar, Judi Marshall. For an account of how she has used these concepts in practice see Marshall (1999).
2 See http://www.youtube.com/watch?v=jyrS0GZdFps (accessed October 29, 2014).

3

Asking artful questions

Attending to your attentional awareness is an essential first step in achieving ethical mastery. However, attending alone is not sufficient. The next capacity this book aims to develop is that of asking good questions. Asking good questions is an important skill for managers, leaders or even just effective human beings in everyday life. Most importantly, the ability to voice an appropriate and sometimes challenging question is the foundation of masterful ethical behaviour.

The following passage from children's book *Hello? Is Anybody There?* by Jostein Gaarder offers an apt, if somewhat fanciful starting point for exploring this territory. In this short passage, the main character meets Mika, a creature from another planet where asking good questions rates as a significant accomplishment:

> I could tell he was looking at an apple for the very first time. At first he just sniffed it, then he ventured to take a small bite.
> 'Yum, yum,' he said. He took a bigger bite.
> 'Do you like it?' I asked.
> He made a deep bow.
> 'What did it taste like?' I asked. I wanted to know what it's like to eat your very first apple.
> He bowed and bowed.
> 'Why are you bowing?' I asked.
> 'Where I come from, we always bow when someone asks an interesting question,' Mika explained. 'And the deeper the question, the deeper the bow.'
> This was one of the silliest things I'd ever heard. I couldn't see how a question was anything to bow about.
> 'So what do you do when you greet each other, then?' I asked.
> 'We try to think of a clever question,' he replied.
> 'Why?'
> I'd asked another question, so he gave a quick bow. Then he said:
> 'We try to find something clever to ask so that other person has to bow.'
> This answer impressed me so much that I gave the deepest bow I could. When

I looked up again, Mika was sucking his thumb. There was a long pause before he took it out.

'Why did you bow?' he asked, sounding rather offended.

'Because you gave such a clever answer to my question,' I replied.

'But an answer is never worth bowing for,' said Mika. 'Even if it sounds clever and correct, you still shouldn't bow for it.'

I nodded, but I was sorry the moment I'd done it, in case Mika thought I was bowing for the answer he'd just given.

'When you bow, you give way,' continued Mika. 'You must never give way to an answer.'

'Why not?'

'An answer is always the stretch of road that's behind you. Only a question can point the way forward.'

His words sounded so wise that I had to stop myself bowing again. (Gaarder, 1997, pp. 30–31)

Part of the aim of this chapter is to encourage you to appreciate the value of good questions as much as Mika does. Perhaps you will even be tempted to bow the next time you hear one!

The importance of questions

Why are questions so important? As Mika suggests in the book excerpt above, questions 'point the way forward'. Questions determine the way in which a conversation will progress. Those engaged with a consulting approach known as 'appreciative inquiry' (Cooperrider and Srivastva, 1987) understand the power of questions in framing and directing the course a conversation takes. For instance, if the first question a consultant poses when engaging with a new organization is, 'So what's the problem here?' people will inevitably focus on everything that is going wrong. This results in energy building around all of the problematic issues in the organization. Those involved in appreciative inquiry point out that such conversations generally leave people feeling worse than they did before the conversation began.

Consultants working from such a problem-based perspective learn a great deal about people's perceptions of what is going wrong but they glean very little about what is going right. Nor do such questions provide insight into the aspirations people may have about what could be done better. Appreciative inquiry practitioners notice that the more something is talked about, the more 'real' it becomes. Following from this, the more people talk about the negative aspects of the organization, the more likely it is that those become amplified and a further focus of people's attention.

Attentional energy shifts dramatically when instead of asking the question 'What's the problem?', the question 'What's working well in this organization?' is posed. A question like this opens up an entirely different conversation. It prompts people to notice what they like about the organization, its strengths and the very reasons they might have for continuing to work within it. As a consulting practice, appreciative inquiry is grounded in the belief that the more people focus on what is going well, the more these positive behaviours and activities become amplified. Organizational transformation can then be achieved through growing the organization's strengths rather than alleviating its problems. The entire process begins with asking the right question.

As the chapter on perception revealed, in any situation, or in fact at any moment, we are bombarded by a myriad of actions, dynamics and sensory stimulations. Any one of those can become a focus for attention. What becomes important is what we choose, either consciously or unconsciously, to notice. Appreciative inquiry highlights the power questions have in directing that attention. In this way, questions carry 'intentionality' with them. Once a certain question is asked, we look for answers to it, whether that is the most important thing we should be attending to or not. This is why questions are so important – they can direct whole inquiries and subsequent interpretations of any situation.

This is important to remember within organizational contexts, because the kinds of questions raised within organizations can determine entire programmes of action. For instance, if the question that everyone jumps to when trying to implement a new strategy is 'How do we do this?' rather than 'Why are we doing this?' or even '*Should* we be doing this?', important issues can be overlooked, particularly from an ethical perspective.

Now that the importance of asking good questions has been established, let's look at the different kinds of questions available. After all, there are questions, and there are questions! Ethical mastery involves asking *good* questions. But what constitutes a good question?

Kinds of questions

Anyone who has been involved in conducting interviews knows that some questions are better than others in eliciting information. This section and the activity in Box 3.1 identify different types of questions and the roles they play in opening up or closing down conversations.

Closed questions

Perhaps the most limited type of question is the 'closed question'. This is the question to which the answer is generally 'Yes' or 'No':

- Do you sell milk?
- Did you pay your taxes?
- Does your organization have a 'code of conduct' in place?
- Have you ever been convicted of fraud?

These questions provide rather limited information; however, they can be a starting point for further questioning. For instance, you may want to find out more about an organization's code of conduct, but you need to establish if one exists in the first place before you can ask further questions about it.

Leading questions

These are the types of questions that are couched in such a way that the person being questioned can infer the answer the questioner wants to hear. Although such questions might appear to be trying to elicit information, in fact the person being questioned often gets the sense that there is only one way of answering the question:

- Are you well?
- Would you agree that if something is legal it is also ethical?
- Would you say it is true that this is a good place to work?
- In what ways are things worse now than they were a year ago?

Opening questions

These are questions that open up the territory being investigated. They are inquiring questions, born from a desire to really understand a situation differently or to find out what the person being asked really thinks. In this way, they prompt the person being asked to speak as freely as possible. The real art of asking questions is to do so in a way that elicits ideas, thoughts or facts which were not known prior to asking the question. This may sound obvious but listening carefully to the kinds of questions that are often asked reveals that many times questions are posed to elicit confirmatory views of the questioner's own perspective.

You can signal that you are asking an open question with prompts such as the following:

- When you've seen this kind of situation before, what were the consequences?
- From your perspective what are the factors that have led to this situation?
- How was it that you first realized there might be a problem with the accounting practices in this firm?
- Why was this interaction of particular interest to you?

Probing questions

Probing questions are questions that seek to dig more deeply into specific situations. There is a real knack in asking probing questions in a way that evokes helpful information, rather than placing the person being questioned on the defensive. This will be explored a bit more in a later section in this chapter concerning 'comportment' but for now the following are offered as starting points for probing questions:

- Can you tell me a bit more about that?
- Could you describe a bit more about what you were thinking when. . . ?
- I'm not quite clear about . . . can you expand?
- Can you explain a bit more about the thinking behind that decision?

 BOX 3.1

INDIVIDUAL ACTIVITY: PAYING ATTENTION TO QUESTIONS

Over the next week, be particularly attentive to the kinds of questions people ask and the effect that those questions have on subsequent discussions. You may find meetings a useful space to do this. Notice how questions are framed and the extent to which they generate new information. Be particularly attentive to those questions that seem to open up discussion and allow for a variety of viewpoints to be shared. How are such questions formed?

You might also notice how questions are used in interviews on the news. When does a question actually allow the person being questioned to reveal something new and how do questions work when they just elicit a defensive response?

See if you can identify two or three new questions that you can use yourself in order to open up discussion.

What do you learn through the process of listening for good questions? Write your reflections in your journal.

Roadblocks to asking questions

So far, this chapter has invited you to reflect on different kinds of questions, and you have also identified questions people use in meetings and other settings that open up or close down the territory for discussion. Before we go on to look at how you can practise becoming an 'artful questioner' yourself, let's consider some of the roadblocks you might encounter as you do so. There are often very good reasons for not posing good questions. It may be helpful to consider those hindrances and plan how you might overcome them.

Fear of appearing 'stupid'

Who among us has not refrained from asking a question because we are afraid of appearing 'stupid'? This is probably the greatest inhibitor to asking good questions. From our early days in school, many of us have learned that it is better to remain silent and appear to understand everything than it is to ask a question and face the ridicule of teachers and peers. Certainly anything written here about this issue is not going to undo years of programming. We 'know' it's important to ask questions and not worry about appearing stupid. Sometimes we will indeed be derided for asking a question (particularly if the person being interrogated doesn't know the answer either!). Given that, what are practical steps we can take when faced with something we don't understand?

Here are some ideas about ways of saving face while pursuing more information or greater understanding:

- Outside of any formal meeting or discussion, ask someone you trust about the situation. If they don't understand it either, pursue your questions together until you have an answer that satisfies you.
- When you are asked to attend meetings in which raising questions will be awkward, make sure you do your homework *before* the meeting. Ask questions before you are in public spaces.
- If you find yourself in a meeting in which you become confused about what is going on or are concerned about the ethical aspects of what is being done, introduce your inquiry with a framing question such as, 'Am I the only one who isn't clear about this?' or, 'Does anyone else have concerns about this?' Often if you are unclear or uncomfortable about something, others in the room will be sharing those feelings. It's important to get support for your questions.

Fear of making someone else look stupid

This is particularly relevant if they have more organizational power and authority than you do! Although we often talk about the fear of appearing stupid ourselves, questions can also put those we are asking on the spot. This relates to the political dimension of questioning; inquiring is a powerful activity. It is critically important to be careful about where and how questions are launched:

- Again, whenever possible, pose your questions 'offline', in informal spaces rather than in public meetings or events.
- Expand the range of the people you speak with. Don't just jump to the conclusion that it is *this* particular person you need to ask about a given matter; there may be others who will be able to give you more information. Entertaining the possibility that there may be others who hold important information may challenge your 'outer arc of awareness'. Do you need to extend it in order to perceive people whose role may not be obvious in a given situation but who are indeed knowledgeable about what is going on? This is particularly important when navigating through the 'grey areas' of ethical issues.
- Be sure you are asking genuinely open questions, rather than leading questions that can often prompt defensiveness in those being questioned.

Remember, however, even with the best method of asking questions in the world, if your inquiries lead to uncovering issues that people want to remain hidden, your questions may be met with defensiveness and resistance. Being in a situation where you could be prompted to 'blow the whistle' on unethical behaviour often arises out of the practice of asking good questions.

Not knowing what question to ask

Even if you are apprehensive about asking a question, but you know what the question you want to ask is, you are at an advantage. Knowing there is a question to ask but not knowing quite how to articulate it is more problematic. Have you ever been in a meeting and experienced a nagging sense of doubt about the way the conversation is going but you've not quite been able to shift that disquiet into an articulate question? If you experience that sort of situation, you may find the following prompts can be helpful:

- 'I'm not sure I understand what's at the bottom of this discussion, could someone say what they understand is going on?'

- 'I'm feeling uneasy about the way things are going, can I check if someone else is feeling uncomfortable?'
- 'Can someone recap the logic that has brought us to this point?'

You will notice that these prompts often originate from a felt, bodily response to what is happening in a given situation. Of course, in order to use this felt sense, you need to notice it in the first place! We will explore the role of the body in ethical knowing in the next chapter but for now it is important just to note that our bodies can alert us to the need to pose a question – even if we are not quite sure what that question is.

The questions we don't quite know how to ask often turn into 'unasked questions'. Unasked questions can have powerful (often negative) affects. The legend of Parsifal explores the power of the 'unasked question' as one of its key themes. Below, I offer a summary of the Parsifal tale, focusing particularly on this aspect of it[1]. Stories like this do more than just point out certain lessons; they reverberate within us. You may find yourself reflecting on different aspects of the story over again long after you are first introduced to it.

The story of Parsifal

Once upon a time, in a land very far away, there lived a young man named Parsifal who dreamed of being a knight. Parsifal lived on his own with his mother as his father had died when he was a child. As he grew up he felt responsible for looking after his mother.

However, Parsifal longed to live a life of adventure. He yearned to visit faraway lands and craved meeting different people. He dreamed of being brave and fighting wonderful wars and generally doing the things it takes to be a man. Although he would worry about his mother, and he knew she would miss him dearly, he resolved to set off on the journey to discover the world, and who he might be within it.

He gathered up his courage to tell her of his plans. She was surprisingly supportive, for she had long known that in order to become himself Parsifal would need to leave home. Together they prepared, and finally the day arrived when he was ready. With all that he would need packed on his horse or slung over his shoulder, he waved goodbye to his mother and set off. He felt full of excitement but also a bit worried and nervous about what he might encounter.

As he travels he meets many different characters and has a range of adventures, but the point I would like to bring you to in the story is when he arrives at the walls of a particular kingdom:

As is the custom in the land, he approaches the walls of the principality and knocks on the big gate that serves as its entrance. When the door yawns open, he is amazed by what he encounters. The entire city seems to be dying. The trees are shrivelling, the people look old and frail and there is a general sense of doom everywhere. By a rather inexplicable string of events that only happens in legends, he is invited to have supper with the King and his family. But at dinner that evening, nothing is very much better within the walls of the castle. The old King is withering away, and his wife looks tired and strained. All that is fed to them is the very mingiest of meat, and everyone walks around looking extremely grim and unhappy. He *wants* to ask what the problem is, what is wrong, but he is too shy to do so. So he spends the night and then sets off again in the morning, without having asked his question.

Parsifal continues his travels, has a great number of adventures, proves himself as a brave knight and develops resiliency and an ability to cope with difficult situations. He slays some dragons, has fun, falls in love and learns what he needs to learn to be a man. After months on the road, he finally knows that it is time to head home again. On his way back, he passes by the dying kingdom that he encountered at the start of the journey. Once again, he is invited to the castle for dinner and to spend the night.

Again he observes how sad everyone is and how no one smiles, and how the King has become even more wraithlike than he was before. This time, however, while dining with the royal family he summons up the courage to ask the question: 'What's wrong, Your Majesty? Why is everyone so sad in your kingdom?' His question has a powerful, magical affect. It is like pouring water on a dying plant, which, through sucking water up through its roots begins to revive.

The old King stirs for the first time in years. 'You ask what is wrong?' he says to Parsifal. Then the King begins to speak of his sadness and his unhappiness at the death of his brother many years previously. In talking of his sorrow, however, the sadness begins to dissipate. Parsifal asks the King to tell him more about his brother, and the old King begins to smile as he recalls his brother's adventurous spirit and how much he loved him. The old King smiles again for the first time in years, and with his smile, the entire kingdom becomes youthful and alive again. The Queen smiles too, and the two of them begin to dance. The waiters and waitresses begin to deliver the food with a spring in their step, and the kitchen cook, hearing the sounds of happiness, begins to cook food with more enthusiasm and love.

The kingdom is magically restored to its former glory. The initiator of this change was Parsifal, having garnered up enough courage to give voice to the unasked question.

Undoubtedly this is a fanciful story. As a legend it holds an archetypal message about the soul's journey and how one becomes who one is. Here, however, we will focus on the 'unasked question', and the role the question plays in revitalizing the kingdom. This question, which Parsifal is finally brave enough to ask as he approaches the completion of his journey, is the key that shifts the energy of the kingdom. It enables stuck, dying energy to move and dissipate. It provides a space for the old King finally to give voice to his grief and despair, and in doing so it frees up and enables life energy to flow through the kingdom again. The story also indicates something important about the nature of human beings in relation to questions; asking good, provocative questions often requires courage. Reflect on the legend of Parsifal by doing the activity in Box 3.2.

 BOX 3.2

ACTIVITY: MAKING SENSE OF PARSIFAL

Legends like Parsifal are very important conduits of human understanding. In order to glean the most from this story, the following activity invites you to linger with it a bit longer to consider the aspects of it that most intrigue you.

Reflect on the story for a few minutes. Which character do you most identify with? Of course it would in some ways be natural to identify most clearly with Parsifal himself as he takes up the central focus of the story. If this is so, you may want to reflect on the aspect of Parsifal that most catches your imagination. Is it his spirit of adventure? It may be his ability to leave his mother behind after having looked after her for so many years. How did he balance the sense of responsibility for taking care of his mother against his own need to leave home to explore the world? Have you found yourself similarly torn by conflicting demands?

You might consider the part of his adventure you were most intrigued by – was it in how he responded to the call of being a knight or perhaps the way he rode off without a clear understanding of where he was going? In your journal, note the answers to these questions and then you might like to write a bit about your response to this aspect. You could, of course, choose another character in the story to attend to: Parsifal's mother, the old King, even Parsifal's horse.

After you have spent some time considering this person, now take another character to consider in depth. What are their motivations? What are they worried about? How do they interact with the other characters?

When Parsifal discovers the dying kingdom when he has just set off, he fails to ask anyone what the problem is. Give some thought to the following questions:

? **QUESTIONS TO CONSIDER**

1 Why do you think that is? Have you ever found yourself in a similar situation?
2 How did you feel after not asking the question you were tempted to ask?
3 If you were able to ask the question, what enabled you to do so?
4 What happens on Parsifal's journey to enable him to ask the question when he returns?

➡

←

What has changed within him that means he is able to do this when he was not able to do this before?

5 Have you ever had a similar experience – of not being able to ask a question, but then some time later finding it within yourself to do so? What happened between those events in order to enable you to do this?

6 What do you learn about the power of questions through this story? Are there 'unasked' questions in your life that you might reconsider asking?

If you do take the challenge and ask 'unasked questions' notice how others react. Does their reaction surprise you?

Turning the tables: asking questions when you are the powerful one

Until now, many of the examples presented have assumed that the questioner is the one with equal or less power than those being questioned. It is apparent that courage is often needed in order to pose questions in these instances. This is true in the case of Parsifal. Many of the warnings given about asking questions concern what can happen if you ask a question that risks making a more powerful person look stupid. But what if you are the one in power – what are the difficulties associated with asking artful questions then? Why did the King, for instance, never ask a question himself, which might have allowed the energy in his kingdom to flow?

When taking up positions of power, asking good questions can require similar bravery. Those in roles of authority risk losing credibility if they appear to not know what is going on. However, there are other hazards associated with asking questions from a position of power, such as the danger of learning things you do not want to hear.

Well-known cases of corporate malfeasance such as those that occurred at Enron, Arthur Anderson and Barclays Bank demonstrate the difficulties associated with CEOs knowing or not knowing what is going on in their firms. Certainly the public expects CEOs to know what is going on and, as in the case of these firms, they have been held liable for the activities of their staff. However, CEOs may not *want* to know what is going on because doing so will mean they will be obliged to take action. In this way there is a double-edged sword for those in power – they may not want to know the messy details – but at some stage they may be held accountable for them.

Of course, a busy CEO will not have the time to know every detail of the working practices of members of their companies. However, a predisposition towards asking questions and a reputation for asking difficult questions can pervade the organization in such a way that its members know such inquiries will be made. This in itself can act as a powerful constraint on behaviour.

Becoming an artful questioner

I hope that the previous theories, stories and activities have 'warmed you up' to begin experimenting with asking more questions yourself. You might start by just taking a moment to think about what you have learned about questioning up to this point. Those lessons might come from what has been written in the book or through your own experiences of searching and listening for good questions. Write your ideas down in your learning journal.

In order to consolidate your learning as well as to catch any points you might have overlooked, the key behaviours associated with becoming a good questioner are summarized below. Hopefully, you will have discovered many of them yourself, and you may have a few more to add:

- *Pay attention to your own embodied responses to what is going on.* Your body will often register the need to ask a question before your mind does. Mental cognition often only occurs in response to a more full-bodied sense of what is happening around you. Being aware of the particular signals your body gives off when it senses there is something not quite right, or at least the possibility that there is something happening that is worth exploring, is critical to developing your skills as an inquirer. In particular, notice those small feelings of discomfort, unease or anxiety that are sending you signals that there is something worth noting and asking about.
- *Listen carefully.* Listening well, like paying attention, is a skill that is often taken for granted. It is very difficult to listen carefully, however. It is very easy to think we are listening but actually to be thinking of the next thing we are going to say in response to what someone else is saying. In the normal ebb and flow of conversation, it is not 'normal' to listen to what someone is saying, pause, connect with how it lands in your own consciousness and only *then* formulate a response. More often we form a response halfway through what the other person is saying! Until everything the other person wants to say has been said, however, it is impossible to connect fully with their intended meaning. Frequently, in order to really understand what the other person means another question needs to be posed, rather than replying immediately with our own reaction.

Because this is so difficult to do on a regular basis, the suggestion here is to try listening well in short bursts to begin with. Choose a person to have a conversation with and just listen intently to what they are saying. Make sure you check their intended meaning before responding with your own reaction. Notice whether or not this feels different from your more habitual way of interacting. Notice the impact of really listening to what another person is saying.

- *Slow down.* This is a natural follow-on from the point above about listening. In order to listen well, you do need to slow down. Once you have slowed down, you need to point the focus of your attention at the other person. Now here is the tricky bit. In order to ask good questions, you need to master the skill of both attending to the other person well, while *simultaneously* noting your own felt sense response to what they are saying. How does what you are hearing 'land' with you? This is the place from which good questions arise, the intersecting point between what is going on outside of you and what is going on inside of you. In fact you could imagine this to be the meeting point of your inner and outer arcs of awareness. You can only do this if you have slowed down and are paying attention well to the unfolding conversation.

- *Have a purpose (but hold it lightly!).* As has been suggested earlier in this chapter, questions are directional. The broader purpose behind a question provides a platform for the conversation, rather than a 'roadmap' in the way 'leading questions' do. Leading questions actually point to the answer the questioner is seeking. Holding in mind a purpose for the question, rather than its 'answer' enables you to elicit new information, while connecting it to the overall purpose of your inquiry. For instance, the overall purpose of a question can be to develop a broad understanding of the thinking that is informing a policy decision or to gain understanding about another's perspective on a situation. It is the difference between asking a question such as: 'How did things end up so badly?' And: 'Can you tell me the history behind where we are now?'

- *Listen to the answer. See if it prompts another question.* Listening well to the answers a person gives you often prompts another question. 'Tell me more about that', 'I'm really interested in that bit of your answer in particular?' 'Why are you coming to that conclusion?' are questions that enable prompt elaboration and further detail of another's views. Questions like these can be key in helping you to understand others' perspectives and can provide insight into their decision-making process. In fact, if you listen carefully enough, such questions can often unearth the 'schemas' of those with whom you are talking.

- *Listen for the schema.* In the previous chapter the importance of identifying your own schemas was suggested. It is equally important to try to identify the schemas of others. Especially when you are trying to make sense of a situation from an ethical perspective, it is critical to understand the frames through which others are reaching their conclusions. For instance, a case of distribution managers who were sending out faulty parts in full knowledge that the parts were defective will be discussed in Chapter 5. They weren't necessarily operating from schemas aimed at maiming or hurting their customers. It is highly unlikely that as they sent the parts out they were thinking, 'Oh great, I hope these products short-circuit and hurt a few people'. It is more probable that they were thinking that the chance of a fault occurring and hurting others was relatively low. Their need to meet distribution targets overruled the relatively small percentage chance that someone would be hurt. My guess is that they were working from a schema of 'need to hit performance targets', whereas the manager who eventually stopped the distribution was coming from a perspective of, 'It is my job to ensure that none of the products sent from this organization could damage another human being'.

These are six general pointers for asking good questions. However, it can often be helpful to have a few good questions in your back pocket when you are developing your skill as an inquirer. The next section and the activity in Box 3.3 offer you just that.

Questions to practise

Questions about the overall purpose of what you are involved in

> What is the purpose of this particular guideline/organizational practice/ meeting?
> What are we trying to get out of this meeting?
> Whose interests are served by this purpose?
> Is this the right purpose?

Questions concerning absent voices

> Who else should be in on this discussion?
> Who knows something about this that we should involve?
> Who will be affected by this action?

Questions to reveal schemas

Why do you think that?
Tell me a bit more about how you come to that conclusion?
Is there a different perspective we can look at this from?
Can you tell me a little bit about the experience you have that suggests this?

Of course, in addition to asking others questions aimed at revealing their schemas and frames for considering a situation, it's also important to be aware of the position you yourself hold in relation to situations (especially those with an ethical component). A few questions to routinely ask yourself include:

What are my motives?
What are my motives *really*?
Have I been in a situation like this before? What happened then?
What am I afraid of as I engage in this situation?

👥 **BOX 3.3**

INDIVIDUAL ACTIVITY: PRACTISE ASKING QUESTIONS

This activity offers you two different situations in which to practise asking questions. In the first, you are encouraged to engage in a meeting you regularly attend with the purpose of posing good questions. The second invites you to strike up a conversation with an individual or group of people you don't normally converse with. You can choose either of these activities to do, or try both of them.

Scenario 1: Choose a particular situation, like a meeting you regularly attend with the intention of asking questions during it. Prepare by reviewing the agenda beforehand. What is the overall purpose of the meeting? What topics of conversation on the agenda do you have a particular interest in? Now delve more deeply as you think about each agenda item. Why is it there? Whose interests will be served by each agenda item? What do you already know about each topic? What would you like to know more about? Formulate questions about two or three different items on the agenda.

Attend the meeting and find points within it that are appropriate for raising your questions. Notice how you feel as you ask these questions. Notice the reaction of others in the meeting. What do you learn by undertaking this activity? Note your reflections in your journal.

Scenario 2: One of the best forums for practising asking questions is with people you don't know very well. In your organization, make a point of striking up a conversation with people you don't habitually speak with. You might start by asking them about a project they

➡

are working on or you could ask their view about a new organizational initiative. Notice the ways in which their viewpoints differ from your own. Rather than trying to convince them of your way of seeing things, be more curious about their point of view. Probe to the point that you really believe you understand their perspective and could retell it to someone else.
   Reflect on what you learn by doing this:

 ?   **QUESTIONS TO CONSIDER**

1 What new knowledge have you gained about the organization?
2 What have you learned about the person or people you have spoken with?
3 What you have learned about the process of asking questions itself?

Keep note of your responses to these questions in your learning journal.

Comportment is everything

The ability to formulate good questions and ask them at appropriate times is the foundational practice this chapter aims to develop. However, it is important to point out that questions can be posed in very different ways. The most innocent question can appear to be threatening depending not just on the words used but on the way those words are expressed.

The general demeanour used in presenting ourselves is called 'comportment'. The philosopher Martin Heidegger wrote extensively about the importance of 'comportment' in the way our being in the world is expressed (Heidegger, 1971). We understand what comportment is more colloquially through terms like 'body language'. The way that I am using the term 'comportment' here, however, goes deeper than surface-level body language, to include the overall energy a person exudes and the quality of that energy (be it, for example, domineering, retiring, sneaky or enthusiastic).

The way in which you comport yourself while you are asking questions has almost as much impact on the quality of the response you are likely to prompt as the actual words you use. If you ask questions in a way that indicates you are trying to 'catch someone out' or make them feel guilty then the likelihood is those you have asked will not be very open in their responses. Of course, the problem here is that much of the way in which we comport ourselves is unconscious. Furthermore, trying to 'act' in a certain way when we actually feel differently doesn't work. For instance, in trying to appear open when in fact we are feeling defensive ourselves, that deeper feeling will generally 'leak' and those we are speaking to will respond to the feeling of defensiveness they are picking up, rather than to the words being spoken. Even if they don't read the undertone as 'defensive', they will be confused at some level by the discrepancy between the words you are saying and the message your body is unconsciously expressing.

Rather than tie yourself up in knots, the main idea here is that it's important to notice the way you are asking questions and the emotions that lie beneath those questions. If you are feeling aggressive and angry but try to comport yourself as open and empathetic, that discrepancy will communicate itself to those with whom you are talking. A more fundamental step forward is to stay with the aggressive feeling you are experiencing for a while. Can you identify the source of the aggression? Is there something you are worried about that you haven't consciously acknowledged? Sometimes, just by staying with an uncomfortable feeling and inquiring into it, the quality of that feeling can alter. Then you will be able to ask your question in a more open manner. The next activity in Box 3.4 enables you to experiment precisely with this behaviour. This activity brings together all the skills you have been working with so far, including paying attention to your inner and outer arcs of attention as well as asking good questions.

 BOX 3.4

INDIVIDUAL ACTIVITY: INQUIRING INTO FEELINGS OF DISCOMFORT

This activity cannot be programmed as easily as others in the book where you can just decide when and where to undertake them. Instead, this exercise requires you to be attentive to your feelings as you go about asking questions and notice if you feel discomfort or unease. For instance, in preparing to ask a question do you feel slightly nervous and have the sensation of butterflies fluttering in your belly? You might feel your throat tighten or your palms become slightly sweaty.

Instead of just moving forward as planned to ask the question, take a step back and pay closer attention to what you are feeling in your body. Now here is the very difficult step. DON'T ANALYSE what you are feeling. Just notice what you are feeling – 'Ahhh, a bit of tightness in my throat', or 'Oh, I feel some tension in my neck'. Now focus, focus, focus on that somatic sensation. Don't try to change it, just notice it. The very interesting thing is, as you focus on it, it will generally begin to shift on its own account.

Now, just acknowledge to yourself what you are feeling. As much as possible, stay with the bodily sense, as well as the interpreted emotion. For instance, you might think to yourself, 'Hmmm, the tightness in my tummy tells me I'm feeling a bit anxious about this', or 'I

➡

←

can tell I'm feeling a bit defensive by the way my throat is constricting'. At this point, just BREATHE OUT. Don't try to change the feeling, just BREATHE OUT.

Now ask the question.

Notice again how you are feeling. Is it the same as before or has it shifted slightly? Notice how the person you are speaking with responds. Notice how the conversation progresses from here. Of course, you will never be able to know whether doing this activity has actually had an effect, as you can't go through the same experience again without stopping to pause, notice how you are feeling and breathing out. But you can notice a general sense of whether or not there is a difference in the subsequent conversation from other times you have had a similar feeling before asking a question.

Reflect on what you have learned and note your observations in your learning journal.

This activity completes the foundational phase of the course. Well done for getting this far! Even if you do not go any further, just practising the skills of paying attention to your inner and outer arcs of awareness and asking questions will provide you with the basic habits by which ethical astuteness can be developed. However, if you want to take these skills to their next level, you are now ready to move to mastery level II: 'Perceptual Practices'.

NOTE

1 For those who are interested in a more detailed account of Parsifal's adventure, you might read Roselle Angwin's account of the legend (Angwin, 1994). Given that these adventures are not the main point of this chapter, here I will summarize them ever so cursorily and offer you the full account in the reference list.

Level II

Perceptual practices

4

Developing moral perception

One of the most chilling illustrations of the absence of moral perception is depicted in the film *The Reader*:

> The story is set in Germany after World War II. Those who had been involved in the worst of the atrocities against the Jews are being tried for their crimes. The film centres on a particular woman, Hanna Schmitz, who is being tried for a crime in which Jews died because the church in which they were being held was engulfed in fire. She is accused of locking the Jews in the burning church. In her account of what happened, she fails to see the wrong in what she has done. Her continual reply to the lawyer questioning her about her actions is: 'But it was my job to stop them from running away'.
>
> One of the complexities of the film is that she is operating within a context in which the Jews she was charged to guard were being transported to death camps. She is a token individual being made to stand for the actions she took within a system that was itself operating in a completely immoral way. Within the logic of that system, adhering to her job of keeping the Jews from escaping made sense. She did not look for a further moral duty; surely if she had done so she would have also questioned the fact that the Jews were being held hostage in the first place.

This capacity, to notice the moral aspects of situations whether or not they are obvious, is a central capacity of moral perception. Lawrence Blum, whose work I will refer to frequently in this chapter, neatly summarizes what is involved when he writes: 'We make choices within the world we see, and what (and how) we see is itself an integral part of the quality of our moral consciousness' (Blum, 1994, p. 4).

Chapter 2 on inner and outer arcs of awareness indicated that perception is not a passive process where we merely perceive whatever is 'out there'. Lawrence Blum's quote indicates the connection between what we choose to see and, in his words, 'the quality of our moral consciousness'. In other words, the choices we make about what we see have consequences for our ability to respond ethically to the world around us.

The solution is not as simple as deciding to be more conscious about what we perceive, however. As the chapter on inner and outer arcs of awareness demonstrated, much of perception operates at a level below conscious awareness. We perceive things and largely remain unaware of the choice involved in perceiving them. In our experience, perception *just happens*. In the film *The Reader* Hanna did not stop to notice what she was noticing about the situation she faced. In her view the most salient feature of the church catching fire was the opportunity it provided the Jews under her guard to flee. She did not think beyond her duty of preventing them from escaping to consider other ethical consequences of her act.

At a more mundane level imagine you are on a crowded train where there are people standing. You may feel very relieved to have found a seat for yourself, and you may very quickly bury your nose in the newspaper or your smartphone to secure yourself a bit of space and the quiet you had anticipated as you stood waiting for the train. In your haste to get yourself settled and comfortable, you may not have noticed the older woman who is standing in the aisle of the train. You may miss the fact that she is rather frail and seems to be a bit pale and is probably in need of a seat more than you are. Because of your own bad day and attention to your own needs, you may overlook the fact that she is very unsteady on her feet and appears likely to fall over.

By not noticing the older woman and her discomfort, you are not committing an ethical 'wrong' like stealing her handbag or knocking her over deliberately. However, your ethical response to the situation is less fulsome than it might be because at the most basic level you don't even notice her. You don't perceive that the situation could call for you to act differently by the mere fact of not noticing a proximate human being in need of care.

Alternatively, you might notice her, but you may also be aware of a very young, fit man sitting immediately opposite to where she is standing. In your judgement, he has a greater obligation to relinquish his seat than you do. In this situation, not only do you perceive the frail woman but you are also observing the young man so deeply buried in the music blaring from his headphones that he fails to take in the significance of the woman swaying in the train's aisle. Two key aspects of the situation are present for you – the frail older woman and the fit young man. In such an instance, you might choose to remain seated and silently bemoan the 'lack of respect young people of today have for their elders'.

Each of these situations demonstrates how perception influences your ability or willingness to extend ethical regard to the older woman. Considering both the train example and that of Hanna Schmitz in *The Reader*, it is possible to identify three different perceptual avenues being taken, all leading to a similar outcome of not acting:

- In the first case on the train, the individual is too self-absorbed to notice the needs of other passengers.
- In the second case the individual notices but decides their own moral duty is less than that of other passengers on the train.
- In the case of Hanna Schmitz, even though she is aware that the Jews will probably die if she locks them in the church, the duty that has more salience for her is not letting them escape.

Each of these modes of perception leads to a similar lack of ethical action, but is fuelled by a different perceptual problem: not noticing at all, noticing but dismissing one's own responsibility, or noticing but acting on a different aspect of the situation that is deemed to be more salient. This chapter elaborates on these and other ways in which perception is crucial to the possibility of taking ethical action. In doing so, it builds on many of the ideas introduced in Chapter 2 about inner and outer arcs of awareness. However, it develops these ideas further by attending more closely to the link between how perception works and its consequences for ethical behaviour.

What does perceiving correctly actually entail?

In his book *Moral Perception and Particularity*, Lawrence Blum details seven different steps that take a person from a given situation to action based on a moral principle. The first two of these, he suggests, constitute 'moral perception'. They are: (1) the accurate recognition of a situation's 'features' – these features are not necessarily presented in a 'coherent' way; (2) the person must be able to recognize the situation as having moral relevance (Blum, 1994, p. 52).

Blum argues that putting these two steps together constitutes a person 'coming upon a situation and recognising its morally salient features' (p. 53). He is adamant that these two aspects should be seen as distinct rather than melding them into one. Of course they are connected but it can be helpful to tease out the subtle difference between them.

The first calls for the 'accurate recognition of a situation's 'features'. As mentioned previously, at any one moment in time we are bombarded by a myriad of sense data. What is perceived is determined by what we experience to be 'salient' within a particular setting. A perception is salient when it comes into focus in a particular way. For instance, in the example from the film *The Reader*, what was salient to Hanna was her duty to stop the Jews under her charge from escaping. For her this was the most important aspect of the situation, despite the fact that doing so meant that they would burn to death.

In the example of being on a crowded train, in the first instance the most salient aspect was the individual's need for comfort after a hard day's work. The presence of the frail woman who appeared to need the seat herself was a second aspect of the situation that could have become salient to any passenger within the train carriage. In the second instance what became salient as an additional component of the situation was the presence of a young, fit man who was interpreted as a more suitable candidate for donating his seat to the frail woman. These examples show that in any situation there are a number of different factors involved. The (largely unconscious) process by which we attend to certain factors and ignore others determines our ability to both see and act on components that require an ethical response.

The key notion here is 'salience'. 'Salience' refers to that aspect of a situation that we recognize as most noteworthy, and is connected to the notions of inner and outer arcs of awareness as discussed in Chapter 2. This concept indicates the way in which certain aspects of the world are important to us. As suggested in Chapter 2, a key influence on what becomes salient to us is our identity. For example, those people who have had to leave their homes to seek political asylum may be more sensitive to the needs of others facing similar plights; those who have physical disabilities will more quickly notice whether or not a building provides ease of entrance for others who are similarly disabled; or those who have been wrongly accused of crimes will perhaps be more aware of shortfalls of justice systems.

What is salient within our perceptual field is central to Blum's first aspect of moral perception. As examined in Chapter 2, our habits of perception generally go hand in hand with what is most salient for us. As Blum suggests, even noticing a situation as a 'situation', that is, a coherent collection of events that coalesces in a particular way, is a prerequisite for then considering its ethical implications. In order for something to become a situation, we need to recognize it as distinctive from the ongoing flow of perceptual input and study its aspects more closely.

Blum's second characteristic of ethical perception highlights the fact that just recognizing a situation as such is not sufficient to foster ethical action. Surely,

Hanna recognized that she was in the midst of a 'situation' – a burning building with people inside. What she failed to do was to take the next step and consider the situation as one with ethical implications beyond those of her duty to prevent the prisoners from escaping.

A less extreme example of blindness towards the ethical aspects of a situation is demonstrated by my own appreciation of climate change issues. Although I have been aware of issues around sustainability for many years (so these issues are 'salient' to me) it was not until I watched Al Gore's film *An Inconvenient Truth* that the ethical component of these issues struck me with full force. When Al Gore pronounced climate change foremost as an 'ethical' issue, I experienced a sense of shock. Certainly, he was correct, because climate change is something that affects others' lives very significantly. This means there is indeed a link between the number of long-haul flights I take each year and people dying from water levels rising in low-lying areas. That is why Gore's film is called *An Inconvenient Truth*; it is much easier not to consider the link between my actions and their impact on others' lives.

A third aspect of moral perception, Blum points out, is the role played by empathy in helping us to understand the impact our actions have on one another. This will be further developed in the next chapter, which looks at moral imagination. For now, you are encouraged to undertake an activity in Box 4.1 designed as a starting point for developing your own ethical perception.

 BOX 4.1

GROUP ACTIVITY: DEVELOPING MORAL PERCEPTION

Generally speaking, ethical issues encountered in organizations don't arrive explicitly labelled as such. As this chapter intends to highlight, work is often required to perceive the ethical aspects of situations. Below, a number of circumstances that arise in the course of organizational life are listed. The first step of this activity is to consider what ethical issues may arise from each of them. After you have formed your own view, discuss your perceptions with others in your group:

- habitually working long hours and because of this regularly missing family commitments;
- providing your son or daughter with business contacts through your own connections;
- spending time surfing the net during working hours;
- ignoring the poor work that an employee does because you know they are undergoing a very stressful time in their private life (their partner is dying, for instance);

➡

←

- suspecting that your boss is having an affair with their personal assistant;
- suspecting that a co-worker is fiddling the accounts.

? QUESTIONS TO CONSIDER

1 How would you describe the ethics of the issue?
2 What are the different ways of seeing this issue?
3 How might other people see the issue?
4 What do you take into account as you debate the issue?
5 Faced with this kind of situation, what options for action might you have?
6 What advice would you give someone in a similar situation?
7 What do you learn from talking over your different perceptions with members of your group?

Embodied perception

Until now within the book, perception has largely been assumed to be a cognitive process operating more rationally than emotionally or viscerally. Perceiving is, after all, often associated with our visual capacity mediated by the brain's interpretations. An alternative perspective about how perception occurs is offered next. 'Embodied cognition' both highlights the critical role played by the body in perceiving, and also provides a link to moral perception.

The notion of embodied cognition (Anderson, 2003; Barsalou, 2008) suggests that rather than chiefly being a rational function led through the brain, cognition results from a full-bodied engagement with the world. In fact, our very ability to perceive is completely dependent on our physical mode of being. At the simplest and most mundane level, two people of different heights will perceive the world differently, by the mere fact that one is taller than the other. Our bodies are our foundational ground point for our perspective. We are always encountering the world from an embodied place and that embodied situation determines what we perceive. From his understanding of the centrality of our embodied nature, the French phenomenologist Maurice Merleau-Ponty argued, 'The world is not what I think but what I live through' (Merleau-Ponty, 1962, p. xviii). In other words, our perceptions happen at the intersection of our embodied selves, our embodied way of being in the world and the world itself.

It is increasingly recognized that our embodied way of being in the world affords us a kind of intelligence that is central to our ethical engagement with that world. In his book, *Ethical Know-How,* the biologist, philosopher and neuroscientist Francisco Varela argues that 'the reference point for understanding perception is not a pre-given, independent world, but the sensorimotor structure of the cognitive agent' (1992, p. 13). That is, perceiving the world is not something that we can do apart from our bodies and their sensorimotor capacities. The implications of this for ethical perception are suggested by his assertion that, 'it is the manner in which the perceiver is embodied that determines how the perceiver can act and be modulated by environmental events' (ibid.).

Returning to the example of being on a crowded train, the fact of our embodied way of being is implicated in all aspects of such a situation. It is because we experience comfort or discomfort in our own bodies, which alerts us to the comfort or discomfort of others. It is the frailty of the elder woman's body that demands our ethical perception. It is only because we too live in bodies that feel tired that we can sympathize with what she might be feeling and thus consider the possibility of relieving her discomfort. At an even more mundane level, it is because we are physically proximate to the frail woman that we can even be aware of her situation. Were we sat in a different train carriage, her situation would not be apparent to us.

Varela goes further than pointing out the role our bodies play in perception, however, by arguing for the immediacy of perception and action. Rather than accepting the oft-cited understanding of ethical behaviour being the result of ethical perception followed by deliberation, which leads to a correct action (see Rest, 1986, for example) Varela points out that in the great majority of circumstances we find ourselves, conscious deliberation plays a limited role. Instead, perception and action are almost simultaneous. For example, imagine yourself standing on a curb waiting to cross a busy street. A teenager stands next to you, wearing headphones and paying more attention to their mobile phone than to the traffic. Absent-mindedly they step away from the curb into the path of a car travelling at high speed. In all likelihood, you would automatically, without deliberation, grab them and pull them back to the curb. In the immediacy of that situation, you act; you do not consider the pros and cons of doing so. Varela's notion of ethical know-how will be explored in greater detail in Chapter 7.

Another aspect of perception relates to the kind of knowing that arises through our emotional response to situations. The British philosopher Mary Midgley has coined the term, the 'yuk factor' to highlight the embodied, emotional reaction that often alerts us to circumstances that are not quite right from an ethical perspective (Midgley, 2000). Midgley describes the 'yuk factor' as our emotional response of disgust to things that don't seem 'right' to us. Elaborating on this point, she suggests that, 'heart and mind are not enemies or alternative tools, they are complementary aspects of a single process. Whenever we seriously judge something to be wrong, strong feeling necessarily accompanies that judgement' (ibid., p. 9). In fact, she drives this point home by suggesting that 'someone who does not have such feelings, someone who has merely a theoretical interest in morals, who doesn't feel any indignation or disgust or outrage about things like slavery and torture, has missed the point of morals altogether' (ibid.).

She is arguing that being able to experience an emotional response to the world is an essential part of perceiving what is 'right' and what is 'wrong' within it. By discounting our emotional embodied response we are neglecting vital information that can lead us to act correctly. Midgley points out the importance of inquiring into strong feelings rather than neglecting them when trying to reach decisions about a way forward. Many times, emotional responses are there because of deep-seated understandings of threats and difficulties that more purely 'rational' approaches might dismiss.[1]

Interestingly, the importance of emotional ways of understanding a situation has been indicated by recent research into how ethical decisions are made. In his study of MBA students, Zhong discovered that when faced with an ethical dilemma, students who immediately responded to the needs of those asking for help, rather than engaging in an elaborate process of deliberation, gave most generously (Zhong, 2011). His study asked students to decide how much money they would give towards certain charities. Without rational deliberation, a significant proportion of the student groups gave on average 20 per cent more to the charity than did groups who were encouraged to engage in deliberative processes. This study points to the way in which an embodied response may indeed lead to greater generosity than a response that is more measured and 'rational'. The activity in Box 4.2 helps you to practise noticing your own emotional responses to the world around you.

BOX 4.2

ACTIVITY: NOTICING YOUR EMOTIONAL/VISCERAL RESPONSE

For this activity you will need to use a camera. Any camera will do; the one in your smartphone or tablet will work perfectly. For the next day or two, take photos of people, places

➡

and situations that you might normally not photograph, but that strike you as possibly being significant from an ethical perspective. Be alert to conversations you might have and although you can't photograph them, you may be able to photograph the person you converse with.

After you have collected ten or more photos in this way, spend a bit of time looking at them all.

? QUESTIONS TO CONSIDER

1 What themes are represented by what you have chosen to photograph?
2 Choose one photo that evokes a particularly strong reaction from you. Why do you react this way?
3 What do the photos you have taken tell you about your own orientation towards viewing the world?
4 How might you enlarge that orientation?

This is an excellent activity to share in your group if you are working in a learning team. Otherwise, it can be helpful to share photos with someone else and compare your responses to these questions. What do you learn from sharing your photos and thoughts with others?

The next part of the chapter looks in more detail at hindrances to perceiving correctly. First, aspects of individuals themselves that can impede this process are introduced. Then aspects of the organizational setting that may hinder ethical perception are discussed.

Aspects of the individual that influence moral perception

There are a number of individually based factors that can hinder the capacity to perceive correctly. In Chapter 2 on inner and outer arcs of awareness, the way in which one's identity affects what one perceives was highlighted. Merely having had a certain experience can alter our response to others with similar circumstances. For instance, a recent death in the family can sensitize us to others' experiences of grief and loss. Alternatively if we have cultivated an identity in which bearing distress without much fuss is central to how we see ourselves, we can lack the ability to sympathize with others' difficulties.

Moving beyond issues of identity, Blum (1994) offers other factors that can hinder the ability to perceive correctly. For instance, he cites 'self-absorption' as one of the most detrimental orientations for ethical perception. Self-absorption or self-preoccupation limits our ability to notice the world around us, and thus restricts ethical awareness (as was apparent in the earlier example of the individual not noticing the frail woman in need of a seat on the train). It is important to note that although some individuals may have a proclivity towards being more habitually self-absorbed than others, self-absorption can affect all of us depending on our circumstances. It is not just those considered to be egotistical who can be self-absorbed; sometimes when we are feeling the most vulnerable and fragile we too can be dispropor-tionately and unhelpfully absorbed with the self.

External factors too, can affect our state of self-preoccupation. If we are in very crowded spaces, like trains or buses or underground transport systems for instance, studies have indicated that there is a tendency to withdraw into the self and not pay attention to the external world (Garcia et al., 2002). In such spaces people commonly avoid eye contact as a way of avoiding unwel-come intimacy or confrontation. At the end of the day when one is tired, it is very easy to sink into a seat on a crowded train – as mentioned previously – and not want to look around for fear of actually recognizing that someone may need that seat more than you do!

A feeling of helplessness can also affect the extent to which individuals look beyond themselves to notice others' troubles. This can be the cause of 'com-passion fatigue', the phenomenon whereby people do not respond in the face of yet another call for aid in crisis-fallen parts of the world. It can be easier to turn off the television when images of famine victims are beamed into our living rooms or turn our heads as we pass people sleeping on the street. What is needed instead is the capacity to 'stay with' the difficult emotions that arise from acknowledging what we perceive. Emotions such as helplessness, guilt, shame, disgust or even horror can be very difficult to feel but such strong emotional responses can be the spur towards ethical action.

A final character flaw that Blum identifies that leads to a reduction in moral awareness concerns our ability to empathize with others. It is only possible to realize the impact of our actions if we imagine how others will be affected by them. This capacity links to the concept of 'moral imagination', which is the topic of the next chapter. It is important to introduce it here, however, because of the role it plays in our ability to perceive the moral aspects of situations. Lack of empathy can result in a person noticing what is going on in a situation but failing to register its moral significance. For instance, I may notice that my colleague seems distraught and upset but if I fail to empathize with them then I may not recognize the importance of their distress and the requirement that I treat them sensitively. In this way both the capacity to notice a situation as a 'situation' and to recognize its ethical aspects are vital in developing ethical astuteness.

So far, moral perception has been explored as a capacity that can be developed by individuals determined to do so. What happens to that determination, however, when a person enters a system that discourages, rather than encourages, moral perception? The next section introduces the idea of 'moral drift', a phenomenon common to many organizational contexts.

Moral drift

'Moral drift' occurs when a person enters a situation where they intend to act from particular ethical ideals but as time goes on, they find these intentions withering away (Heugens et al., 2008). Rather than acting from their own ethical standards, they begin to adopt those of the organization they are a part of (which may be significantly lower than the person's own standards). This is illustrated by the story of Sally:

Sally joined the pharmaceutical company Zelco as an enthusiastic sales representative just out of University. She eventually planned to go to medical school, but she decided to take a break before continuing with her studies to earn money for her tuition. The pharmaceutical industry, she believed, would provide her with helpful insights into how medicines were developed and became available to the public.

When she joined Zelco she was given guidance on how to develop her contacts and she was also set monthly sales targets to reach. They were stretching targets and she found herself working very hard to achieve them. She began to feel very stressed as her salary was dependent on her hitting her sales targets. One day over lunch she spoke of the difficulty she was having with a co-worker. 'Oh, he said, you don't know about "the system."' She looked at him blankly, and he went on to explain that everyone knew the sales targets were vastly optimistic. If you did everything 'by the books' he said, you would never get a bonus. He told Sally about a number of 'dummy accounts' which had been established which he and a number of other colleagues used to generate sales when they needed them. He assured her that no-one got hurt from this activity, and if she would like, he would add her to the group.

Sally was appalled, and considered reporting what she had been told. For two weeks she did nothing, and struggled on to make sales. Then however, a major client went bankrupt, and Sally's one stable account collapsed. She began to tell herself over and over how crazy the sales targets were. How was she ever going to save up the money for Medical School? She contacted her colleague and asked if she could join 'the system'. Where was the harm in it really? Surely if she just used the dummy accounts every once in awhile, she would be fine and no ill would come of it?

What happened to Sally is frighteningly common. It is one of the key means by which 'good people' end up doing 'bad things'. We know that perception, and particularly perception of what is right and wrong, is influenced by circumstances and the norms of those around us. As the business ethicist Edmund Hartman counsels young graduates as they enter the world of work and organizations: 'if you want to remain ethical in your actions, be sure to work for an organization or industry sector that operates from an ethical base' (Hartman, 2006, p. 79). Box 4.3 helps you to reflect and explore how moral drift occurs.

 BOX 4.3

ACTIVITY: TO EXPLORE HOW MORAL DRIFT OCCURS

Reflection: Can you recall an occasion in which you found yourself doing something you never thought you would do, from an ethical perspective?

 QUESTIONS TO CONSIDER

1 What was the situation?
2 How did it arise?
3 When did you first realize something was not as you might have expected it to be?
4 What action did you take?
5 In retrospect, what would you do differently in the future if faced with a similar situation?

Activity: Write a story, in the form of a legend, fairy-tale or myth, with you as the central character that depicts the situation.

? QUESTIONS TO CONSIDER

1 What helpers might you give yourself in the tale?
2 What would be the key turning points?
3 What would 'the moral of the story be?'.

Organizational influences on moral perception

As the example of moral drift above illustrates, there are forces beyond the individual that can influence how she or he perceives what is right or wrong from an ethical perspective. Increasingly, business ethicists are exploring the relationship between an individual's moral perception and aspects of the organization. For instance, Jones and Ryan (1998) suggest that organizations influence individuals' perceptions in two ways: first, through determining the composition of an individual's 'referent group' (that is, generally speaking, organizations determine where an individual is situated within it, and therefore the group of people they will spend the most time with); and second, through affecting the level of responsibility that an individual attributes to themselves. For instance, organizational structures can inhibit individuals from 'putting together' the full impact of something they are doing in terms of its moral consequences, just by the mere fact of the organization's structure. In this way, an individual's direct understanding of the effects of their actions can limit their sense of ethical responsibility. For instance, if I am a fitter in a factory, my job is to see that the component parts I am assembling do so as they are meant to, not to consider the fact that the end product is a bomb that will be used to kill thousands of people. The role an organization's structure plays in hindering moral perception will be explored in more detail in Chapter 8.

Victor and Cullen (1987) have developed the concept of 'ethical work climate' (EWC) as a way of describing the overarching ethical orientation within an organization. Based on Kohlberg's work on cognitive moral development (1984), Victor and Cullen have created a diagnostic instrument that can be used to assess whether an organization's culture fits more within 'pre-convention' (ego-based), 'conventional' (relationally-based) or 'post-conventional' (principle-based) reasoning around ethical issues.

Developing on Victor and Cullen's work, VanSandt et al. (2006) have conducted research that indicates that a relationship exists between an organization's ethical work climate and the moral perception of individuals within it. Their study of six organizations in a range of industry sectors within the USA showed that individuals within organizations with a pre-conventional ethical work climate were worst at identifying the ethical components of situations as compared with their counterparts in organizations with conventional or post-conventional orientations. An implication of their work is that exercising a high level of ethical perception if you find yourself in an organization with an impoverished ethical work climate may be something of a challenge.

A first step in recognizing the effect of your organization on your ability to exercise ethical perception well is to have some sense of what your organization's ethical work climate is. This is possible, without distributing Victor and

Cullen's questionnaire by considering the following aspects of your organization's culture and their implications for its ethical work climate.

Organizational 'set pieces'

Each organization has its rituals and practices and these will support or create its culture. Here, such habits are categorized as 'organizational set pieces'. These are occasions, such as the weekly staff meeting, the monthly publication of a newsletter or the Christmas party, which are taken-for-granted rituals of organizational life. Often these set pieces reveal a great deal about what is important to the organization and correspondingly, what is salient to it. In particular, it is interesting to note the way in which such practices embed understanding of 'how we do things around here'.

Let us take a look at the weekly staff meeting, for instance (also see the activity in Box 4.4). In terms of the implications for the ethical climate of an organization the following questions are interesting to pose:

- Who is invited to attend?
- Who sets the agenda?
- How is time allocated on the agenda?
- Are questions of purpose addressed?
- What is the overall tenor of the meeting?
- What is the level of discussion and interaction and engagement?
- What kinds of questions are asked?
- How is information from the meeting disseminated?
- How are agreed actions followed up?
- How is accountability exercised?

In order to exercise ethical perception well, the broadest group of people available should be invited to such a meeting. It is only through having the broadest representation of different views that the ethical consequences of difficult decisions can be debated fully. Setting the agenda is also central to ethical perception because the agenda articulates what is considered important for the organization at a given point in time. What stays off the agenda, what stays on it? The agenda indicates those things that are legitimate to talk about (but a deeper question concerns who legitimizes what is discussed). What is always at the head of the agenda? How often do we think about the ethical aspects of agenda setting?

Meetings play a crucial role in legitimizing information within an organization. The way that this connects with issues of ethical perception is how inclusion or exclusion of certain agenda items signals what is and what is not seen to be important for organizational operations. For instance, many businesses never question who they work with as clients. Generally, clients are accepted no matter what product they are involved in selling. This can have ethical implications, for instance, if your clients are arms dealers equipping governments to exterminate various minorities within their own countries.

 BOX 4.4

ACTIVITY: OBSERVING YOUR OWN ORGANIZATION AT WORK

Examine the agenda from the last three meetings you regularly attend in your organization. From that agenda, consider the following:

 QUESTIONS TO CONSIDER

1 What can you discern are the most salient issues for the organization or team?
2 What gets the most attention?
3 If you can remember back to the meeting, what were the things that took up the majority of the time?
4 How was discussion facilitated within the meeting?
5 Were perceptions from the broadest range of people attending actively sought?
6 How was confrontation handled? (Ethics is not about not having confrontation, by the way, it is often about raising issues of confrontation so that debate can openly occur.)
7 What are issues that you believe should have been included on the agenda that were not, but that might lead to broader ethical perception within the organization?

What and who is responsible for what?

Within their very way of structuring, measuring and allocating accountability organizations signal those things that are considered to be important and those things that are thought to be less important. In-house newsletters, media announcements and externally focused promotional material all reveal what organizations really place at the centre of their attention. Similarly, by measuring their impacts solely in terms of their financial indicators, an organization clearly broadcasts its primary focus.

Perhaps an even more insidious means by which organizations enable or prohibit moral perception is through the very way in which they are structured. The nature of organizing itself tends towards diffusing responsibility, thus weakening the need to perceive ethically, suggest Jones and Ryan

(1998). They go on to explain how organizational hierarchy desensitizes individuals to their own ethical responsibilities if they feel their actions are insignificant in the face of rigid organizational structures. In othere words, if someone senior is always responsible, then taking the time to perceive a situation outside the borders of one's direct responsibilities can seem pointless. Deconstructing production processes functionally or geographically can also obscure 'the entire picture' and the way in which interconnections can lead to ethically suspect situations. A good example of how the size and number of contributors to the food chain has resulted in an ethically questionable situation is seen in the 'horse meat' scandal in the UK in 2013. The large number of suppliers located in geographically distant parts of the world has resulted in no one really being held responsible for the fact that horse meat has been traded as beef and used in many ready-meal preparations. Ever-increasing globalization of production means that deliberate work must be undertaken to ensure ethical standards are maintained throughout an organization's supply chain. Chapter 9 will attend to these issues in more depth.

Language: euphemisms and moral muteness

The very language that an organization uses to describe its activities can obscure the impacts of those activities (see Box 4.5). Labelling the deaths of civilians as 'soft targets' or 'collateral damage' has been a hallmark of recent conflicts in Iraq and Afghanistan by American and European militaries, for instance. Speaking of fallen soldiers as 'body bags' rather than as dead young men and women somehow eases our sense of ethical responsibility; after all, 'body bags' are not due 'moral consideration' in the way that a killed human being might be.

The ability of an organization to engage in discussion about what it is noticing from an ethical point of view is an essential aspect of its ethical work climate. In many organizations, 'moral muteness' is the state of affairs. Without recognized forums in which it is possible for organizational members to exchange their perceptions of what is going on and to discuss whether or not what is happening is correct from an ethical perspective, much ethical knowledge goes underground and is only whispered about. In the aftermath of great ethical catastrophes such as those witnessed at Enron, Arthur Anderson or Bhopal, it is always amazing to notice how many people knew what was going on but were silenced by the prevailing culture.

BOX 4.5

ACTIVITY: CONSIDERING THE LANGUAGE OF WORK

Pay attention to the everyday language common in your organization:

 QUESTIONS TO CONSIDER

1 Can you identify any key euphemisms used that somehow obfuscate the processes, products or benefactors of those process or products? For instance, do you use the term 'headcount' rather than 'people' when you are considering your organization's payroll costs?
2 In your organization, how are the profit and loss accounts organized?
3 If your organization claims that 'our people are our greatest asset' but in fact they are counted within the organization's costs, what messages are conveyed?
4 How easy is it to talk with others in your organization about any issue of an ethical concern that you may identify?
5 Are there senior managers you can confide in about difficult issues?
6 How are ethically suspect issues handled in the organization?
7 Given your reflections on this, how would you rate your organization in terms of its ethical climate?

Codes of conduct

One response to the need to increase ethical behaviour in organizations has been the proliferation of 'codes of conduct'. These general principles that organizations adopt can indeed serve the purpose of bringing greater ethical clarity to decisions. However, there is a small body of research that indicates that sometimes the presence of a 'code of conduct' can actually prevent organizational members from perceiving ethical aspects of situations themselves.

A contemporary example of how such codes actually inhibited ethical perception is seen in the case of the British Members of Parliament (MPs) expenses scandal that I studied together with a colleague, Kim Turnbull-James (see Ladkin and Turnbull-James, 2009). In the spring of 2009 one of the UK's daily national newspapers broke the story that MPs had been making questionable expenses claims. Up until that point, only the MPs themselves, their administrators and the HM Revenue & Customs had known what the MPs had been claiming. In the eyes of the public a significant amount of what had been reimbursed was considered outrageous and sometimes of dubious morality.

As we wrote:

> Previous scandals involving MPs – sleaze, sex scandal, corruption – have involved individuals found to be acting out of line with public expectations. The difference this time was that as the scandal unfolded so many Members were revealed in a new light. Many MPs were truly horrified: a Radio Four programme on 21st July reflecting on MPs' experiences during this crisis revealed 'MPs have privately told me they are dismayed, angry, even embarrassed'. They were in state of shock and horror at what people were doing – people couldn't look each other in the eye. Whilst it is important to remember that many Members were *not* caught up in these revelations, the scale of involvement indicates that something beyond individual corruption (of which there may have been a few cases) was likely to be involved. (2009, p. 3)

From our research involving archival material of public reports in the aftermath of the scandal, we identified three themes that served to explain how the scandal had occurred. Issues of moral perception are implicated in each of these:

- First, the MPs did not construe the situation they were in as having a moral component. This could be because they did not attend to data that would have indicated that a question of morality might be involved or because they did not then interpret that data as having moral significance.
- Second, their perceptions were affected by the fact that the standard by which they were judging their behaviour was different from the standard being applied by their constituencies in judging their behaviour.
- Third, and in this case most importantly, their moral awareness was impaired because the system they were operating within repeatedly asserted that they were working within a 'legal' framework. In this way MPs failed to perceive the important distinction between acting 'legally' and acting 'ethically'.

This finding concurs with others, such as Ten Bos (2003), Dillard and Yuthas (2002) and Jones (2003), whose work suggests that sometimes codes of practice can blind organizational members to their responsibilities of seeking out the ethical component of a situation. This is particularly true the more senior a person is in an organization.

Concluding considerations

This chapter has described ethical perception in some detail, in an attempt to help you notice what you notice and, perhaps more importantly, to notice what you do *not* notice as a key step to ethical mastery. You have been invited to consider your own habits and predispositions that impact on your ability to perceive 'correctly' from an ethical perspective. You have also been prompted to consider the features of your organization that will affect that capability, a topic to which we shall return in Chapter 8.

As has been hinted at throughout the chapter there is another critical dimension of ethical perception: its imaginative element. The next chapter turns to this essential aspect of ethical mastery.

NOTE

1 For more information about Mary Midgley's view of the role of emotions in ethical decision making, see her book *The Myths We Live By* (2003).

5

Developing moral imagination

The last chapter introduced moral perception and the idea that being able to recognize ethical aspects of situations is critical to being able to respond ethically to the world around us. A number of steps important to developing this capacity have been introduced:

- identifying the schemas through which your perception is organized;
- stretching your perceptual boundaries to include the viewpoints of others who you might not normally consider;
- proactively searching for ethically salient aspects of any given situation.

The notion of 'moral intensity' was also briefly introduced. Moral intensity is the tendency to give more moral 'worth' or 'value' to those psychologically closest to us or to those who have been particularized in some way (Jones, 1991). This idea provides a conceptual bridge to the aspect of ethical mastery elaborated in this chapter: moral imagination. Moral intensity speaks to a kind of emotional connection between the perceiver and who he or she perceives. If there is a particular connection or empathy between the perceiver and the perceived, the degree of moral intensity tends to be higher. This ratcheting up of moral intensity is only possible because of an empathetic move between perceiver and perceived. That empathetic move is only possible because of the power of imaginative engagement.

The kind of imaginative process involved is not a whimsical, 'untruthful' way of using the mind. In the Western world's intellectual climate imagination can be dismissed as a merely playful type of cognition. Yet, many ethicists argue that it is only because of our imaginative capacity that we can experience the sort of empathy required to appreciate how our decisions or actions might affect one another. For instance, I would not only refrain from stealing money from a colleague who has left her wallet on top of her desk because I believe to do so would be 'wrong', but also because I understand through applying my imagination, how distraught she would feel to be robbed.

Imagination enables empathetic understanding to be made; it is the means by which we connect with the experience of another and how they might experience a given situation. It is at the heart of the ability not only to perceive stakeholders other than those we might normally think about but it also enables us to put ourselves into their shoes in terms of how a decision or situation might affect them. In this way moral imagination is the crucial step on from moral perception. Unless we can have some sense of the affect our behaviour has on another human being, we cannot truly engage with him or her except from a rule-based perspective. Even utilitarian-based approaches require the ability to imagine the relative pleasure or pain of those affected by decisions. The philosopher Hannah Arendt saw imagination as so critical to our ability to function ethically that she famously suggested that those who committed the horrific crimes during the Nazi rule in Germany did so through a 'failure of imagination'. In this way she highlights the central role imagination plays in the way we engage with ethical terrain.

This chapter invites you to explore the notion of moral imagination and offers activities intended to enhance your own capacity in this regard. Four different orientations towards moral imagination will be introduced: that of the Scottish philosopher Adam Smith and his idea of 'moral sympathy'; the role metaphor plays in moral imagination offered by the contemporary philosopher Mark Johnson; the notion of the 'caring imagination' developed by the philosopher Maurice Hamington; and finally we will explore the intersection of moral imagination and systems thinking as proposed by the business ethicist Patricia Werhane. Throughout the introduction of theoretical material you will be invited to try out activities designed to help you develop your own moral imagination.

The chapter introduces a particular organizational case study as a touchstone for exploring key ideas. It is a generic case, representative of an issue senior managers almost always have to deal with at some point in their careers – that of making decisions about who to make redundant at the time of necessary organizational downsizing. Making people redundant is often couched as a correct action to take from a utilitarian ethical perspective. It is regularly framed as a means by which an organization can survive when it falls upon difficult financial times, and by staying in business, can at least provide some people with further work (rather than everyone losing their jobs should the business fail completely). However, utilitarianism doesn't provide very much guidance about *who* to make redundant from an ethical perspective or how that decision should be taken. Case Study 5.1 provides the opportunity to engage with this type of dilemma from an imaginative viewpoint in order to explore how the use of moral imagination might assist you in making such decisions.

CASE STUDY 5.1

Brite Technologies

Brite Technologies is a relatively small, owner-operated firm that has run into difficult times financially because a major client of its technology has closed down. Thirty per cent of Brite's output was bought by this client, resulting in their margins being badly affected. After a good deal of consideration and hand-wringing about how to handle this, the decision has been made to let one of the senior people within the Brite team go. But which one? Here is a thumbnail sketch about each of the four people Brite is considering making redundant. As you read each sketch, imagine yourself as the 'boss' of Brite who will ultimately make the decision about who to let go:

Nico (Head of Sales): Nico has been with the company since it began ten years previously. Enthusiastic and hard-working, Nico knows a good deal about the business and is largely responsible for building the firm's portfolio of clients. Lately, however, Nico has been exhibiting signs that he may not be as committed to the business as he once was. He has been coming in late and also there have been times when he has taken much longer at client lunches than might be expected. You are also concerned that Nico did not have any forewarning of the client who has gone bankrupt; you would have expected him to have had some idea of that possibility and to have alerted you to the issue. Although you know the mess you are in is not Nico's fault, you can't help but blame him a bit for having his 'eye off the ball' and perhaps for not pursuing other clients as vigorously as you may have liked.

Sally (Designer): Sally is new to Brite but has been a very good addition to the business. A highly skilled computer engineer, she has spearheaded two of Brite's leading new components. She is highly enthusiastic and shows great commitment to the company. She is often in to work before you arrive and greets you with a raft of suggestions for new products and improvements to your current line. She is also rather 'high maintenance' and has been known to get into embarrassing arguments with some of the other engineers who she has accused of being sexist. You know very little of her private life, although you assume she is rather 'married to her job' as she spends so much time in the office.

Alper (Computer Programmer): Alper is one of your most steady and conscientious pro-grammers. He has been with Brite for three years and in that time he has never missed a day's work. Everyone in the firm likes Alper and clients often go out of their way to tell you how much they have enjoyed working with him. He is one of those relatively rare computer programmers who works well at the technology/client interface. The only difficulty that you face with Alper is that he does not have residency rights and you have had to work hard (and pay a good deal of money) to secure his working permit. This permit is coming up for renewal within the next six months.

Chris (Client Manager): Chris is one of the older employees at Brite and works closely with Nico as Head of Sales. Chris has a mixed reputation at Brite. He is troubled by depression and can miss many days off work without explanation. Having said that, the clients who are in Chris's portfolio love him and you suspect that were Chris to join a competing firm, those

> **CASE STUDY 5.1** (continued)
>
> clients might follow him. Chris has been hinting that he would like a promotion but you have reservations about giving him a job that might create additional stress in his life.
>
> Based on the above situation and the characters described here, make an assessment of what you would do and why. We will return to the case, and to your decision, as we work through ideas of moral imagination.

The historical figure often most associated with the notion of moral imagination as it relates to the notion of 'sympathy' is the Scottish philosopher, Adam Smith. The next section introduces the central role that 'sympathy' plays in his ethical framework and how it relates to moral imagination.

Adam Smith's notion of 'sympathy'

Adam Smith is most widely known for his book the *Wealth of Nations* (Smith [1776] 1863), which is often cited as a justification for reliance on the 'invisible hand' at the centre of free market capitalism. Lesser known is an earlier book, *The Theory of Moral Sentiments* (Smith [1759] 1982), which lays out a theory of ethics grounded in the notion of 'sympathy'. Another Scottish philosopher, David Hume, had introduced the concept of 'sympathy' in his earlier writings, particularly in his *Enquiry Concerning the Principle of Morals* (Hume, 1751). For Hume, sympathy is a 'disposition to communicate and thus share feelings'. Smith builds on this idea, saying that imagination provides the means by which human beings can feel the pain of others. He writes, for example:

> As we have no immediate experience of what other men feel, we can form no idea of the manner in which they are affected, but by conceiving what we ourselves should feel in the like situation . . . it is by the imagination only that we can form any conception of what are his sensations . . . By the imagination we place ourselves in his situation, we conceive ourselves enduring all the same torments. (Smith [1759] 1982, p. 2)

It is important to note that for both Hume and Smith, such imagination was not a 'special' capacity; it was something that by virtue of being human, we share. Although neither of them drew particular attention to the role our bodies play in this kind of knowing, it is often clear in the examples Smith uses that our experience as sentient, embodied beings is the basis of sympathetic understanding. For instance, in a graphic passage Smith describes the general response to watching a man die by hanging (a not uncommon occurrence in Britain in the nineteenth century). He writes of how when watching a person hang, perceivers' bodies themselves twitch in sympathy. Another less extreme example would be illustrated by physical feelings of discomfort we can feel when encountering others who are badly injured. The following activity in Box 5.1 invites you to explore similar experiences you have had yourself.

 BOX 5.1

INDIVIDUAL ACTIVITY: ENGAGING WITH ART TO DEVELOP MORAL SYMPATHY

This activity invites you to visit an art gallery. Ideally, you would physically go to a gallery, but if for any reason that is impossible for you to do, most galleries have online facilities that enable you to view art online. You can spend as long as you like with this activity, but at a minimum you should expect to spend 30 minutes doing this.

Once you are at the gallery, have a walk around and see if there are any artworks that grab your attention. If you are doing this online, browse through the gallery's online collection. Identify one artwork that draws your attention, for whatever reason, and study it carefully. It does not have to be a 'famous' piece of art; in many ways, it is helpful if it is not a well-known painting that many people have views about.

? QUESTIONS TO CONSIDER

1 What is it that you notice about the artwork? For instance, are you captured by the story it conveys to you? Are you riveted by its colours? Is there a sense of energy or peace that it represents? Jot down these first reactions to the work.
2 Now think a bit more deeply about the artwork. Can you imagine what prompted the artist to create it? What do you think they were trying to express, or show to the viewer? What is the emotion behind the work? Can you imagine how it would have felt to create the work?
3 After you have answered these questions, reflect again on how you feel about the artwork. Are you still drawn to it in the same way? Has anything changed about the way in which you see it?

Jot down your experience of doing this. What have you learned about your own process of perception by doing this? What have you learned about your own process of imagination?

This activity aims to provide you with some insight into how your own imagination works. It might reveal to you something about the kind of situation or people that most easily attract you. Generally, there are people and situations that each of us can more easily identify with. For instance, you may find it easy to give money to people begging on the street, or you may even regularly go to a shop and bring that person a sandwich or cup of coffee. Someone else might never consider giving them money or engaging with them in any way, perhaps because they are too far removed from the person and their situation to even imagine responding in such a way. The important point is not whether it is right or wrong to take either action but to notice your habitual response to such a situation. Pay attention to who you find it easy to sympathize with and those who evoke not a shred of sympathetic understanding. Let's return to the Brite Technologies case study in Box 5.2 to explore how your habitual inclinations to sympathize with some rather than others might be influencing your interpretations and judgements in that case.

 BOX 5.2

INDIVIDUAL ACTIVITY: RECONSIDERING BRITE TECHNOLOGIES

Consider the Brite Technologies case study:

 QUESTIONS TO CONSIDER

1 Do any of the characters remind you of people you know in your life?
2 Which of the four characters do you naturally have the most 'sympathy' with? Why is that?
3 Think again about the person you have chosen to make redundant. What is your level of sympathy with that person? What is that sympathy based on?
4 What assumptions go into your understanding of the person, and what are those assumptions based on?

Once again, note your answers in your journal – we will be returning to them throughout the chapter and it is helpful for you to have a record of your thinking process as we go along.

Sympathy in action: the case of the Japanese firm EISAI

As highlighted in the previous section, most of us habitually find some people and situations easier to sympathize with than others. Is it possible to change our 'sympathetic' habits and learn to extend sympathy to those we normally exclude from sympathetic engagement? In an effort to enhance its understanding of patient needs, the Japanese pharmaceutical company Eisai began an initiative which involved sending its staff on 7-day workshops in nursing homes, as well as undertaking medical care observations (Moberg & Seabright 2000). Rather than concentrating efforts on understanding physicians who bought their products, Eisai wanted to better understand end-users' needs. Getting staff out to meet the elderly and ill patients for whom products were bought led to a greater sense of their humanity. Additionally, getting close to the end-users enabled Eisai staff to have a better understanding of how they could improve their products; for instance by making tablets easier to swallow.

The programme expanded until over 1000 of Eisai's employees had taken part in the workshops. Through inviting staff members to meet their products' end-users face to face, the company created a higher level of sympathetic understanding between them which resulted in products which better met patient needs

Although very important, sympathy is just one aspect of moral imagination, however. The next section of the chapter introduces another facet of it, that of metaphorical thinking. In considering what metaphors are and how they enhance the practice of moral imagination, I turn to the work of the contemporary American philosopher, Mark Johnson.

Johnson's view of moral imagination

Moving on to more contemporary ideas concerning moral imagination, the work of Mark Johnson spans the fields of embodiment, philosophy and cognitive science. His book, *Moral Imagination* (Johnson, 1993) provides a thorough explanation of what moral imagination is and how it operates from an embodied perspective. In the early part of his book, Johnson explains in some detail the notion of 'metaphor' and the role it plays in developing moral imagination. In fact, for Johnson, metaphor plays a role more generally in our cognitive understanding, as he suggests that 'our fundamental concepts are metaphorical' (p. 10). What does he mean by this?

A metaphor is a concept that enables us to understand something in terms of something else. You might think that metaphors only exist in the realm of poetry: 'Love is like a red, red rose', but it only takes a bit of reflection to see how often we use metaphors in everyday language. For instance, in describing a person's personality, we might remark: 'She was as cold as ice' or 'He was always operating on a short fuse'. By this we don't mean that she was indeed made of ice or that there was a fuse hanging from his leg that would go off at any moment, but that her way of operating was cold or that he was tense and apt to 'fly off the handle' (another metaphor!) at any time. We regularly use metaphors to convey information, elaborate on things in terms of their qualities or suggest meanings that work 'below' precise description. Gareth Morgan demonstrated the power of bringing metaphorical thinking to the realm of organizations in his book, *Images of Organization* (Morgan, 1986) in which he likened organizations to eight different metaphors, ranging from gardens to psychic prisons. The book powerfully demonstrated that although the overriding metaphor for organizations has been the 'machine' since the Industrial Revolution, other metaphors bring vital, often overlooked aspects of organizations and organizing to the fore. Such alternative views are critical to discovering new ways of dealing with organizational challenges.

Returning to the connection between metaphorical thinking and the ability to act ethically, Mark Johnson suggests that metaphors aid our moral imagination in three key ways:

- They provoke different ways of construing situations and in this way different metaphors provide additional insights to the same phenomenon. For instance, it is possible to notice different aspects of organizations if they are thought of as 'gardens' rather than 'machines'.
- They provide the actual means by which we can understand the nature of morality as such. It is only through metaphorical reasoning that we come to know constructs such as 'justice', 'purpose' or 'compassion'.
- Through metaphor, we can comprehend the differences and similarities between circumstances and thus make judgements about how to approach a specific case. It is interesting to speculate, for instance about how rules about not invading others' privacy might be imagined differently in a time of perceived terrorist threat and possible attack (Johnson, 1993, p. 10).

Underpinning each of these possibilities is the idea that metaphors provide 'a way into' comprehending another's world and circumstances. Returning to the notion that ethics is a way of regulating relations with one another, doing this well requires the capacity to comprehend how your actions might affect another person. We can never know another's experience directly and therefore we must rely on metaphorical thinking to ascertain what a situation is 'like' for the other person.

The next activity in Box 5.3 invites you to work with metaphorical thinking by applying it to the Brite Technologies case study.

BOX 5.3

INDIVIDUAL ACTIVITY: USING MORAL IMAGINATION TO RECONSIDER BRITE TECHNOLOGIES

Consider each of the four people who are potential candidates for redundancy. Could you think of a metaphor to represent each character? For instance, you may think of them each as a different kind of animal. Or you may think of them as a different kind of science fiction character. You may emphasize the time of life they are at by thinking of them as a different representative of an age. You may consider what they contribute to the company by thinking of them in terms of treasures or jewels. You may want to mix your metaphors. Try several different metaphors for each person until you arrive at one that 'fits' each person but that also provides you with a way of regarding the four of them together.

? QUESTIONS TO CONSIDER

1 What additional insight do you gain by thinking of them in this way? What aspects of the situation are revealed that were not revealed before?
2 Do you notice different things if you use different 'types' of metaphor for each person (e.g., if you think of one person as a tree and another as a forklift truck rather than if you imagine them as different examples of the same type of metaphor; for instance, what happens if you think of them all as trees but each as a different type of tree)?
3 Thinking of the circumstances of the case more broadly, what does it mean to you to be made redundant? What would it be like for you to be made redundant (or in fact, if you have been made redundant, what was the experience like)?
4 Have you made others redundant before? What was it like to do so? What is your experience and how does it affect how you view the situation?
5 What do you learn about your own assumptions by doing this exercise?
6 If you are working with other people, compare your responses to this activity. What do you learn from the metaphors others use and how they have worked with them?

There is another way in which the imagination can be used when encountering difficult issues and that is as a means to tap into the ethical wisdom of others. By using your imagination, you can conjecture 'What would (insert the name of the wisest person you know) do in a situation like this?'. Although it is impossible to know precisely how they would handle the situation, just imagining what their response might be can be helpful, and provide options to consider before acting. Referring to others imaginatively in this way can also help lessen the sense of isolation often associated with taking difficult decisions of an ethical nature.

Moral intensity

An idea that works alongside that of metaphorical thinking, which is also critical to moral imagination, is that of 'moral intensity'. This concept was mentioned briefly in the introduction to the chapter. Moral intensity is the experience of having a heightened awareness of how others (either humans or more-than-human agents) might experience a situation from a moral perspective (Jones, 1991). Generally, we tend to experience a higher degree of moral intensity for family members and those with whom we most closely identify. It is easy for us to 'imagine' how our own elderly mother would feel were she standing on a fast-moving train and thus we might more easily extend moral consideration to another elderly woman we encounter in such a situation. Case Study 5.2 demonstrates how one senior manager experienced moral intensity in relation to a situation in her work place.

CASE STUDY 5.2

Eon Group Technologies

Janice, a senior distribution manager, with Eon Group Technologies discovered that one of the key warehouses she was responsible for was sending out goods with faulty electric wiring. Although it was relatively unlikely, the fault could potentially cause injury or, in an extreme case, death, to potential users. On investigating the situation further, she discovered that those packaging the goods and making them ready for shipment knew about the problem but were not alerting senior managers because of their fear of not meeting their shipping targets and thereby losing their bonuses. Janice reported, 'I was appalled by what they were doing! I have two young children, and I kept thinking that if one of my children were hurt – or potentially killed – by a faulty part, how terrible that would be'.

Janice promptly escalated the matter and the faulty products were recalled. The spur for Janice's action was clearly the imaginative leap she took in asking the question, 'How would it be for me if one of my children were hurt by a faulty part?' By imaginatively bringing the affect of such a calamity squarely into her own life, the moral intensity of the situation was heightened. The 'abstract' statistical possibility of such an event occurring was trumped by the imagined possibility of the injury one of her children might suffer. That understanding propelled her into taking action to have the distribution of the product stopped, regardless of the financial cost to the business.

Now reflect on the Eon Group Technologies case study in Box 5.4.

BOX 5.4

REFLECT

 QUESTIONS TO CONSIDER

1 What do you think about the actions Janice took and her reasoning behind them?
2 Have you ever found yourself in a similar situation?
3 Have you ever found that you were the only one who felt strongly about the moral issues involved in a certain situation because you could imagine how the outcome of a decision or action might affect you or those close to you? What did you do in such a situation?

The concept of moral intensity brings us to another aspect of the kind of imagination needed to navigate ethical territory with mastery and that is the notion of the 'caring' imagination. It is, after all, not enough that one can just 'imagine' all manner of catastrophe or danger that our actions (or inactions) might set into motion. We must actively care about those outcomes, an idea that is introduced in the next section.

Developing a caring imagination

In his book, *Embodied Care*, Maurice Hamington focuses on the importance of developing what he calls 'a caring imagination' in order to engage well with ethical situations (Hamington, 2004). This involves going beyond 'just imagining' to bringing a caring orientation to that imaginative process. In particular, it means considering the impact of our actions on others from an affective perspective. What will the felt sense of those affected by particular actions be? From an organizational perspective, a caring imagination would take into account not just the financial impact of a decision but also the impact it will have on the well-being of staff as well as other internal and external stakeholders.

Hamington identifies three key roles of the caring imagination:

- It creates the possibility for empathy.
- It creates the possibility for critical thinking.
- It provides the opportunity for critical application.

Summing these roles up he argues that crucially, 'The caring imagination allows the mind to carry out possibilities in the moral context of a given situation, thus transcending the moment' (2004, p. 68). It is important to highlight that within Hamington's framing of the term, it is also possible to care for the self.

Hamington suggests that engaging the caring imagination involves speculating about what another person's life is like and in this way it 'animates' morality (2004, p. 60). Hamington clearly positions our ability to imagine in this way as an embodied capability. Just as Adam Smith suggested with his idea of 'sympathy', Hamington explicitly argues that the ability to use a caring imagination is grounded in our bodies. We first ask ourselves, 'How would this particular situation "feel" for us?' Then imagination enables us to project ourselves into the space of how it might be for another in the same or a similar situation. This insight intimates that ethics are not just regulated by conscious, cognitive processes but are also intrinsically rooted in our embodied reality as physical beings. The idea that physicality itself is an important source of ethical information will be developed in the section of this book concerning 'taking ethical action'. However, the next activity in Box 5.5 aims to provide you with an experience that will engage you at a more 'embodied' level, thus deepen your appreciation of the power of moral imagination.

 BOX 5.5

GROUP ACTIVITY:
ROLE PLAYING THE BRITE TECHNOLOGIES CASE

Ideally, this activity would take place within a classroom setting, in which there are sufficient people to play the roles of the four characters who might be made redundant, as well as an audience who watch and listen to what is said and done in order to provide additional views.[1]

The role of each of the four people in danger of being made redundant from Brite Technologies needs to be taken up by a member of the group. That is, one person will play the role of Nico, another would be Sally and so on. It is not necessary for roles to be played by individuals of a corresponding gender; in my experience the case reveals additional complexities when men take up the role of Sally, for example, or when women play Nico, Alper or Chris.

Each person taking up a role is invited to create a 'back story' for his or her character. In the back story, they may, for instance, explain the anomalies of their character mentioned in the brief introduction to the case given on page 84. For instance, the reason that Nico is now late and having to take long lunch hours may be because someone in his family is very ill and he has to visit them in hospital or assume additional child care responsibility. There is no 'right' back story here; the important thing is for each character to imagine themselves into a back story which would make sense of the data presented.

Once each character has created his or her back story, they are then invited to share it with the rest of the group as well as to express their experience of working at Brite Technologies. It is critical that each character speaks from the first person perspective and in this way assumes the *persona* of the character they are portraying.

➡

After each person has had the opportunity to present his or her back story and experience of Brite Technologies, the discussion can open amongst the characters or be open to the full classroom for questions. The point of this discussion is to try to understand the motivations, desires, fears, anxieties and hopes of each character.

After you have discussed their motivations with each character, pause now to reflect on how you are feeling about the case and about the decision that needs to be made:

? | **QUESTIONS TO CONSIDER**

1 Given your insights into each of the characters, what is your view about what you should do now?
2 Is there any further information (from the larger organizational system, for instance) that would be useful to have?
3 What insights have you gained that you had not considered before?
4 For those people who 'acted' in the case, what did it 'feel' like to take up this role?
5 What new insights have you developed through doing so?
6 Has your viewpoint changed as a result of undertaking this activity?

As it is written, the Brite Technologies case study provides little in the way of information about the larger organizational system or indeed the wider industry of which it is part. Would different ethical considerations be made, for instance, if the economy a redundant person was facing was robust and thriving as opposed to one in which unemployment is high and generally people are struggling to find work? The business ethicist Patricia Werhane brings our attention to the larger dynamics of the situation in which ethical dilemmas are embedded in her work on moral imagination and systems thinking. We examine her ideas in the next section and consider the additional insight they bring to moral imagination and its practical applications.

Moral imagination and systems thinking

One of the important developments that Patricia Werhane and a number of other business ethicists bring to the field of moral imagination is their systems thinking perspective. A systems thinking orientation encourages us to account for the wider system in which any action rests. As Werhane suggests, 'systems thinking requires conceiving of management dilemmas as arising from within a system with interdependent elements, subsystems, networks of relationships, and patterns of interaction' (Werhane, 2002, p. 33). In other words, in order to understand the full impact of any action or decision, its impact, not just on one part of the system but on how the system works as an intersection of all of these different concerns and realities, needs to be comprehended. In doing so it is important to remember that few systems are 'linear' in the way that they work. Fewer still are actually 'closed'; that is, most systems draw from the environment and emit waste products into it. These characteristics of systems introduce a good deal of complexity when trying to decide what is 'right' or 'wrong' in relation to them.

For instance, let us take an example that many of us would consider being indicative of a morally 'good' act – that of building wells in African countries where water supplies are low and people (often women and children) have to walk many miles each day to access water. Certain aid agencies and NGOs encourage the giving of money to increase the numbers of wells built near African settlements. On first glance, this looks like an ethical action to take.

However, sociologists and anthropologists working in such villages over time can tell a different story. For instance, in her PhD study examining the impact of aid in Africa, Patta Scott-Villiers (2009) demonstrates how in the communities she studied, water wells built by well-meaning charities often disrupted traditional relationships within villages and communities. Her research revealed that people in these communities had long understood how to regulate their water use and how to deal with the impacts of drought and heavy rains. They knew how to manage water within the environmental system of which they were a part. Scott-Villiers' work demonstrated that rather than bringing well-being to African communities, these wells often brought discord, strife and paradoxically, less water resources to communities in the longer term.

This is a striking example of how the desire to do 'good' and to act ethically, within a system that is not deeply understood, can cause more trouble than good. Crucial to creating ethical 'good' then is an appreciation of the history, interrelationships and deeply held knowledge within any system one wishes to influence.

Taking a 'systems thinking' approach demands checking assumptions and asking good and probing questions. Werhane notes the following steps to take to begin to develop a systems orientation:

1. Understanding the history of a place or situation and gaining insight into how the issue being considered has developed.
2. As with moral perception, getting as broad an understanding as possible of who the different stakeholder groups are in the situation and how they

view it. There is usually some kind of rationality behind the way things are done in any system; it is important to understand what that rationality is.

3. Recognizing which stakeholders' views within the system are being prioritized and considering how things might look differently if other stakeholders' views were given priority.
4. Understanding how interactions between different agents in the system work and how they go about reading the system.
5. Always bearing in mind the question of what values are at stake (and whose interests they represent) (Werhane, 2002).

In considering these steps it is important to note that none of them leads to neat answers about what to do next. Returning to the example of African women and children walking many miles to collect water (which means, for instance, that many children do not go to school) – is the solution just to walk away and not intervene in any way? One of the points systems thinking highlights is that we can never *ever* know all of the impacts of any decision we take. This can be paralysing itself. Through systems thinking, what is being offered is the challenge to problematize situations in order to reveal ethical aspects that otherwise remain obscured. This can result in more informed choices in relation to subsequent actions taken.

There is never one way of solving the kind of ethical dilemmas that such problematization raises. Taking ethical action can itself be an imaginative act, as Patricia Werhane points out by highlighting the role imagination plays in finding alternative solutions to seemingly insoluble problems. Case Study 5.3 on the Grameen Bank and its founder Muhammad Yunus is a good example of what can happen when moral imagination and systems thinking align.

CASE STUDY 5.3

The Grameen Bank

The Grameen Bank was established in Bangladesh in 1976 by Dr Muhammad Yunus to provide small loans to the poorest of people who would otherwise not have the capital required to establish their own small businesses. Educated in economics at Vanderbilt University in the USA, Dr Yunus returned to his native Bangladesh and was confronted by the discrepancy between the economic theories he had studied and the reality of the poverty-stricken villagers living near where he taught at Chittagong University.

Through interacting with the villagers, he soon discovered that the amount of finance needed for them to start their own enterprises was minute. He explains that in the first instance, he and his economics students made a list of villagers known to them and the amount of money they needed. Their tally indicated that 40 villages would benefit from a mere $27.00. Dr Yunus loaned the money to them himself. He found this was quickly repaid, and began making further loans, which were also returned. The mounting evidence he began to collect indicating the willingness and ability of the villagers to repay money lent to them was not enough to convince the banks to follow suit. Instead, Dr Yunus established his own bank, the Grameen, or 'village' bank, in 1983. The bank works in drastically different ways from most banks, in that (1) it seeks out the poorest as borrowers; (2) it lends to people who have no collateral; and (3) borrowers join in self-formed groups of five who are together responsible for the repayment of loans taken by their members.

The bank has gone from strength to strength, operates in more than 2500 locations throughout Bangladesh and has spawned similar micro-financing operations throughout the world. Dr Yunus and the Grameen Bank were awarded the Nobel Peace Prize in 2006 for their work in relieving world poverty.

What is interesting about this case from the perspective of moral imagination is how the idea of the Grameen Bank began not from a great imaginative insight, but in a small action aimed to alleviate an immediately apparent situation. In this way it shows that using moral imagination does not necessarily require a grand gesture or a great creative leap. It can come from just asking the question, 'How might I be able to intervene helpfully in this situation, here and now?'

Having been introduced to the Grameen Bank example, let's turn in Box 5.6 to the case of Brite Technologies to consider the extra insight that might be gained by examining it through a systems thinking lens.[2]

BOX 5.6

INDIVIDUAL ACTIVITY: USING SYSTEMS THINKING TO REFLECT ON THE BRITE TECHNOLOGIES CASE

Returning to the case of Brite Technologies, let us consider the decision to make someone redundant from a systems base perspective. Frequently in organizations the decision to make people redundant is taken using the rationale that in making some people redundant, the rest of the system will be able to thrive. Engage your imagination to consider the following:

 QUESTIONS TO CONSIDER

1 From a systems perspective, what questions might be asked that could lead to a different conclusion about the way forward – that is, is there a different way of thinking about the situation that would lead to a different outcome for the firm?
2 From a systems perspective, what will be the impact of letting any one of these four employees go? What knowledge does each of them have that will be absent from the system once they leave?
3 How will making these people redundant affect the larger system and the motivation of those left behind? What skills and knowledge will be lost? How will this affect Brite Technologies' ability to do business?
4 Given these considerations, can you imagine a different way forward for the company?
5 If not, given these considerations, who is now your candidate for redundancy? Why?

Concluding reflections

This chapter has introduced a number of different aspects of moral imagination and how it can assist you in navigating ethical dilemmas. It started by considering Adam Smith's concept of 'sympathy', moved on to the role that 'metaphor' plays in moral imagination, spent time with the idea of the caring imagination and finally, explored the role of systems thinking. This final section of the chapter offers a few summary points and suggests ways in which you might continue to develop your own moral imagination.

Fundamentally, our imaginative capacity enables us to transcend the 'distance' between our own reality and that of others. This can be geographical distance but temporal and cultural distances can also be bridged by this capacity. It allows us to find a way of relating to others we do not know, who may live in lands we have never visited. In this way, it can assist us in answering the question, 'How do I come into the "right relation" with the other especially if the other is from a culture I don't know or understand?' 'How do I develop an appreciation for its norms and why people act in a certain way within it?' Moral imagination provides the means by which we can begin to sympathize with others based on our shared experience of being human (or by projecting ourselves into more-than-human creatures and entities as well).

Second, the imagination enables us to reflect on the moral context of a situation. This allows us to discern that actions that might be wrong in one context may not be wrong in another. A simple example is that of war, in which the taboo against killing another human being is released in the context of armed combat. Similarly, most ethicists would believe that when faced with a situation in which one's life or the lives of one's family members are being threatened, one has the ethical right to 'fight back' and to defend oneself. It is the imagination that enables us to engage in a situation and think of the context in which it is situated. That is why it is so difficult, if not impossible, to create moral laws that can be applied generally which will be correct in any situation. Moral imagination enables us to see how actions and their consequences can be different in varying circumstances.

By enabling us to explore the implications of a particular context, moral imagination broadens any particular field of inquiry. In a similar way to being more aware of the impact of your own identity on how you perceive situations, engaging your imagination when faced with complex situations encourages you to view the situation from many perspectives. It also enables you to 'move things around' and consider different combinations of stakeholders and how they interrelate and influence one another. This is a critical capability in navigating ethical territory well.

Finally, it is important to remember that working with one's imagination means working beyond the goal of trying to find 'one right answer'. The aspiration of engaging moral imagination is to reveal the myriad of different possibilities offered by a given situation and to uncover possible consequences one has not seen before. The task then often becomes choosing between alternatives, none of which is ideal (as in the Brite Technologies case). Calling on the imagination when faced with ethical dilemmas allows for a helpful orientation; it is a way of engaging in 'serious play' around seemingly intransigent issues. It is born from a curiosity about how things fit together and how a decision in one part of the organization may have quite unintended consequences somewhere else. This is especially true when you try to impose one moral system on a different culture where there are different mores and ways of operating in the world. We will discuss cultural influences on ethical understanding in Chapter 9. However, to complete this chapter, let's turn to the case of Brite Technologies one last time in Box 5.7.

BOX 5.7

ACTIVITY: USING MORAL IMAGINATION TO MAKE MORAL CHOICES

Throughout the chapter you have been invited to undertake activities aimed at bringing your attention to a particular aspect of moral imagination. Once again you were prompted to consider how your identity affects what you perceive and your ability to empathize with different people. You were encouraged to consider how using metaphor can extend your understanding of other people or situations. You were encouraged to think of the entire system within which a particular problem sits, and to consider how thinking of the unintended consequences can have an ethical impact on others, even those not yet born. You have considered how the 'caring imagination' works and you have attempted to extend a caring imagination to people you do not normally consider in this way.

This final activity invites you to reflect one last time on the case of Brite Technologies and the answer you gave at the beginning of the chapter about who you would choose to make redundant. Given what you have thought about and worked with as you have gone through this chapter, how do you now see the options about who to make redundant? Have you changed your view? If so, how has this come about? How are you seeing that situation differently from the way you saw it at the beginning of the chapter?

Going beyond that case, reflect on the following:

 QUESTIONS TO CONSIDER

1 What has surprised you about what you have learned about yourself from the information in this chapter?
2 Are there any new habits that you will try to foster, such as asking yourself who else is involved in problematic situations and how will they be impacted by any decisions you make?
3 What have you learned about your capacity to empathize with those you do not know?
4 Who do you find it easy to empathize with? How might you extend your circle of empathy just a little bit more?

Discuss your answers with your learning group or with a friend. What have you learned from revisiting this case on a number of different occasions?

Having completed Chapters 4 and 5, you have built another layer of foundation on the way to ethical mastery. As we move to the next level, you will continue to use these capacities but they will not come to the fore as much as they have here. In the next section, we begin to consider the possibility of ethical action; both through decision-making processes but also through embodied enactments. An exploration of these capabilities opens the door to the next stage of ethical mastery.

NOTES

1 The idea for enacting this case as a role play originated with an MBA project undertaken by Mark Grenfell-Shaw, Ilan Pragaspathy and Evgenia Asimova, who I am grateful to for the idea and also for permission to use their work in this chapter.

2 For more information about the work of Dr Yunus and the Grameen Bank, see his book, Banker to the Poor: The Story of the Grameen Bank (Yunus, 1998).

Level III

Practices towards action

6

Building blocks for ethical action

The first half of this book has concentrated on the importance of perceptual processes in your ability to engage with situations from an ethical perspective. The notion of 'moral perception' was introduced and the role that cognitive schemas play in how situations are framed and understood was considered. 'Moral imagination' and the role it plays in enabling you to become aware of the impact your actions may have on a variety of others were explored. In this way you have been introduced to the notion that moral imagination 'closes the gap' between you and your understanding of others across geographic, social and even temporal divides. All of this work has been primarily concerned with the cognitive aspects of ethical engagement: noticing, imagining and seeing the connections between actions you take and how those actions affect others.

This kind of perceptual awareness is critical to ethical engagement. However, sooner or later, ethical engagement demands decisions and subsequent actions (even if that decision is positively to 'do nothing'). How do you make good ethical decisions and take appropriate ethical action? This chapter introduces three key building blocks for moving into this territory: 'negative capability', 'timing' and 'practising caring habits'. Let's begin by considering what 'negative capability' is and how it connects to taking ethical decisions and action.

Negative capability

The term 'negative capability' sounds slightly paradoxical; in what way can something that is 'negative' be a good thing? Here, the term 'negative' relates to the ability to 'not do' and especially to 'not do' in a reactive way. The English poet and philosopher John Keats describes it as: 'The ability to live with uncertainty and not knowing and to do so without grasping after action, without irritability' (Keats, 1970, p. 43).

The British management academics Peter Simpson, Robert French and Charles Harvey have written extensively on the topic and suggest that 'negative capability' is a key capacity for managers and leaders to develop in order to deal effectively with difficult and unknown situations (Simpson et al., 2002). In contrast to the 'positive capability' of decisive action, they suggest that 'negative capability' enables a person to engage in 'reflective non-action'. In many ways then, one needs 'negative capability' to enact much of what has already been introduced in this book. Without it, it would be impossible to pause sufficiently to engage in the inquiring and imagining required of moral perception and moral imagination.

It will be dawning on you that 'negative' is not used here in the normal sense, where something categorized as negative is 'bad' or to be avoided. Instead, it may be helpful to think of the term 'negative' here as analogous to that of the 'negative' charge within a magnetic circuit. You need both positive and negative charges to create such a circuit. Similarly, both positive and negative capabilities are required to enact effective ethical action. Whereas much attention generally goes on the activities of decision-making and enacting those decisions within ethical debates, here we shall dwell on the benefits of not deciding and not acting in the first instance when confronted with an ethical dilemma.

Does 'negative capability' mean doing nothing at all? No, that's not a useful position either. In fact, when engaging in 'negative capability', one is perhaps at one's most attentive and alive. This is because it involves actively observing, listening and waiting. As intimated in previous parts of the book, waiting or inquiring, especially if one is feeling pressure or has framed the situation as being critical, can be very difficult. It often means containing strong emotions and impulses, rather than immediately acting on feelings of anxiety, uncertainty and fear. This is not a passive kind of relaxed stance to take. A good deal of psychological work is often required in order to contain anxieties and emotions and reflect on a situation well.

Perhaps a way into thinking about what negative capability requires, is to consider its opposite. Drawing on the work of Needleman (1990), Simpson et al. suggest that the opposite of 'negative capability', or containment, is 'dispersal', which represents itself in 'explanations, emotional reactions and physical action' (2002, p. 1221). Often, behind such behaviours is the need to 'be right', to 'save face' or to protect one's ego. Of course, these are all 'normal' reactions, especially when fear and uncertainty are around. Exercising 'negative capability' often requires humility and the ability to put one's ego to the side in order to do what is best for the situation. Along similar lines, Hutter writes that it requires the capacity to 'tolerate a loss of self and a loss of rationality by trusting in the capacity to recreate oneself in another character or another environment' (Hutter, 1982, p. 305).

'Negative capability' is a very different kind of competency than that prized by most leaders and managers of organizations. After all, managers and leaders are paid 'to do', to sort things out, to solve problems, rather than *not* to do. The ability to say nothing, Simpson et al. point out, is not readily cultivated in Western societies in particular.

How do you *do* 'negative capability'?

What are the behaviours associated with 'negative capability'? Simpson and his colleagues suggest three: waiting, observing and listening. Although at first glance these appear to be relatively passive pursuits, what makes them more active is the *way* you engage with them. Waiting does not mean just sitting back and doing 'nothing'; instead it involves concentrated attention. This kind of waiting creates space in which new information can emerge and the possibility for new patterns to be seen. This leads naturally to Simpson and his colleagues' second behaviour – 'observing'. The previous chapters on perception have already signalled the importance of observing what you are observing. This way of observing is an active process, especially when you try to become aware of what you are *not* seeing as well as what you are seeing.

Finally, listening is absolutely critical. In a case study introduced by Simpson and his colleagues in order to demonstrate how 'negative capability' works in practice, people from four different nationalities are trying to create an organization together. Although translators are used to help individuals to communicate, the central figure in the case study highlights the importance of listening to the meaning *behind* the language spoken. He mentions how easy it is for language to obscure, as well as to reveal meaning. The kind of listening required of 'negative capability' attends to meanings below the level of words, to the emotional content of what is going on as well as to the contextual resonances that underpin interchanges. Once again, in this kind of listening, it is important to be able to put one's own frame to the side, to listen wholeheartedly to what the other is trying to say, without a judgement about what they 'should' be saying.

An historic example of 'negative capability' in action is portrayed in the case of the Cuban missile crisis that occurred during the Kennedy administration in the USA in 1962. Let's use that event in Case Study 6.1 as an example to explore how negative capability works in practice.

CASE STUDY 6.1

The Cuban missile crisis

The Cuban missile crisis refers to the escalation in tensions between the USA and the Soviet Union during October 1962. The particular event that sparked the crisis is often cited as US surveillance intelligence that revealed the placement of missile launchers on the island of Cuba with the ability to strike the USA mainland. The US government, headed by President John F. Kennedy and his National Security Council had to decide what action to take in response to what they perceived as an aggressive act on the part of the Soviets.

It is important to elaborate on the broader context within which the Cuban missile crisis was situated before diving into the detail of those particular 13 days. First, this event occurred within the context of the Cold War between the United States of America and the Soviet Union. Within the USA there was a general fear of the spread of communism. Fidel Castro's rise to power and his commitment to Marxism fostered a sense of unease within many American citizens. Prior to the Cuban missile crisis the Kennedy administration had been embroiled in a failed attempt to support 'freedom fighters' within Cuba to overthrow Castro's government – an event known as the 'Bay of Pigs Invasion'.

Given the heightened tensions during this time, a question that historians and political philosophers who have studied the case ponder is: 'How did American leaders manage to stay cool-headed enough for the demands of nuclear crisis diplomacy?' (Guttieri et al., 1995, p. 601), for indeed, this was a crisis of potentially epic proportions. As Graham Allison wrote in his article concerning the conceptual models with which the Americans approached the crisis: 'this was a "seminal event" with a higher probability that more human lives would end suddenly than ever before in history with over 100 million Americans threatened, as well as 100 million Russians, as well as Europeans who would be caught in the cross fire' (Allison, 1969, p. 689).

Part of the answer to how they managed to 'keep cool' in this crisis was the 'negative capability' demonstrated by President John F. Kennedy and his advisors.[1] Certainly, however, Kennedy and his team did not just 'sit there' and 'do nothing'. In his article outlining the key events of the crisis, Allison recounts how one of Kennedy's first actions was to assemble his Executive Committee, known as ExComm, who were told to 'set aside all other tasks to make a prompt and intense survey of the dangers and possible courses of action'. Most of the action then taken was involved in 'canvassing all the possible tracks and weighing the arguments for and against each' (ibid., p. 696).

Together, ExComm developed six possible courses of action, from 'do nothing' (which was ruled out because it would make America more vulnerable to the possibility of attack from the Soviet Union) to a surgical strike aimed at disabling the missiles that were being established (which was ruled out due to the likelihood of the confrontation being escalated and lives being lost in Europe) to declaring a 'quarantine' around Cuban waters, thereby not allowing the landing of any further missiles. (The US administration chose the word 'quarantine' rather than 'embargo' as to embargo the waters would have been seen as an act of war.) The latter action

CASE STUDY 6.1 *(continued)*

was chosen, which indeed represented a 'middle way' in responding to the threat – it was not doing 'nothing', but it was not engaging in armed conflict either.

President Kennedy made his rationale clear in a speech given to American citizens on 22 October 1962 in which he said:

> Above all, while defending our own vital interests, nuclear powers must avert those confrontations which bring an adversary to a choice of either a humiliating retreat or nuclear war. To adopt that kind of course of action in the nuclear age would be evidence only of the bankruptcy of our policy and of a collective deathwish for the world.[2]

There are a number of aspects of the USA's response that are important to note in relation to 'negative capability'. First, Kennedy did not try to manage this issue on his own. He assembled a team of people with various expertise and perspectives to come together to present and discuss their differing viewpoints. He made it clear that their purpose was to 'explore all possible courses of action' and 'weigh each one against the other' before acting.

Much was at stake, and there were many unknowns. Understanding the situation from the Soviet viewpoint was critical. Just why was the Soviet Union flexing its muscles in this way? Prior to the installation of the missiles, the USA and Soviets had been enjoying a spell of relative détente. How would the Soviets respond to any military show of strength? How accurate was the surveillance? How far could the USA push without forcing Khrushchev into a position in which he would need to 'save face' in a strong way in order to appease his own population?

After a very tense 13 days, Soviet ships did indeed turn back and did not infringe on the American quarantine of the island. This was after a number of nail-biting events that included the shooting down of an American surveillance plane and the death of its pilot, as well as a period of time in which it appeared that a Soviet ship was breaking the embargo. On each of those occasions, Kennedy and his team had to exercise the 'negative capability' of waiting to see what would happen next instead of responding with knee-jerk reactions. This was despite there being pressure within ExComm itself to meet the crisis with military force.

In the end, military conflict was avoided and Khrushchev managed to save face in a way that facilitated the missiles being removed from Cuba. However, in retrospect Kennedy's choice of non-action, rather than action, was seen to be courageous and wise. In all likelihood, his ability to exercise negative capability enabled the world to pull back from the brink of a globally catastrophic armed conflict.

Box 6.1 helps you to reflect further on the benefits of non-action.

  BOX 6.1

INDIVIDUAL ACTIVITY: REFLECTING ON NON-ACTION

Can you recall a circumstance you have faced in your life (either at work or home, or in other social situations) in which the best action was 'non-action'?

? QUESTIONS TO CONSIDER

1 What were the circumstances?
2 How did you identify that the best thing to do was to wait?
3 What was the result of your waiting?
4 What enabled you to wait?
5 How did you know in the end that this had been the correct action?
6 Can you recall a similar situation where you wish you would have waited, rather than acted?
7 What were the circumstances in this situation?
8 Were you under pressure to take a certain course of action? Where did this pressure originate and what were the agendas of those applying this pressure?
9 What were the consequences of your action?
10 In retrospect, what would you do differently if faced with a similar situation?

Note your reflections down in your learning journal. What do you learn from re-evaluating these situations?

Hopefully, your reflections will allow you to see that perception plays a pivotal role in being able to 'activate' 'negative capability'. This is because you need to be able to take a moment and *notice* that the situation you find yourself in requires or could benefit from time 'not acting' or 'not deciding'.

A note of caution

All of this attention to the importance of being able to 'not act' brings to mind a story told to me by an MBA student about how he had experienced 'ethics' operating in his organization:

This company had recently established a comprehensive code of conduct for its operations, which the student saw as a helpful step in formalizing its stance on particular matters. However, it soon became apparent to him that the high-profile 'ethics' in the firm could also be misused. In particular, one senior manager seemed to cite the code of ethics as an excuse for not taking any action at all. When faced with difficult decisions, he began to suggest that there were 'ethical issues' involved and the ethics committee had to take a look at the implications. In this student's view the manager was using the ethics committee as a delaying tactic for decisions he did not want to take. Sometimes, this delaying had ethical implications itself, for instance when decisions that had an impact on others' ability to move forward inhibited good customer relations. As the student summed up his concern: 'How do you know you are not hiding behind ethics [or in this case 'negative capability'] as a way of avoiding doing your job?'

This question points to a concept introduced by Greek philosophers attending to a similar issue – that of *akrasia*. *Akrasia* is 'moral laziness'. It amounts to knowing what you 'ought to do' in a situation but not doing it. A very simplistic example is when you find yourself walking down the street and you are confronted by trash left by someone else. Do you pick the rubbish up and deposit it into the nearest waste bin or do you leave it there for someone else to deal with? A more significant example of *akrasia* is when you know you ought to alert someone to the peculiar accounting practices appearing in your firm's books but you decide to ignore them.

The difference between *akrasia* and 'negative capability' is that in a situation of *akrasia*, you *do* know what needs to be done from a moral perspective. For instance in the example above, picking up the trash is the correct act. Doing *something* with your observations about the accounting practices – if only making inquiries about what is going on – shows greater ethical mettle than turning a blind eye. In truth, only you yourself can know whether your response to a given situation is borne from 'negative capability' or moral laziness.

Box 6.2 helps you to reflect on a time when non-action was not the best response.

BOX 6.2

ACTIVITY: REFLECTING ON NON-ACTION AGAIN!

Reflect on a situation that you recognized as having an ethical dimension that you should have responded to, but you did nothing.

 QUESTIONS TO CONSIDER

1 What were the circumstances that led you to do nothing?
2 In retrospect, are there actions you wish you had taken?
3 What has been the impact of your lack of action on others? How has your lack of action affected you?
4 Presented with a similar situation in the future, what would you do differently?
5 What advice would you give to someone else faced with a similar situation?

Note your responses to these questions in your learning journal. If you are working within a group, discuss these issues with them. It is often extremely helpful to exchange these sorts of stories and learn how others have dealt with or not dealt with similar issues.

The next section of the chapter turns to the second building block for taking ethical action: developing a sense of 'timing'.

Choosing your moment: the ethics of 'timing'

The Cuban missile crisis shows how John F. Kennedy and his team successfully enacted 'negative capability' in their handling of that situation. Of course, he and his ExComm did take action; however, another critical aspect of their actions concerns *when* they decided to act and with what level of force. '*Kairos*' is the Greek notion of 'timing', which speaks to this aspect of judging how and with what force to act in response to situations.

Kairos is a central concept in much of Greek philosophy, where it underpins approaches to ethics, aesthetics, epistemology and the practice of rhetoric. It comprises two aspects, each of which informs appropriate ethical action: 'right time' and 'right proportion'. More elaborate versions of the concept include definitions such as, 'a significant moment of crystallisation, a turning point or things coming together in a specific, particular way' (Hoskin, 2004, p. 744) or 'the cosmic force bringing opposites into harmony for a particular moment in time' (Bartunek and Necochea, 2000, p. 104). For the Greek philosopher Pythagoras, *kairos* is 'the most important thing in every action' (Untersteiner, 1954, p. 2). Indeed, Plato made *kairos* an essential aspect of the ability one has to act with virtue and Aristotle developed this notion further with his concept of the virtuous act being positioned between two extremes.

Kairos involves both knowing the moment to act and also apprehending how the act should be carried out. For instance, it may be the right time to prevent a child from hitting another child but the force one uses to do so will depend on a number of contextual factors: the age difference between the children (a different approach might be used to stop a toddler from hitting her teenage brother, for example, than would be appropriate if the hitting is going on between two teenagers), the potential harm that could be caused, the way in which the conflict arose in the first place, and even the psychological disposition of the children themselves. Being able to assess all of these aspects of the situation and then respond appropriately is an act of *kairos*.

Knowing the 'right time'

How does one know when 'the right time' is? Amelie Frost Benedikt tackles this question in a book chapter called 'On doing the right thing, at the right time'. In it she suggests that becoming apt at working with 'kairotic moments' first requires an effort to 'recognise opportunities and become more sensitive to the "critical character" of particular moments' (Benedikt, 2002, p. 227). The ability to do this often calls on imagination because the 'facts' are often not laid out clearly and unambiguously. For instance, in assessing the 'right moment' to act, you might ask yourself questions such as:

- What have been the significant instances that have led to this particular moment? What is their rhythm and frequency?
- How will various options for action I am considering taking fit into the overall pattern of engagement to date? For instance, if there is a pattern of stand-taking and withdrawal, how do my actions feed into that pattern? Will they exacerbate and agitate a system that has its own rhythm of interaction?
- How might the action I am about to take be judged in years to come? Or, in fact, what will the headline in the newspaper be tomorrow?

Being aware of *kairos* helps you to consider the temporal nature of any decision and to ask the critical question, 'Is this the right time to undertake this action?' This question played a key role in another moment in US history; the case of the FBI's conflict with the Branch Davidians in Waco, Texas in 1993. Let's look at this in a bit more depth in Case Study 6.2 in order to understand the role 'timing' played as events unfolded.

CASE STUDY 6.2

The Branch Davidians in Waco, Texas

Even 20 years after the FBI's storming of the 'Branch Davidians' compound near Waco, Texas there is no definitive account of events leading to the conflict that resulted in the death of 76 people, including 20 children. However, most sources seem to agree on the following chronology of key happenings:

- On 28 February 1993, officials from the Federal Bureau of Alcohol, Tobacco and Firearms (ATF) served warrants on the Branch leader, David Koresh, to investigate claims that firearms were being stockpiled in the compound. Instead of allowing the premises to be searched, a gun battle broke out between the federal officials and sect members, resulting in the deaths of four federal agents and six 'Davidians'. (Interestingly, the ATF had chosen 28 February to serve its warrant as, being a Sunday, it believed the Davidians would have locked away their guns in respect for Sunday as a day of rest and prayer.)
- The Federal Bureau of Investigation (FBI) took over from the ATF, as it was deemed to be more skilled in handling 'hostage negotiations'. The situation was reframed as one where hostages were involved, particularly given the number of women and children living within the compound. At this point in time, negotiations between the FBI and Koresh began.
- On 1 March, ten children were released from the compound.
- Koresh promised to surrender twice, on 3 and 7 March, but did not emerge from the compound.
- Koresh's mother hired an attorney to defend him on 12 March. The attorney began to contribute to the negotiations.
- On 1 April, the attorney concluded that negotiations had achieved all that they could. Koresh announced that he would leave the compound after Passover, which would end on 13 April.
- Koresh did not exit the compound, claiming he needed another 14 days to finish the interpretation of the Seven Seals he was working on.
- On 19 April, the FBI stormed the compound, leading with tear gas. Fires broke out and all of those within the compound perished.

In reading through both journalistic and academic accounts of this conflict, the role 'timing' played on both sides is very apparent. From the FBI's perspective, it was imperative to resolve the conflict as quickly as possible within 'chronological', rather than 'kairotic' time. The fact that agents from the ATF had been killed exacerbated the felt need for those responsible to be brought to account quickly. Each time David Koresh set a date to leave the compound but did not do so, ratcheted up the mounting pressure for 'justice to be done'.

It also seems that each time Koresh reneged on his promise, he was seen to be 'in control' and setting the time scales for events. It could also be assumed that the FBI were keen to avoid the conflict extending to 28 April, which would have been the two-month mark of the conflict, again in relation to 'chronological' time.

In their paper, which analyses the situation from the perspective of music theory, Steven Albert and Graham Bell (2002) suggest that David Koresh could be interpreted to have been operating from a different sense of time, one more aligned with kairotic, Biblically-based cycles. His choice of 'after Passover' as a date by which he would leave the compound indicated his connection to such kairotic moments from a Biblical perspective. His request for an additional two weeks after the end of Passover could have been aligned to Ascension Day, which would have occurred on 28 April. Had the FBI been more aware of key Biblical timings they might have insisted that the interpretation should be carried out within 40 days, which is timing associated with Biblical figures ranging from Moses to Jesus himself (who spent 40 days fasting in the desert). Another alternative kairotic reframing would have been to suggest that the Davidians needed to be released by 15 April, which is 'tax day' in the USA. Such a suggestion would have highlighted a different kairotic cycle and may have altered the temporal dynamic of the conflict.

It is, of course, impossible to know if a different outcome would have resulted if the FBI had acted from a sense of kairotic, rather than chronological timing. However, the question remains as to whether or not the FBI got their 'timing' right in this circumstance.

In Box 6.3 is a series of questions that will help you reflect on your own sense of timing.

BOX 6.3

ACTIVITY: REFLECTING ON YOUR SENSE OF 'TIMING'

Think of a situation you have been involved in where 'timing' played a key role, such as asking for a raise, telling your partner you want to separate from them, deciding to look for a new job or deciding to go travelling: ➡

QUESTIONS TO CONSIDER

1 What aspects of 'timing' were you aware of?
2 If other people were involved, how aware were you of their time horizons and key moments?
3 Did you take these into account as you planned your own action?
4 Is there anything about the timing of your action you wish you had done differently or that you think was particularly apt?
5 What did you learn about timing from this experience?

Developing a sense of timing

In their article Albert and Bell suggest that timing involves 'understanding the mechanisms which create and release tension, that generate a sense of movement and pattern, and that stimulate the need for and produce closure and rest' (2002, p. 574). Prior to writing about the Branch Davidian case, Steven Albert wrote an article in which he offers five key points to consider when trying to judge when the 'right time' to act is. They are:

- *The person* (or the decision-making unit). The 'right time' should be determined by *who* is doing the acting as much as by the act itself. People with different levels of power within organizations, for instance, can affect actions in different ways and therefore need to be aware of the level of effect they might have in a situation. For instance, it may seldom be the right time for a CEO to admonish an organizational member located at the bottom of the organization's hierarchy.
- *The properties of the action.* What kind of action is called for in the situation? Is it continuous or will it unfold in a series of events? How long will it be necessary to maintain the action? How quickly will it develop to its full effect and how will it tail off? These aspects are what Albert calls the action's 'signature'.
- *The plot.* What are the different 'story lines' that are coming together to create the situation? How do they interact? Recalling the Cuban missile crisis once again, a key plot element that underpinned that event was the 'Bay of Pigs' failure that had occurred shortly beforehand. Kennedy would have wanted to avoid a similar outcome. What he had learned from that experience would have informed his actions in October 1962. The plot lines affecting Khrushchev would also be important to take into account, as well as the burgeoning relationship between the Soviet Union and Cuba. Understanding the logic of the plot as it unfolds is

critical to deciding where you might be in it, and what appropriate action might accompany your role.

- *The purpose.* What is the overall purpose to be achieved? Different actions would have been suitable – for instance, if ExComm's overall purpose had been framed as demonstrating their military might to the Soviet Union, rather than preventing the loss of millions of lives around the globe. In the case of the Branch Davidians, it was unclear what the prime purpose of the FBI was; was it to save as many of the people in the compound as possible or was it to end the conflict as quickly as possible? As the FBI discovered, these two purposes proved to be irreconcilable.

- *Positioning rules.* This is an understanding of the way in which the previous four aspects interact. For instance, if I am CEO and my purpose is to grow the company that I lead, then particular activities need to be done at specific times. Amelie Frost Benedikt summarizes this idea by suggesting that: '[it is a question of] the right person doing the right thing at the right time and for the right reasons' (2002, p. 233).

Although the final point suggests a formulaic quality that itself seems in conflict with *kairos*, what is clear is the requirement for person, action and purpose to align in order to create appropriate action. The following activity in Box 6.4 invites you to play with the applicability of Albert and Bell's framework by using it to analyse an ethical dilemma you have previously faced.

 BOX 6.4

ACTIVITY: MAPPING A TIMELINE

Identify an ethical dilemma you have had to resolve in the past. Write down a brief summary of the event, the people involved, what was at stake and if it is an event that has finished, how it was concluded.

Now consider the timing involved with the event. What were the critical points within the event's unfolding that you can now recognize in retrospect?

? QUESTIONS TO CONSIDER

1 Map the event out on a timeline. What were the significant incidents as the situation unfolded? What was their 'signature'; that is, how often and regularly did they occur? What was the temporal space between them?
2 What were the underlying 'plots' informing the situation? What were the different stories that underpinned people's engagement with the issue?
3 How long had the situation been developing?

➡

←

4 What was the quality of its development (had it happened very quickly, was it sprung on you suddenly or had it been simmering for some time)?

5 In terms of the possible solutions, what was the quality of their timing (i.e., would they have to happen in a very short period of time, could they themselves evolve)?

6 What was the overall purpose to which any action was directed? Was the purpose shared by all of those involved in the situation?

7 What role did timing play in the eventual outcome? How might you have timed your own involvement differently? How did you make a decision about when to act, as well as what to do?

Discuss the situation with someone else, either in your learning team or with another individual who was not involved in the situation. Notice in particular, those 'choice-point' moments when you could have done one thing or the other. How did they arise? Did you recognize them at the time, and if you did, how did you do so?

What do you learn about ethical action by considering your own ethical dilemma through the lens of *kairos*? How will you take this learning forward into the future?

Note your reflections in your learning journal.

The second aspect of *kairos*: appropriate quality of action

As has been mentioned previously, *kairos* is not just about 'timing'; it is also about *how* you respond in a given situation. You can get the timing right but if you overplay or underplay the action, an ethically undesirable outcome can still occur. Returning again to the Cuban missile crisis, the USA could have responded 'at the right time' but if that response had been overly aggressive, a negative outcome could have resulted. In particular, the USA did not want to back the Soviets into a corner that meant their only way of saving face would have been to attack.

Considering the Branch Davidian case, it could be argued that the force used by the officials was excessive (especially given the number of women and children still located within the compound). However, given that federal agents had died in a previous gun battle with Davidians, and the amount of firepower stockpiled, the FBI would have made assumptions about the force required for them to defend themselves.

How does one determine the quality and force needed to resolve ethical situations? The answer to that question depends on one's discernment. The first step in developing such judgement is to become acutely aware of the quality and force of others' interventions, and particularly to notice those that are accomplished with appropriateness and grace. The USA-based management scholar, Steven Taylor, offers an idea that I think is useful here – that of 'little beauties'. 'Little beauties', writes Taylor, are '[t]hose small moments when an office wit makes a particularly cunning remark, when a tempered radical (Meyerson, 2001) speaks truth to power in a perfectly elegant way, when some small thing works perfectly' (Taylor, 2012, p. 72).

Achieving 'little beauties' requires a particular kind of knowledge, Taylor argues – that associated with 'craft'. That is, in order to be able to judge an intervention 'perfectly' so that it has the quality as well as the timing inherent to *kairos,* you need to practise doing the sort of intervention you want to perfect. The office wit practises their timing and learns to pick up the dynamics associated with jokes 'falling flat' rather than provoking laughter. They learn how to judge the mood of a room full of people and how to ease back when a crowd becomes too rowdy. The mediator practises working with opposing sides and learns how to judge when to push, when to back off, when to speak and when to keep silent. We will discuss different behaviours that can be practised in more depth in the final part of this chapter. For now, however, the important point is that developing the aspect of *kairos* involved with making judgements about the correct quality of a response is only possible through practice, through attending to situations and their points of tension and release.

Leading on from this, Bartunek and Necochea point out that both Greek and Biblical perspectives on *kairos* suggest that 'a person who experiences what seems to be a *kairos* moment usually does not know exactly what must be done in response. However, it is clear that it is urgent to respond in some way, even without knowing the ultimate truth of the situation' (Bartunek and Necochea, 2000, p. 105). In other words, you do not need to know exactly what to do in response to a kairotic moment. Finding some way of taking advantage of such moments *is* crucial, however. Otherwise, as Benedikt points out 'opportunities really do come and go, whether anyone sees them or not, or seizes them or not' (p. 227).

The Cuban missile crisis demonstrates this point precisely. Neither President Kennedy nor his ExComm team knew the 'ultimate truth' of their situation but at key points action was necessary. The choice to create a naval blockade preventing the landing of further missiles was one of the strategic actions taken, and history suggests it was taken at the right time and with the correct level of force. In this way ExComm fashioned a middle-road response – one that enabled Khrushchev to save face while at the same time protecting American interests. Crafting actions that are delivered with 'just the right amount of weight and force' is a talent that needs to be cultivated, as any person who works at mastering a set of behaviours knows.

The final building block for ethical action highlights certain behaviours that can be practised on a day-to-day basis, thereby forming a solid underpinning for taking ethical action.

Practising caring habits

The capacity to act ethically in a particular circumstance is based on a foundation of more broadly based ethical behaviour. In his book *Embodied Care*, the American philosopher Maurice Hamington offers three 'caring habits' which serve as the basis for an ethical orientation in one's dealings with others (Hamington, 2004). They are: active listening, seeking out the other, and practising participation. The final part of the chapter reviews each in turn.

Active listening

The work of the American writer and activist Jane Addams and her social project, Hull House in Chicago, serve as the basis for much of Hamington's understanding of caring habits:

> Hull House was launched by Jane Addams and her friend Ellen Gates Starr in Chicago in 1889. Initially established to provide art and literary education for Chicago's less fortunate citizens, the activities offered by the house soon expanded to include practical classes intended to help immigrants integrate into American society. It soon developed into a key meeting place between those of different socio-economic classes, faiths, races and nationalities. It became a central resource for the less advantaged and socially destitute of Chicago to receive practical care and assistance in times of need.
>
> One of the most important day-to-day practices undertaken within Hull House was active listening. Addams supported the idea that people needed to know one another intimately in order to develop sympathy towards each other, and the most basic way in which such sympathy was formed was through active listening. She herself spent many hours listening to the stories of prostitutes and others who found themselves in difficult life positions. Through listening, she developed practical ways of helping, ranging from providing no-interest loan schemes to establishing soup kitchens to taking care of children or helping out in homes when people were sick.

Active listening is, just as it says, an engaged process that requires the listener to attend not just with their ears but also with their heart and emotional response to the other. It requires letting go of the judgements we might have of the other in order to really put ourselves in their shoes, and, as much as possible, to experience the world as they do. As was suggested in the previous chapter concerning moral imagination, it is only through such active engagement that the requisite quality of sympathy toward the other can be developed, which subsequently leads to an increased ability to make sound ethical judgements in relation to them.

Before we can actively listen to another, however, we must first 'seek them out', and this is the second habit that Addams and Hamington offer.

Seeking out the other

In our day-to-day lives it is easy to move from one group we feel comfortable with and know well to another group we are similarly at ease with. This may make for a contented way of living but it also results in seldom encountering those from different backgrounds or who experience the world differently from the way we do. Addams was adamant that in order to develop sympathy towards the other, we had to *know* others, as it is impossible to care for those we do not know. Her philosophy emphasizes the need for those who want to develop their ethical awareness to seek out those different from themselves in order to extend their circle of ethical awareness.

There are a number of ways of achieving this. For instance, Addams advocates the use of literature and theatre for understanding the plight of others. Today, she might have recommended Alice Walker's *The Color Purple* for its insights into the plight of African American women in the early twentieth century or Khaled Hosseini's book *The Kite Runner* for the window it offers into the world of those living through the conflicts in Afghanistan. In today's context, she would probably have also recommended film as a powerful medium for engaging emotionally in others' worlds. For instance, Steve McQueen's film, *12 Years a Slave* provides a potent and emotionally gruelling encounter with one man's experience of slavery.

As powerful as books or films can be, however, Addams is clear that they are no substitute for the information gained through being physically present with the other. Only through such proximity is it possible to pick up the subtle embodied cues that inform us of what the other's situation is 'really' like. The shudder of pain that runs through the young mother's body as she talks about her sick child or the lacklustre heaviness that accompanies her loss of hope are transmitted through bodily presence. It is through such lived encounters with the other that sympathetic knowing is developed at a visceral level.

Furthermore, rather than just waiting for others to approach us, Addams encourages us to actively seek out those we would otherwise not meet. She goes as far as to suggest that actively seeking out the other is a core ethical practice, for without it we cannot develop the requisite capacity for sympathetic engagement. This recommendation on Addams' part leads to the final caring habit: practising participation.

Practising participation

Finally, after the previous five chapters, which may seem to be more about 'not' taking action rather than acting, it must be admitted that ethics (at the end of the day) only come to life through their lived enactment. Jane Addams accentuates this point, writing: 'the sphere of morals is the sphere of action . . . that a situation does not really become moral until we are confronted with the question of what shall be done in a concrete case and we are obliged to act upon our theory' (Addams, 2002, p. 119). In particular, she suggests that ethics is ultimately about taking social acts and that becoming skilled within this domain can be developed through practising participation.

How can participation be 'practised'? Isn't participating something you do when you are called forward to do so rather than being something one can practise? Addams argues that on the contrary, getting involved with others in pursuit of mutual interests can be deliberately undertaken. Through such engagement, it is possible to learn how to assert influence, how to give and take and, most importantly, how others see the world and the particular situation at stake. Actively going out of one's way to get involved, particularly with people you might normally not meet, is an activity that builds your capacity to relate to others through the sympathetic knowledge such interaction fosters.

Practising participation on a regular basis builds the foundation for the kind of understanding required for making sound ethical decisions in relation to others. When subsequently faced with a difficult ethical dilemma, such practice enables you to draw from a well of experience in order to find an appropriate way forward. The next activity in Box 6.5 provides you with the opportunity to practise participation.

BOX 6.5

ACTIVITY: LEARNING FROM NEW 'OTHERS'

Identify a socially oriented cause that you feel some affiliation to. It could be anything from helping to save the dwindling bee population to supporting community development in your local area, to supporting the cause of women and children in a war-torn or disease-stricken area in a country other than your own.

Once you have focused on a particular cause, investigate the ways in which you might get involved. Do a bit of study about the history of the particular cause and the circumstances it arose from. Find out about the different groups or charities that are engaged in the cause. Find out if there is any local branch of the group or people who are working alongside it.

Connect with that group in some way. Notice I am not necessarily suggesting that you need to join that group, only that you find some way that fits into your way of living that enables you to contact the group and find out a bit more about it. Is there any way you can engage with the people in it that fits into your life? Is there any limited activity that you can take on that would enable you to support the group in whatever way fits into your life?

? · QUESTIONS TO CONSIDER

1 What do you learn from this experience?
2 How do you see the issue in a way that might be different from the way you originally viewed it?
3 Who have you met through this journey, and what have you learned from them? What have you given to them?
4 How will what you have learned through undertaking this affect you in other aspects of your life?

Note down any reflections that occur as you undertake this activity in your learning journal. If you are working with a group, be sure to share your experiences with one another.

Putting together the building blocks for action

This chapter has covered a good deal of territory 'on the way to ethical action'. Paradoxically, the chapter opened with the notion that the first step towards ethical action involves *not* taking action, through practising 'negative capability'. Negative capability enables you to be reflexive about a situation and your role in it before responding with a knee-jerk reaction. It is about quickly assessing whether or not a situation requires an immediate response and if it does not, it enables you to step back and observe what is going on from a number of different angles. The case study of the Cuban missile crisis was offered as a touchstone to demonstrate how John F. Kennedy and his

ExComm's ability to wait and act with calm deliberation might have saved the world from a cataclysmic military battle.

The idea of *kairos* was introduced next. *Kairos* highlights the temporal dimension of 'the right time' and the aesthetic dimension of 'the right amount' in responding to situations. It offers timing as a meaningful dimension subject to judgement, rather than the more abstract linear time associated with chronology. The case study of the Branch Davidian conflict in Waco, Texas was used as a touchpoint story for examining this concept in action.

Finally, the third building block towards masterful ethical action involves 'practising caring habits'. If all of this 'waiting' and 'reflecting' has been a bit tiresome and you find yourself keen to go on and *do* something, practising caring habits builds a behavioural foundation for taking masterful ethical action. Practising the habits of active listening, seeking out the other, and participating provides you with bedrock capabilities vital to taking the next step of acting astutely in relation to ethically challenging situations.

I hope these building blocks have demonstrated that coming to the point of taking action that you judge to be ethical is not as simple as 'knowing the right thing to do and then acting on that knowledge'. Much background work goes into deciding what the 'right' thing to do is. The *intention* to act ethically is not sufficient for acting ethically. For instance, finding an ethical way forward in the case of the Cuban missile crisis or the Waco massacre did not rely on merely 'wanting to do good'. That intention is a taken-for-granted prerequisite; the work begins once that proclivity is in place. This chapter has provided you with ideas and activities that form the foundation for being able to move beyond good intentions towards sound ethical action.

Before taking that next step, take a moment to reflect on the key learning points you want to remember from this chapter in Box 6.6:

BOX 6.6

ACTIVITY: REFLECTING ON YOUR LEARNING

Reflect, either individually or in a group, on the following questions:

 QUESTIONS TO CONSIDER

1 What are the key learning points you have gleaned from this chapter?
2 What have you done differently as a result of this chapter?
3 What has been the most surprising idea you have encountered?
4 What has been the most difficult activity to DO? What significance does this difficulty have for you?
5 What will you take forward into your daily life as a result of engaging with the chapter?

Write down your key reflections in your learning journal.

Having considered the 'building blocks' towards ethical action, let's now turn to ethical action itself, which is the topic of Chapter 7.

NOTES

1 The events of the crisis are well documented in the film *Thirteen Days*, directed by Roger Donaldson, which presents an account of the Cuban missile crisis. The film illustrates some of the tensions JFK was under to act but also his ability to put off action in such a way that eventually resolved the crisis. It's a compelling example of 'negative capability' in action.

2 See http://www.youtube.com/watch?v=EgdUgzAWcrw – JFK's "Cuban missile crisis" speech (complete and uncut); accessed 20 November 2014.

7

Taking ethical action

The previous six chapters have been preparing you for the 'moment of truth' of ethical mastery – taking action. Taking action is critical, because it is what you *do* that ultimately indicates your ethics. As Maurice Hamington paraphrases the political philosopher Jane Addams' thinking, 'when one acts, morality can no longer be abstract . . . to act is to confront a reality and generate an experience' (Hamington, 2004, p. 119). The German philosopher Hannah Arendt also focuses on the importance of action in ethics writing in her text, *The Life of the Mind*: 'it is how we act in the world that matters. If one wants to act ethically, one must be consistent in word and deed' (Arendt, 1971, p. 19).

In this chapter we will consider two aspects of acting ethically. The first concerns what to do when you don't know what to do. That is, what do you do when you want to act in the 'best' way possible but you are uncertain of what 'the best' way is? How might you find the optimal way forward? The second concerns knowing what the right thing to do is (or at least having a fairly good idea of what it might be) and developing the resolve or courage to act on it. Ethical action only results when both of these occur. Without the action there is only ethical intent (which is, in the final analysis, of questionable value). How does one muster the courage to act on ethical intent?

Let's begin exploring this territory by examining how a fictional character engages with the need to make a choice about how to act when faced with an ethical dilemma in Case Study 7.1. The film *The Scent of a Woman* provides an apt example of such a 'moment of truth'. In it, an individual is forced to make a decision when faced with an ethical dilemma and act on that decision. If you have the opportunity to view the film before reading this chapter please do so, as it will serve as way of illustrating many of the chapter's key points.

CASE STUDY 7.1

The Scent of a Woman

There are two main protagonists in the film. The first is a young man called Charlie who is a student at a prestigious boys' school on the East Coast of the USA. Having come from a lower-income home in Oregon, he is studying there as a scholarship student and supplements his finances by working at the school's library. He is a quiet, studious young man who seems rather unsure of himself. Socially, he is situated on the edge of a popular, 'in crowd' of other boys.

The second main character is Frank Slade, a blind ex-military commander who lives with his daughter and her husband and their young family. He is cantankerous and wild. The first time Charlie encounters Frank he is yelling abuse at his daughter and grandchildren. Prior to meeting him, Charlie has agreed to look after Frank for a weekend while his daughter and her family go away for a brief holiday.

The critical incident around which Charlie's ethical dilemma is centred occurs on the Friday night prior to Charlie moving in with Frank for the weekend. He is working late into the evening at the library. He leaves the library accompanied by one of the boys in the 'in crowd', Freddie, and as they exit the building they are met by one of the school's female faculty members. They begin to chat but are disturbed by noises and look up to see a number of other boys who are in the 'in crowd' contriving a contraption hanging from a tree, which dumps a pail of paint on the new car owned by the headmaster of the school, Mr Trask. Because of the darkness and the way in which she is situated the faculty member can't see who the boys are but is aware that given their positions, Charlie and Freddie could probably see well enough to positively identify them.

The next day Mr Trask calls a meeting of the entire school, asking for those who committed the prank to make themselves known. Everyone is silent. He then calls Charlie and Freddie into his office and once again demands that they tell him who they saw rigging the bucket of paint. . They refuse to do so. Mr Trask says he will give the boys until the next week to reveal the perpetrators of the prank or they themselves will be expelled from the school. Additionally, in private Mr Trask hints to Charlie that if he exposes those responsible he will pave the way for Charlie to win a scholarship to Harvard in the coming year.

The film follows Charlie over the ensuing weekend as he tries to decide what to do, while at the same time caring for Frank. Frank has his own agenda for the weekend, which includes travelling to New York City for two days of fine dining, carousing and, as it turns out, Tango dancing. As the weekend progresses, Charlie discovers that Frank plans to kill himself rather than return to his daughter's home. In other words, there is a lot going on for Charlie as he navigates the weekend's events.

Reflect on this case study by answering the questions in Box 7.1.

BOX 7.1

REFLECT: CONSIDERING CHARLIE'S SITUATION

Before continuing, pause for a moment and consider the following questions:

? QUESTIONS TO CONSIDER

1 What are the ethical issues that Charlie is facing in relation to the situation at school?
2 Who are the different 'interest groups' that Charlie is trying to negotiate between?
3 What do you see as the alternative actions that Charlie might take?
4 Have you ever been in a similar situation? What did you do? How did you decide to do that?

We will return to the story of Charlie but first let us stop for a moment to explore this moment of 'action' in relation to ethical mastery. We'll begin by once again turning to Aristotle to examine his advice on the matter.

Aristotle: action based on virtue

Aristotle's advice about how to act ethically is deceptively simple, while at the same time frustratingly vague. He suggests that the means by which one can discern right action from an ethical perspective is 'to be a person of high virtue'. A person of high virtue will necessarily know the correct way to respond to a given situation. The question of how one might become a person of high virtue is therefore extremely important and much of this chapter elaborates on how that can be done. Before turning to the question of how one develops a virtuous character, let's consider two other slightly more pragmatic suggestions Aristotle makes about how to decide on the correct way to act in relation to ethical dilemmas.

Finding the 'mean'

In his *Nicomachean Ethics*, Aristotle introduces the notion of 'the mean' as a guide to discerning ethical action. According to this notion, ethical action involves identifying a mid-path between extreme reactions to situations. As described by the Aristotelian scholar Francis Eterovich, 'the mean is not simply a middle of the road position, but the most reasonable course of action man can take in a given situation. Avoiding two extremes is the high point of practical wisdom' (Eterovich, 1966, p. 33). Aristotle provides three rules for attaining the 'mean':

- First, avoid the extreme that is most contrary to what the mean would suggest. So, if you are given the choice between damaging a human being or damaging a thing, choose to damage the thing.
- Take into account your own inclinations and how they will affect what you might habitually do in a given situation. If you tend to avoid conflict, consider the possibility that 'the mean' might require you to assert yourself, whereas if you are a person who habitually turns to aggression, taking a more passive approach may be more appropriate.
- Be aware of the effect of 'immoderate pleasures' on your choice: habitual drinking, greediness or self-dramatization can lead to immoderate action.

As a general guide to give you more of a feeling for how 'the mean' works, Aristotle also provides a list of moral virtues and their corresponding 'vicious extremes' as outlined below (ibid., p. 34).

Feeling	Virtue	Defect	Excess
Confidence	Courage	Cowardice	Rashness
Fear	Courage	Fearlessness	Cowardice
Pleasure of touch	Self-control	Insensibility	Self-indulgence
Anger	Gentleness	Spiritlessness	Irascibility
Shame	Modesty	Shamelessness	Bashfulness

Of course, this list of emotions is not exhaustive – people feel a whole array of things beyond confidence, fear, pleasure of touch, anger and shame! However, the extremes that Aristotle highlights provide some way of thinking about the mid-point of ethical action, given one's emotional response to a situation.

Finding the middle path is also dependent on the particular situation in which you are operating. What is courageous in one situation might be reckless in another or indeed indicative of cowardice in a third. Let's get more of a feel of how finding the mid-point might work by reconsidering Charlie's dilemma about what to do in relation to the headmaster and his schoolmates.

Some of the relational dynamics between Charlie and the headmaster and Charlie and his schoolmates include:

- The headmaster is almost universally disliked amongst the boys at the school. In particular, his vanity and the way it is expressed through the parading of his new car has irked the boys and is partly the reason that they decide to pour paint on it. This is not to excuse their actions but to point out that the headmaster himself and the way he manages his relationship with the boys are also implicated in the situation.

- Another ingredient is that the headmaster is pressurizing Charlie to tell him what he knows in ways that could be interpreted as coercive. For instance, he suggests that if Charlie does reveal what he knows, he could use contacts to secure him a scholarship at Harvard. Rather than making Charlie more inclined to divulge what he saw, this has the opposite effect. Because of Mr Trask's offer, telling on his colleagues would mean literally 'selling himself' out.

- Charlie's relationships with his colleagues are also not completely straightforward. The boys in question are 'well to do' and their behaviour is brattish. They regularly hand out the possibility of friendship to Charlie but then retract it. There is nothing really in their history together that inclines Charlie to be loyal to them, apart from the fact that he is 'one of them' in terms of being a student of the school.

In Box 7.2 are some questions that will help you reflect on Charlie's dilemma.

 BOX 7.2

REFLECT: EMPATHIZING WITH CHARLIE

 QUESTIONS TO CONSIDER

1 Bearing these aspects of the situation in mind, what do you imagine Charlie's overriding emotional response to be?
2 What do you think Charlie's 'natural' inclination would be in this situation? How would a 'middle path' response differ from this natural inclination?
3 What do you think are possible actions he could take? What are the most extreme versions of these?
4 Can you think of three possible actions Charlie could take that would sit between the two extreme actions you have identified above?

Finding the 'middle path' often involves identifying a 'balancing point' between extreme ways of being. One of the best ways of discovering such a balancing point is to experience balance within one's own physical body. It is very difficult to find the mid-point of an action when one is literally, physically, out of balance. The following exercise in Box 7.3 aims to provide you with the physical sensation of being 'in balance'. As such, it is a helpful starting point for finding the mid-point when facing difficult ethical decisions.

👥 BOX 7.3

ACTIVITY: FINDING YOUR PHYSICAL POINT OF BALANCE

For this activity you will need a space large enough to bend over and also to be able to swing your arms around your body and above your head without hitting anything. The best way forward is to read these instructions through first and then go through them from memory rather than read them and try to do them at the same time. It is also best if you can do this exercise in bare feet. It is also wonderful if you can do this exercise outdoors on the grass.

First, find a comfortable standing posture, with both feet on the ground – standing as you normally do. Just notice how that feels – how do your feet feel, can you sense where your feet meet the floor or ground? What is their temperature? Just notice other parts of your body, your arms, the back of your neck. You may want to scrunch your shoulders up towards your ears to release any tension that has accumulated there.

Now very carefully, bend your knees and let your body begin to fold towards the earth. It's helpful if you pull your tummy muscles in towards your spine as you do this to protect your lower back. Don't worry about touching the ground or your toes, just let yourself bend over your body, very slowly. If it is comfortable for you to do so, take hold of each elbow with the opposite arm's hand. Keep your knees bent.

Hang in this position for a moment or two.

You are going to uncurl back to a standing position from here, but the very important aspect is to do so VERY slowly. Imagine if you can, that you are uncurling one vertebra in your back at a time. Keep your tummy muscles pulled in tightly as you do so. As you uncurl, see if you can notice what you have to do in order to keep your balance. Generally, in order to keep your balance you have to continually make micro-adjustments. Making such small adjustments allows you to come up in a balanced way. See if you can notice how the weight shifts very subtly from one foot to the other or from the front of the foot to the back of the foot as you move to a standing position.

Let your head fall forward as you rise up, so that it is the last part of your body to come upright into a standing posture. Tuck your chin in slightly so that you feel a slight stretch at the back of your neck. Tuck your tummy in and make sure your bottom is not sticking out. Keep your knees slightly bent. Now just scan through your body, noticing how you are holding this balanced standing posture. What needs to work so that you can maintain this stance? Do you notice the very tiny movements your body needs to make just to stay 'still'?

❓ QUESTIONS TO CONSIDER

1 What do you learn about balance from doing this simple physical activity?
2 How is this stance different from your more habitual way of standing?
3 What do you notice about your breathing when you are in this balanced position?
4 What do you notice about your mind? In particular, has it stopped racing around in a way that might be more common to you?

A very simple practical activity you can do when faced with the difficulty of finding the mid-point of behaviour is to steady yourself and find the balancing point of your body. If you do not have space or time to do the complete version of the exercise above, once you have done it a couple of times, you will be more able to find your balancing point by taking up the posture as known by your body's memory. Merely taking up this posture can foster a state of being that is more conducive to finding a balanced way through ethical dilemmas.

Aristotle's second guideline: converse with wise others

For Aristotle, learning from the community in which one is situated is essential to developing ethical discernment. He suggests that only by engaging with wise ethical others can we become wise ourselves. In this way, the ability to act ethically is something we learn. Left to their own devices, Aristotle suggests that children would not be able to act ethically, as they would only ever act from self-interest. Children learn to regulate their selfish impulses by being part of a community and discovering the behaviours acceptable within that community and those that are not. In a similar way, in order to find 'the mean' in any activity, we must notice how those wiser than ourselves react in situations we find troubling.

In the event that you do not have such a 'wise other' close at hand when you run into ethical difficulty, it can be helpful to bring to mind someone whose opinion you would seek and imagine the advice they would give you. The wonderful thing about engaging your imagination in this way is that you can draw on the wisdom of anyone who has ever lived. You could wonder what Martin Luther King would say, for instance, or Mother Teresa or Aung San Suu Kyi or some other exemplar of ethical behaviour you would like to emulate. This is the power of role models; not necessarily that they are always perfect but that through wondering what they would do in similar situations a way of navigating difficult ethical terrain can often be found.

Another important wellspring for ideas about handling difficult ethical situations resides in the many legends and myths central to every culture. Such myths and legends serve a critical purpose in providing cultural guides to morality that work on both conscious and unconscious levels of awareness. They are also often richly textured and can be ambiguous about prescribing 'right action'. In this way they can also serve to hone the reader or listener's capacity to reason well from a moral perspective. For example, let's consider the following legend, which comes from the Hindu tradition, in Case Study 7.2.

CASE STUDY 7.2

Krishna on the battlefield

One of the most important books from the Hindu tradition is the *Bhagavad Gita*, part of the great epic poem the *Mahabharata*, which tells the story of the climactic battle between family members contesting the rule of a kingdom. The story is told from the perspective of Arjuna, who fights on the side of his elder brother, the rightful heir to the throne. However, Arjuna is in conflict when he fully realizes that the war is between members of his own family: 'And Arjuna, standing between the two armies, saw fathers and grandfathers, teachers, uncles, and brothers, sons and grandsons, in-laws and friends. Seeing his kinsmen established in opposition, Arjuna was overcome by sorrow' (Easwaran, 2007, p. 80).

   He asks his chariot driver, who is the god Krishna in disguise, for advice about what he should do. Krishna responds that in making his decision, Arjuna must consider what his *dharma*, or purpose, in life is. To act against this purpose is to commit a wrong, explaining:

> Considering your dharma, you should not vacillate. For a warrior, nothing is higher than a war against evil. The warrior confronted with such a war should be pleased, Arjuna, for it comes as an open gate to heaven. But if you do not participate in this battle against evil, you will incur sin, violating your dharma and your honour. (Ibid., p. 92)

In other words, Krishna is advising Arjuna that in deciding between possible actions, in order to avoid evil he must align his action with his ultimate purpose. This is the case even if the outward action (in this case killing his own family members) appears to be unethical. Following one's purpose is the means by which 'the war within' can be mastered. Now reflect on the questions in Box 7.4.

 BOX 7.4

REFLECT: THE IMPACT OF FEELING IN CONFLICT

? **QUESTIONS TO CONSIDER**

1 Consider an instance when, like Arjuna, you felt in conflict about how you should respond to a given situation. How did you go about deciding what action to take?
2 Would your response have been different had you consciously worked to align your response with a larger purpose that you are committed to?
3 What is your greater purpose?

Reflecting on these questions leads well into the next recommendation from Aristotle about how you can decide right action – building good character.

Building good character

So far the chapter has introduced two practical actions you can take when you want to do the 'right' thing but are unsure of what it is. That is, you can identify the 'middle path' of possible responses and you can converse with wise others about your dilemma (either literally or metaphorically by referring to historical or mythological characters). These are perhaps stepping stones to achieving the kind of character that, according to Aristotle, would enable you to navigate ethical dilemmas with mastery. How does one become such a person of good, or to use Aristotle's language, 'virtuous', character? The underlying question underpinning this concern is 'What kind of a person do you want to *be*?' This is at the heart of any action you might take, either consciously or unconsciously. What you *do* determines the kind of person you become. This is why personal ethics are so important: through the actions we take and our behaviours we become the ethical or unethical people we want to be.

Let's return to the film *The Scent of a Woman* for a moment, to consider this interrelationship between what you do and what you become more carefully.

Charlie's moment of truth

In the final scenes of the film, Charlie and Freddie are brought before the assembled students and School Board to once again be given the opportunity to reveal who the perpetrators of the paint crime were. During the middle of this encounter Frank appears and takes a seat next to Charlie, announcing that he is present in order to support Charlie (as Freddie's father is there to support Freddie.)

Freddie avoids Mr Trask's direct question about who he saw by arguing that he didn't have his contact lenses in at the time and therefore is unable to make a positive identification. When given a final ultimatum about disclosing the names of his fellow students who paint-bombed Mr Trask's car, Charlie admits that he saw who did it but that they looked like 'any students of the school'. In other words, he does not 'snitch' on his school mates. Immediately the headmaster declares that Charlie will be expelled.

It is at this point that Frank interrupts the proceedings. Among the tirade of accusations he makes to the shocked gathering is a quote that is particularly pertinent to the question of how good character is built. He says:

> I don't know if what Charlie has done is right or wrong. But I do know that he won't sell anyone out to buy his future. That, my friend, is called 'integrity', that's called courage, that's the stuff that leaders should be made of . . . When faced with tough decisions, I always knew what the right thing to do was. But I never took it . . . because it was too damned hard. But to do so is the path of principle, and that is what builds character.

This quote is interesting in at least two ways. First, Frank suggests that what is critical here is not whether Charlie's action was 'right' or 'wrong'. Although acting ethically is often framed as discerning between the two and acting according to what is 'right', what Frank points out is that there is an alternative way of looking at how to take such decisions, that is, through anticipating the kind of person a certain course of action will lead you to *be*. If you want to build a virtuous character, you have to do things that build virtue. In Charlie's case, whether or not revealing the identities of the offending schoolboys was right or wrong, the action he took required courage. It placed his own future academic career in jeopardy. It was a selfless, rather than self-serving act. In this way, it would build in Charlie the qualities of courage and selflessness indicative of a virtuous character.

The second key aspect of Frank's diatribe is what he says about courage and how it is built. As Frank suggests, we often, in our heart of hearts, know what the 'right' thing to do is, but knowing what the right thing to do is and actually *doing* it are two different matters. This points to the importance of moral courage, which will be explored in more depth in the last section of this chapter. Before examining moral courage in more depth though, a final theory of ethical action is briefly introduced – that of 'ethical know-how'.

Francisco Varela's idea of 'ethical know-how'

Let's take a step back for just a moment to consider an idea offered by the Chilean biologist, Francisco Varela, most widely recognized for his work on autopoiesis, which refers to a system that is capable of reproducing and maintaining itself. In his later years, Varela's work extended beyond biology to the field of neurophysiology and, along with his colleagues Evan Thompson and Eleanor Rosch, he made important contributions to our understanding of embodied cognition. His book, *Ethical Know-How: Action, Wisdom, and Cognition* (Varela, 1992) is a collection of three lectures given in 1992 that offer a radical take on ethical action and how it links to cognition.

His starting point for considering ethical action is the view that the vast amount of ethical behaviour we engage in each day is not reflected upon, deliberated or consciously chosen. It just happens. It is apparent in our everyday, seemingly unmediated response to those around us. For instance, if you are driving along the road and witness an accident, you stop and offer help. Your colleague has forgotten his wallet so you pay for their lunch. You are directly behind someone walking down the street when they trip and fall and you stop to help them up, even if it means you will be late for your appointment. This spontaneous ethical response occurs because you have done the background work of perceiving the ethically salient aspect of the situation, but still, your response happens without conscious thought. This, Varela calls 'ethical know-how' and, from his perspective, is the ground from which the vast majority of ethical behaviour occurs.

This notion is elaborated in the first of his three lectures, entitled 'Know How and Know What'. In it he argues that 'most of our mental and active life is of the immediate, rather than "deliberate" variety' (p. 19). This insight seems to oppose much of what is suggested in this book as well as the majority of other business ethics texts. It indicates that in the majority of cases, we respond to situations we find ourselves in without 'thinking'. Key in this statement is the notion of 'finding ourselves in a situation'. Borrowing from Heidegger's philosophy, Varela argues that as human beings, we 'always operate in some kind of immediacy of a given situation' (p. 9). He labels these immediate situations as 'micro-worlds'. Micro-worlds play a key role in our propensity to both perceive a situation as having an ethical component and to respond to it, as explained in the following section.

Becoming aware of the impact of the micro-world you inhabit

Being able to identify the micro-world in which you are situated is crucial to discerning an appropriate ethical response to it. Varela's argument is based on the idea that we always take action within specific rather than general-ized situations. In this way, as has been argued throughout this book, critical to astute ethical action is the ability to perceive a situation in its concrete, embodied particularity. He suggests that 'the ability to take appropriate action is in some sense how we embody a stream of recurrent micro-world transitions' (p. 10). This requires the ability to read the demands and dynam-ics of each situation we encounter as we go through our day and to be able to respond to those demands appropriately.

What are the implications of this idea for the busy person who is attempt-ing to navigate the ambiguous territory of ethical dilemmas within organizations? First, it means understanding and recognizing the micro-world you are a part of as you engage with the variety of situations you find yourself in, and becoming more aware of how that micro-world dictates your way of seeing the world. For instance, the way in which executives in Enron just 'did what others around them were doing' in terms of turning a blind eye to accounting irregularities has been well documented elsewhere. In the Enron micro-world, certain accounting practices became 'the way things were done' rather than 'unethical'. Being able to see beyond one's micro-world, particularly to recognise how those outside may regard it, is essential if you are going to be able to take conscious, correct ethical action.

The way in which you are physically located has a significant impact on how you experience the micro-world you are inhabiting. Returning to Jane Addams' work for a moment, this is why actively seeking out others and their 'micro-worlds' is such an essential part of being able to relate to them ethically. If you always remain within the confines of your own micro-world, there is a diminished chance of encountering others in ways that help you develop sufficient sympathetic knowledge towards them. From an organizational perspective, this highlights the importance of being physically present with others throughout the organization and their 'micro-worlds'. Being physically present in an office where secretaries are run off their feet or on a factory floor where workers' boredom is palpable, provides otherwise inaccessible insight into their micro-worlds.

What Varela is working towards in this first lecture is the idea that sound ethical action has an *immediacy* to it. This does not mean we are destined only to respond in unconscious ways, however. By becoming more aware of the impact of the micro-world we are situated in and by actively engaging with others' micro-worlds, we can begin to extend the range of our unconscious ethical sympathy and response. The next reflective activity in Box 7.5 is designed to help you become more sensitive to the different micro-worlds that are part of your daily routine.

BOX 7.5

ACTIVITY: NOTICING MICRO-WORLDS

Consider the day you have had so far before coming to this point of reading this book:

 QUESTIONS TO CONSIDER

1   What are the different micro-worlds you have inhabited? Notice the micro-worlds you might routinely ignore, such as the micro-world of being a commuter, either by car or by public transport.
2   What are the unconscious 'rules' of each of these micro-worlds?
3   What impact do these 'rules' have on your ability to perceive the ethical aspects of each micro-world?
4   What might you do differently as you engage with each of these micro-worlds to become more aware of their ethical components?

Developing ethical expertise

The second lecture in Varela's book is devoted to the notion of 'ethical expertise'. In it he stresses that rather than actively deliberating about the vast number of ethical issues we face daily, most of the time we use immediate 'ethical expertise'. The critical question then becomes, how do we develop this 'ethical expertise'? Echoing many of Aristotle's ideas about how a virtuous character is developed, Varela argues that this kind of ethical 'know-how' arises through our engagement with the society we grow up in. He turns to the Confucian writer Mencius (fourth century BCE) to further elaborate on how such ethical expertise is developed.

The starting point for Mencius' approach to developing ethical expertise is the requirement for three capacities: extension, attention and intelligent awareness. The first two are very similar to the notions of moral imagination and moral perception covered in the second level of the book. However, it is worth reiterating them here and adding the particular flavour Mencius brings to them:

● *Extension* is the capacity to transfer the feelings and responses from one situation to an analogous situation. For instance, when encountering the suffering of children who are malnourished due to war or extreme drought, one can experience the compassion and desire to alleviate their pain as if they were one's own children. In brief, extension is the ability to put oneself in another's shoes and feel the effects of our actions on those others. Mencius writes of the way feelings 'break through' to the new situation.

- *Attention* underpins the ability to extend an emotional connection between situations. As an aspect of moral perception, unless you first notice that a situation calls for a compassionate response, you will be unable to extend compassion into it. Mencius, like Aristotle, calls for the need to 'perceive clearly (in order to) identify corresponding affinities' (quoted in Varela, 1992, p. 28). In trying to see correspondences and affinities, 'the situation at hand becomes much more textured' (ibid.). What is important here is the emphasis that is placed on paying attention to specific circumstances and their 'texture', rather than attempting to abstract them into broader generalities. However, this does not mean that rationality plays no part in discerning ethical action.
- *Intelligent awareness* is where rationality comes into play and results from the intersection of rationality with an appreciation of 'the texture of the situation at hand' (Varela, 1992, p. 31). In this way, ethical action does not result from obedience to rules and procedures but through 'balancing a spontaneous response to the particular with rational calculation' (ibid.).

Varela goes on to describe how such 'intelligent awareness' can result in truly creative responses, likened to acting from a position of 'crazy wisdom'. The notion of 'crazy wisdom' will be explored in more depth in the final chapter of this book. For now, however, think of 'crazy wisdom' as an approach to ethical dilemmas that can appear unorthodox or counterintuitive but that somehow reveals itself to be wise. The Old Testament story in which the judge suggests dividing a baby and giving the two women contesting its ownership one half each is indicative of 'crazy wisdom'. On the surface, it looks absurd and even unethical, but in this story, it reveals the identity of the child's true mother (who cries that the child should go to the other woman, rather than be split in two).

In summary, according to Varela, the great majority of ethical dilemmas we navigate are resolved through 'ethical know-how', which does not rely on deliberation or balancing different options for moving forward. Instead, he suggests that we only 'fall back' on deliberation when the situation we encounter disrupts our 'normal' way of operating and we cannot readily find a response. For Varela then, the pertinent question is not so much 'How do we deliberate to create ethical action?' but 'How do we build the kind of "ethical know-how" that enables us automatically to navigate our relations with others in an ethically sound fashion?'

Like Aristotle before him, Varela suggests that building this capacity is a process of learning in which we reflect on experience, observe wise others who we would like to emulate and become ever more open to and sensitive towards 'the other'. He suggests this journey is akin to developing the Chinese virtue of '*wu wei*'. It is 'a process of acquiring a disposition where immediacy precedes deliberation, where non-dual action precedes the rational distinction between subject and object' (Varela, 1992, p. 35). This is a difficult process because it involves honesty in self-reflection and alertness both to the outer world and our inner response to that world. Acting ethically is also difficult because, just as Frank argued in the film *The Scent of a Woman*, often doing the 'right thing' is just plain old 'hard'. This is where moral courage steps in.

Moral courage

> Courage would not be courage if the courageous person did not sometimes pay a price for it. (Hartman, 2006, p. 71)

Absolutely critical to taking good ethical action is the extent to which one exercises moral courage. Cheffers and Pakaluk define courage as: 'a trait that enables a person to act appropriately, that is, reasonably, in the presence of something fearful. In this way it is a virtue of character' (2005, p. 73). In other words, courage is the ingredient that enables you to take the leap into action that you know may have painful consequences for you.

Most people writing in this area agree that moral courage is not something that can be taught. Going back as far as Aristotle, his view was that to develop honesty, you must practise being honest, and if you want to act justly, you need to practise acting justly, and most importantly, if you want to be courageous, you must practise being courageous.

Although it may not be possible to develop courage in any way other than being courageous, research indicates that it is possible to develop what is known as 'moral resolve'. Moral resolve is the *intention* to act courageously. In their empirically based study of accounting students exposed to different levels of exemplars in terms of moral courage, Christensen et al. (2007) found a relationship between students exposed to others who had exercised moral courage and their own commitment to be courageous from a moral point of view. Discussing vignettes in which people acted courageously was deemed to have an even larger impact on their resolve to be courageous themselves in relation to ethical action. It seems that being aware of others' courageous behaviours (Box 7.6) can act as a spur to wanting to be courageous!

BOX 7.6

REFLECT: EXEMPLARS OF MORAL COURAGE

? QUESTIONS TO CONSIDER

1 Who is the most morally courageous person you know?
2 What have they done that you admire?
3 What have they taught you about moral courage?
4 How do you emulate them in your own life?

In his book *The Cheating Culture*, David Callahan suggests that in order to exercise moral courage, you often have to be 'a pain in the ass' (2004, p. 2). In other words, being morally courageous, especially within organizations, often requires behaviour that stands out from the crowd. It often means developing the willingness to confront colleagues when they are doing something you understand to be ethically wrong. He notes that for most of us, confronting others with judgements they do not want to hear is not easy, but it is critical to do. This requires taking a courageous stance. He writes, furthermore, that for many of us, the incentives for acting unethically are much more apparent than those for acting ethically. He suggests that in many organizations there are three factors that mitigate against acting ethically:

- The possibility of losing one's job – even though there are laws to protect whistle-blowers, they often suffer from speaking from their conviction.
- Many people don't really care deeply enough about unethical behaviour in their organizations to actually do anything about it. If you are going to take an unpopular stand on something, you have to care deeply about the situation. It is often easier to just ignore what is going on in order to have a 'quiet life'.
- The issue of efficacy – if unethical behaviour is rife in an organization and is even encouraged by senior management, taking a stand against it can seem futile.

Given these realities, what can a person wanting to act ethically do within organizations? Again, Callahan offers some practical steps that people can take when faced with unethical behaviour in their firm or as ways of increasing the possibility of ethics being a more central focus for behaviour:

- Learn the ethics of your industry or profession and also any pertinent laws and remind colleagues of these points. Raising these issues in a general way, at team meetings or retreats, and giving people the opportunity to discuss the profession's ethics is a way to open up dialogue on the subject of organizational ethics.

● If your organization is large enough, encourage your senior management to hire a Chief Ethics Officer, who can help develop a more formal ethics system. Putting the resource behind such an appointment will send an important signal to the larger organizational system. The downside of this is that the Ethics Officer can be seen to 'be responsible' for ethics in such a way that other organizational members may feel it is no longer their responsibility.

● Get involved in a professional organization that may uphold the ethics of your profession and in which you can discuss and get support for your own stance.

Now reflect upon your own experiences in Box 7.7.

 BOX 7.7

REFLECT: YOUR EXPERIENCE OF ACTING COURAGEOUSLY

Identify an experience you have had where you wish you had behaved in a more coura-geous manner. What were the circumstances? Note down all that you can remember about the situation and what you did.

 QUESTIONS TO CONSIDER

1 Is there someone you admire in terms of how you imagine they would have handled a similar situation? How do you believe they handled it?
2 What might you have done differently in the situation now that you have reflected on it?
3 What would you like to do if a similar situation arises again?

Let's return to Charlie in *The Scent of a Woman* for one last time before ending this chapter. Certainly, most people would agree that by not telling the headmaster who he had seen the night of the car paint-bombing, he was acting courageously. By taking that action his future at the school was put into jeopardy, as was his chance of being admitted to Harvard. When I watch the film, I often wonder what motivates Charlie to do what he does, especially since he is not a great friend of the boys he ends up protecting:

● What questions do you still have about the action that Charlie took?
● If you see his action as courageous, where did this courage come from?
● What do you learn from reflecting on his actions?

Finally, do the activity in Box 7.8 to identify your ethical 'touchstone'.

 BOX 7.8

FINAL ACTIVITY: IDENTIFYING AN ETHICAL 'TOUCHSTONE'

What virtue would you particularly like to be known and remembered for? Find some kind of symbol or representation for the person you aspire to be from an ethical perspective. Perhaps find an object that in some way represents that virtue for you. It could be a photo of the person you want to emulate or whose actions you find exemplary. It could be some kind of material object that reminds you of your commitment, for example it could be a particular stone or seashell. Make sure you place this object or photo in a place where you will encounter it on a regular basis to help you remember and practise this virtue.

So far we have considered ethical action in relatively abstract terms, outside of specific organizational contexts. The next chapter highlights the specific challenges of navigating ethical dilemmas within organizational settings and invites you to bring many of the skills introduced so far to life within your own context.

Ethics in the organization and beyond

8

Navigating organizational systems ethically

Taking ethical action is easy enough in an abstract sense. It may be possible to discern the 'right' thing to do in a certain circumstance. You may even garner up the moral courage to take that action. However, when working within an organization, its context and culture inevitably interact with any action you take. Your actions will both be affected by and, perhaps more importantly, will prompt a response from the organization. As countless whistle-blowers know, that response can often be more damaging to the person taking the action than to the system. Alternatively, the action you believe to be correct may prove to be problematic within the larger organizational context. It can generate unintended consequences that you could not have anticipated.

This chapter addresses the question of what you need to take account of when you attempt to act ethically within organizations. In particular, it highlights the importance of the political and systemic nature of organizations when you are endeavouring to hold your own ethical line.

Attending to these aspects of organizations falls within the sphere of moral perception and the foundational chapters indicated the importance of watching for the 'invisible' facets of organizing. This chapter takes an in-depth look at the nature of organizations themselves and identifies the characteristics that can make acting ethically within them a challenge. Not to make ethical action an impossible aspiration, the chapter also offers some generic strategies for navigating this difficult territory.

The nature of organizations

On joining an organization, it becomes the micro-world in which you operate. Each organization has its own rituals, language, rules of engagement and taken-for-granted assumptions about what is 'right' and what is 'wrong'. Different micro-worlds create different rules of play and what is fine in one micro-world is not acceptable in another. A first step in navigating the ethical terrain of an organization, therefore, is to be aware of its micro-world and its intrinsic ethics.

The American scholar Robert Jackall conducted one of the most sustained and thorough studies of ethics in organizations in the 1980s. Jackall interviewed over 100 executives in three large-scale USA-based organizations. His study examines the particular micro-world of the bureaucracy – an organizational form that has come to dominate working lives. His study shows how this very form itself, which distributes responsibility and authority through hierarchies and splits production processes, gives rise to particular ethical issues.

A sociologist by background, an overriding theme of Jackall's findings is captured in the following quote:

> Bureaucratic work causes people to bracket, while at work, the moralities that they might hold outside the workplace or that they might adhere to privately and to follow instead the prevailing morality of their particular organizational situation . . . What is right in the corporation is not what is right in a man's home or in his church. What is right in the corporation is what the guy above you wants from you. That's what morality is in the corporation. (Jackall [1988] 2010, p. 4)

In other words, Jackall found that people behaved very differently within organizational settings, particularly within bureaucracies, than they would do or would espouse to do in their homes or neighbourhoods. The need for achievement and promotion almost uniformly outweighed any impulse towards ethical consideration in those he interviewed. This was true at both the macro-level of how the organization interacted with its competitors, suppliers or the communities in which they existed, or at the micro-level of interpersonal relationships within the firm. When a manager was demoted, for instance, rather than offering help or support, other managers were more likely to snub this person lest they be associated with someone regarded as a 'loser' by senior managers.

Jackall attributes many of the issues he discovers to the nature of bureaucracies themselves. Rather than merely being technical systems of organizing, his research demonstrates the extent to which bureaucracies are also systems of 'power, privilege, and domination' (ibid., p. 10). Rather than being driven by logic, many decisions within the organizations he examined were taken without real rationale, including the degree to which performance targets were understood to have been met. The managers he spoke with were convinced of the arbitrary nature of much that affected them. For instance, markets were seen to be by their very nature capricious. Political manoeu-vrings meant that those people one had allegiance to could be fired and then one would be left with few contacts. Furthermore, promotion decisions were often based on the degree to which one was known, rather than on objective measures of performance. All of these factors contribute to the creation of an uncertain, anxiety-producing context within which many managers work. Without a sense of security where so much is tenuous, ethics can easily be discarded in an effort to protect oneself. Jackall's research indicates that in the struggle between security and integrity, the perceived need for security is likely to win out.

The next three sections elaborate on aspects of organizations that impact on both the capacity of the individual to exercise ethical awareness and to take value-based action. These are:

- organizational culture;
- organizational structure;
- compensation and performance management practices.

The important point about these aspects is that taken in isolation, each is seemingly 'ethically neutral'. In other words, there is seldom anything inherently 'unethical' about an organization's culture or structure or how it measures performance. Performance management systems are often estab-lished in order to provide desired levels of customer service. The ability to hit such targets could have ethical implications itself (think, for instance, of waiting time targets for those visiting accident and emergency departments). However, such measurement systems can also inadvertently result in unethi-cal outcomes, as will be illustrated. Let's start, however, by considering the impact organizational culture can have on individuals' capacity to recognize and act on ethically salient situations.

Organizational culture

The part that an organization's culture plays in people's perceptions has already been touched on in Chapter 2. Here the concept is considered in more detail, particularly by identifying aspects of the organization that con-tribute to the creation of its culture. First, just what is organizational culture? Organizational culture has been defined as the taken-for-granted modes of operating that inform any group of people, whether that group is a dyad or a large organization (O'Reilly et al., 1991). O'Reilly and his colleagues go on to suggest that organizational culture is a set of values that is reflected in both informal norms and the formal organizational system. The American organizational behaviour scholar Edgar Schein is known for his work in identifying three 'levels' of an organization's culture: (1) its 'artefacts', which are those material 'things' and identifiable processes that operate at the most transparent level; (2) its attitudes and beliefs that are not easily seen but are reflected in the organization's ways of operating; and (3) at the deepest level, the organization's values and assumptions (Schein, 1992).

It is at the level of 'values and assumptions' that the interrelationship between an organization's culture and how individuals within it are prompted (or not!) to identify ethical aspects of situations is both most powerful and most problematic. Assumptions cannot, after all, be identified in the same way that the office layout, bonus schemes, car parking arrangements or any other organizational artefacts can be identified and manipulated. Yet research has indicated that the extent to which an organization's underlying assumptions are experienced has a significant impact on the moral imagination of those working within it (Caldwell and Moberg, 2007). Those assumptions are themselves influenced by other factors, including the industry or organizational sector that the organization is a part of, its enacted as well as espoused purpose, the values held by the top team and/or founder, and the 'socio-material' practices embedded in how work gets accomplished. Let's take a look at each of these in more detail.

Industry or organizational sector

The American business ethicist Edmund Hartman suggests that those wishing to lead ethical careers should start by considering the very industry or organizational sector they join. Some industry sectors are recognized as being inherently problematic from an ethical perspective. For instance, the tobacco industry creates products that are known to shorten human lives and the pharmaceutical industry has been criticized for questionable pricing practices resulting in the poor being prohibited from receiving medicines they need. Hartman (2006) advises young business students that a crucial step in their ability to exercise virtue within organizations is to be aware of the ethics inherent in the industry they join.

Furthermore, this is not a static judgement. Sectors such as banking have had their ethical reputations tarnished by the 2008 financial crisis, which revealed less than sound practices both in the USA and in Europe. This is not to say that all banks and financial services firms are ethically questionable, it is just to highlight the changing views concerning the inherent ethics (or not) within various sectors.

Underlying the ethical difficulties inherent to particular industry sectors is the purpose towards which those industries' activities are directed. 'Purpose', another seemingly ethically neutral aspect of organizational life, can have a significant impact on how ethics are perceived and acted upon, as considered in the next section.

Purpose

Apart from tobacco companies, munitions manufacturers or pharmaceutical companies, the purpose towards which an organization's activities are directed largely remains unquestioned in terms of whether those activities are ethical or not. Change is afoot however, as industry sectors that have been left relatively unscrutinized in terms of their products face increasing inspection. For instance, manufacturers of sugary drinks are beginning to feel public pressure to reduce the levels of sweeteners used as the health implications of their products are revealed. Fast-food firms increasingly come under fire for the levels of salt and saturated fats present in their products. In these instances debate is on the rise concerning the ethics of organizations selling products that contribute to customers' ill health.

These cases reveal a deeper-seated issue of 'purpose' that speaks to what an organization is actually trying to do in the world. An organization's espoused purpose is often enshrined in its mission statement, that official document declaring what the organization is about. Seldom does an organization's mission statement explicitly articulate the organization's desire to act unethically. However, the extent to which a mission statement provides unwavering commitment to a particular cause can blinker organizations from recognizing the effects of single-minded determination to achieve a particular goal. Case Study 8.1 – Amazon – illustrates this point.

CASE STUDY 8.1

Amazon

At the time of writing this book in 2014, Amazon is the world's largest online retailer. Launched as an online bookstore by Jeff Bezos in 1995, the company operates in 17 countries worldwide and in 2013 had revenues of $75 billion. It now sells everything from digital goods to clothing to furniture to jewellery. Amazon's mission statement states: 'Our vision is to be the earth's most customer centric company; to build a place where people can come to find and discover anything they might want to buy online.'[1]

From an ethical perspective it is difficult to see what is wrong with that! Bezos claims that the mission statement has been a guiding principle for the company's growth and is used as a benchmark for making strategic and tactical decisions. Amazon is recognized for the ease with which items from its website can be purchased, its cut-down prices and for its speedy delivery times. Once again, there is nothing inherently unethical about fulfilling customers' desires as inexpensively as possible and doing so quickly.

Ethical questions begin to be raised, however, when the cost of this singular focus on customer experience is exposed. The need to keep prices low in order to please customers from a cost perspective has had consequences for the company's hiring policies and its treatment of staff. Permanent staff are kept to a minimum, with large numbers of temporary workers being brought in for the heavy demand period in the run-up to Christmas, in particular. Once hired, workers are subject to challenging targets for 'picking' items from shelves in huge warehouses, where their every move is monitored. Warehouses in the USA and in the UK have been criticized for their near 'sweatshop conditions' in which ambulances are stationed outside to deal with staff who faint when temperatures climb over 38°C (100°F). Undercover journalists have noted the sense of stress and sheer physical fatigue inherent in working for the company, especially for those on temporary contracts.

In its aim to be a place where customers might 'find and discover anything online', Amazon has also been treading a questionable ethical line. In 2013 the company was attacked by the World Jewish Congress for selling 'Holocaust-denying books' and there are ongoing legal battles concerning its selling of books of questionable content (such as those promoting dog- or cock-fighting, paedophilia and books containing libel).

In these ways, although innocuous in itself, Amazon's purpose as enshrined in its mission statement can be seen to unwittingly lead to actions of questionable ethics (without considering the company's alleged approach to tax avoidance!).

Box 8.1 helps you to examine the ethics behind a company's mission statement.

BOX 8.1

ACTIVITY: SCRUTINIZE AN ORGANIZATION'S MISSION STATEMENT

Identify the mission statement of a company you regularly buy from, such as Nike, Apple, Walmart or MacDonald's. What is the purpose of the organization as articulated in that statement? What are the implications of the mission statement from an ethical perspective? What new insights result from asking these questions?

An aspect of organizations that might more clearly influence its ethical practices concerns its leader and leadership team, which we turn to next.

How leadership and authority are exercised

The relationship between an organization's leadership and the extent to which its culture supports ethics has been examined by a number of scholars (see, for instance, Brown and Treviño, 2006; Neubert et al., 2009). The USA-based organizational theorist Daniel Palmer suggests three ways in which this relationship becomes apparent:

- how the personal ethics of the leader themselves influence others in the organization;
- the way in which leadership is enacted and how authority is exercised; and
- the purposes towards which leadership and organizational activity are directed (Palmer, 2009).

Much of the 'leadership and ethics' literature is based on Palmer's first point. It seems logical that the personal ethics of the 'leader' will in some part influence the way in which their subordinates discriminate between 'right' and 'wrong' behaviours. For instance, a manager within one of Germany's largest distribution companies talks about the way in which the CEO's attention to finance influences the ways in which employees behave. Stories circulate throughout the organization about how the CEO never tips taxi drivers and always returns change from 'petty cash' he takes when travelling. This sets the standard for how others within the organization account for their expenses and trickles into an exacting code by which finances are handled throughout the company.

In his book *The Moral Capital of Leaders: Why Virtue Matters*, Alejo José Sison argues that the long-term viability of an organization is directly impacted by the ethics of its leader and leadership team. Those leaders who exhibit ethical standards encourage others in the organization to do so as well. This in turn, Sison argues provides the basis for long-term organizational strength even when making ethical choices means losing out on short-term gains (Sison, 2003).

Although there is intuitively a link between the personal ethics of an organization's leader and how the organization operates from an ethical perspective, the connection may not be quite as straightforward as suggested. Palmer's second category alludes to the importance not just of the personal ethics of the leader but also to how they enact them through the way in which they exercise authority.

Robert Jackall's work supports this point precisely. In the three organizations he researched, the way in which authority was exercised played a central role in resulting ethical action. In particular, he noted the endemic understanding that, above all else, subordinates were expected not to contradict or go against their boss. Simultaneously, there was a propensity within these organizations to 'push down' the details of what it took to get tasks accomplished. The implications of these two tendencies included the following:

- Senior people often did not deal with 'tedious' details.
- The consequence of not getting involved in details left those in senior positions free to criticize subordinates after they had done something (because they were just told the end point, not *how* to get there).
- Not getting involved also relieved senior people from 'knowing too much', especially knowing things that might be morally questionable (Jackall [1988] 2010, p. 22).

In other words, in Jackall's study, authority was exercised in such a way that senior managers often expected successful results without ever knowing about the messy complications involved in achieving them. Pushing the level of detail fixing down often created real pressure on middle managers who could then be 'fall guys' if and when things went wrong. A key practice among almost all of the managers Jackall interviewed was the development of 'CYA' ('cover your ass') strategies. A common 'CYA' tactic was not to take decisions, or to diffuse responsibility associated with decisions in such a way that accountability was impossible to determine. All of these actions, neutral enough in themselves, often led to inadvertent unethical behaviour.

Socio-material practices

A final aspect of organizational culture considered here is that of 'socio-material practices'. The concept of 'socio-materiality' points to the ways in which social and material worlds are inextricably interlinked or 'entangled'. The American scholar Wanda Orlikowsky is credited with developing this notion, primarily through her research on how technology and social processes become interlinked in organizational worlds (see Orlikowski, 2006, 2007). Socio-material practices are habits and routines undertaken by people in organizations as they go about their day-to-day lives which shape their experiences and ways of understanding the organization. The socio-material world accounts for not just the meetings, routines of handling email and habits of interaction but the way in which these activities are undertaken. For instance, there may be designated meetings during which 'ethics' are discussed but the way in which these are conducted, who is present, how discussion takes place (whether or not there even *is* discussion) will significantly impact how 'ethics' are understood more broadly through the organization.

Keen to understand the socio-material practices of organizations recognized for embedding ecologically sustainable practices into their operations, I conducted research with two 'eco-hotels' in the Southwest of England, the Bedruthan and the Scarlet. A number of unique socio-material practices were apparent in both hotels, which assisted staff in making sense of the term 'sustainability' and provided ongoing means by which sustainability was further embedded into the organizations' ways of doing things. For instance, staff were given time off to do volunteer work in the local community and were expected to do at least an hour of such work a year. A 'beach clean' was included in their interviewing processes to demonstrate both the organization's commitment to the local ecology but also to assess candidates' willingness to join in with this kind of work. Each year staff across all of the hotels' functions met to recreate the 'philosophy balls': a mobile in which the key principles of the hotels' mode of operating were represented by papier-mâché 'balls', talked over and ceremoniously added to the mobile.

Through the entanglement of materiality – the rubbish on the beach, the papier-mâché balls, making bird boxes for the local environment – and the social – the meetings during which these activities were undertaken, talking with one another while picking up detritus on the beach – staff of the two hotels not only learned what working sustainably meant within their context but also created sustainable ways of operating. This mutual interdependency of the social and the material is an area of study that is in its earliest stages, but has significant potential for bringing insight into how organizational culture works and how socio-material practices influence it.

Let's move on to another seemingly ethically neutral aspect of organizations, their structure, to see how it affects the way in which ethics are understood and acted upon.

Organizational structure

The very way in which an organization is structured can influence how its members can respond to ethical issues. Let's pause for a moment to consider what organizational structures actually do that can lead to this claim. Ostensibly, an organization's structure provides the means by which work is broken down into component parts in order that it can be efficiently handled. There are many ways of dividing work: through functional speciality, through geographically recognized markets or through types of product or component parts of products. As well as being divided 'vertically' in these thematic ways, organizational structures provide a means by which authority can be distributed between different levels of hierarchy. Greater levels of complexity in terms of numbers and types of products or services, larger distribution networks or supply chains can lead to ever more complex structures.

The more complex and diffuse the structure is, the more difficult it is for any one person to understand how everything fits together. In this way, the implications of what is being done by the organization overall are totally understood by only a few people. Following from this, organizational structures designed to create efficiency and facilitate the very possibility of work being accomplished can simultaneously obscure what is being done.

Jackall's work (Jackall [1988] 2010) indicates that organizational structures can influence the possibility of ethical perception and action in at least three ways. First, as noted above, organizational structures *affect transparency* by obscuring the impact of what the organization is doing overall. This is particularly apparent within bureaucracy as an organizational form. Bureaucratic structures often separate people in such a way that they do not fully comprehend the impact of what they are doing. When you are operating at a relatively junior level of an organization's hierarchy, it can be difficult to understand how your job fits into the overall machine and therefore what the impact of your action is. Without sight of the full picture, people can engage in behaviours that aren't in themselves 'wrong' but that add up to something that is.

Second, organizational structures can *dilute responsibility*. Individuals working within bureaucracies in particular can feel far removed from any individuals their work might negatively affect. Moral intensity can be weakened when individuals feel separated from remote stakeholders who are never imagined as 'real' people. Furthermore, within the legal structures of public limited companies (PLCs), responsibility for ethical wrong-doing can be offloaded to the abstract 'organization', rather than ascribed to.

Finally, organizational structures can *split authority for decision-making and expertise*. This means that sometimes those who have the most information about the ethical aspects of situations can be hierarchically situated such that they have limited influence on the way decisions are taken. A good example of this is the case of the United States space shuttle *Challenger* disaster in 1986. Engineers warned leaders within NASA that the cold weather temperatures forecast for the lift-off day were likely to result in an O-ring malfunction, which could result in the craft exploding. These warnings were overruled by the leadership of the organization who were under political pressure to launch the shuttle. The shuttle did indeed explode 73 seconds into its flight, resulting in the deaths of all seven crew members.

In light of the influence organizational structure can have on individuals' ability to perceive and take ethical action, the USA-based ethicist Harvey James suggests that it is far more important to create a structure that does not inadvertently undermine individuals' ethical sensibilities than to create elaborate codes of conduct or ethics training programmes (James, 2000). Interwoven with an organization's structure is its performance management practices, which James also cites as playing a key role in individuals' behaviours (ethical or otherwise!) in organizations.

Compensation and performance management practices

Another crucial aspect of the way an organization can help or hinder ethical behaviour within it concerns how people are compensated and how their performance is measured. Compensating employees appropriately and monitoring their performance are both important, and if not undertaken with care can themselves lead to ethically questionable situations. Both how people are compensated and how their performance is measured broadcasts what is really important in the organization. This can have inadvertent consequences for how the organization operates. As Robert Jackall notes:

> Whenever structural inducements place premiums on immediate personal gains, especially when mistakes are not penalized, there seems to be a sharp decline in

the likelihood of men and women sacrificing their interests for others, for the organization, or for the common weal. (Jackall [1988] 2010, p. 101)

The impact of business performance targets on ethical behaviour is well documented (for instance, see Jansen and Von Glinow, 1985; Metzger et al., 1993; Treviño and Nelson, 1995). Targets that are given to employees will always influence the schemas through which they perceive salience in any situation. In the UK for instance, government-generated targets concerning hospital waiting times have produced a plethora of unintended consequences relating to how hospital staff manage to achieve targets, from failing to admit ill patients and keeping them waiting in ambulances to 'stacking' them in ward corridors.

One of my favourite stories indicative of how creative individuals can be at meeting performance targets was revealed through a student's research project into hospital waiting time targets:

> While conducting ethnographic research in a waiting room of a doctor's surgery, he noticed that although there was a ticket machine that people could take a ticket from and thus be served on a first-come, first-served basis, there was also a man at the door indicating to people when they could take the ticket. This system was working fine until two people disagreed about who had actually come into the doctor's surgery first. At this point, the question was raised as to why they just couldn't take a ticket when they first arrived, as that was the entire purpose of the ticket machine. The person giving people permission to take tickets explained that each ticket was timed and would show the length of time people spent waiting. In order to hit the target set for the surgery concerning waiting times, his job was to only let people take a ticket when the time on it would keep the surgery within the targeted waiting time.

This is an amusing example perhaps, but it becomes more serious and an issue of more ethical importance when such targets affect care delivery or even the well-being of those trying to adhere to those targets.

Another aspect of performance measurement targets is their generally short-term focus. Short-term focus on profitability or productivity can work against the longer-term health of both plant and people in organizations. For instance, Jackall illustrates how managers keen to show short-term return on their capital assets (RoAs) would delay much-needed upkeep or replacement of large capital items. A commonplace practice was to 'milk' the plant, that is, to take it to its leanest operating possibility and then move on to another job, leaving a starved plant for the incoming manager to deal with. The actions encouraged by this type of short-termism do have ethical consequences, particularly if they mean safety standards are compromised. Box 8.2 encourages you to reflect on the practices of an organization you know well.

 BOX 8.2

REFLECT: CONSIDER AN ORGANIZATION YOU KNOW

Think of an organization you have worked in or where you currently work. How would you describe it in terms of its culture, structure, means of monitoring performance and the way in which authority is exercised? Reflect on the way in which these aspects impact on:

- how accountability works;
- how the details of business are handled;
- the level at which different people know different things.

 QUESTIONS TO CONSIDER

1 What implications does all of this have for the working of ethics in this organization?
2 What do you observe about the way in which the organization is structured and how this influences ethical perception within it?
3 What kinds of discussions about ethics are there in the organization?
4 How would you describe the ethical micro-world of this organization?

These three factors then – the organization's culture, structure and how performance is measured – will have an almost invisible effect on the way that ethics are both perceived and acted upon. I say they are 'almost invisible' because these aspects of an organization are generally taken for granted. They provide the frames within which organizational work is accomplished. However, in navigating the ethical terrain of an organization, it is important to recognize how they operate and the role they are playing in your ability to see and act on ethical aspects of your work.

We move now to what could be considered a form of behaviour where you actually *do* navigate this territory – the domain of 'political behaviour'. Political behaviour may seem antithetical to acting ethically but the following section indicates that acting politically can be accomplished ethically. In fact, the argument is made that in order to bring a more value-based way of operating into the organization, understanding the organization's politics and finding ways of acting within them is crucial.

Acting ethically and acting politically

Although one of the earliest theorists of organization, Max Weber, characterized organizational politics as a 'breakdown of rationality', the inevitability of organizational politics is being increasingly recognized within the organizational theory domain. Similarly, although 'playing politics' is often associated with unethical behaviour, researchers also recognize that acting with political astuteness has the potential of furthering ethical, as well as unethical ends. The following part of this chapter introduces a model that offers the possibility of aligning ethical and political behaviour. It stresses that without political astuteness, actions intended to be done for 'good', may miss their mark and can potentially result in unintended, unethical consequences.

Before introducing that model, the next activity in Box 8.3 invites you to articulate your own assumptions about organizational politics and how they function.

 BOX 8.3

ACTIVITY: IDENTIFYING A POLITICALLY SKILLED PERSON

Think of the most 'political' person you know. This may be a boss or colleague you have previously worked with or it may be someone in your current organization. He or she might also be someone completely outside of your organizational context; for instance, she or he could be a member of your family or someone you know through a club or other leisure-time pursuit. Reflect on the following questions in relation to this person:

 QUESTIONS TO CONSIDER

1 What is it about them that makes you think of them as 'political'?
2 What ends do they achieve through their political behaviour?
3 Are there aspects of the way they engage politically that you would like to emulate?
4 Are there aspects of the way they engage politically that you would like to avoid?

If you are working in a group, share your reflections with one another. Whether you are working with other people or on your own, what have you learned about political behaviour by focusing on this person?

Let's move on now to how the subject of organizational politics is considered by those researching the topic.

Organizational politics

Although there are still organizational theorists who believe politics in organizations to be inherently 'wrong' (including, for instance, Henry Mintzberg, 1983) there are others who suggest this is not actually the case. For instance, the British organizational theorist Ian Mangham explains that 'reasonable people often disagree with regard to both ends and means and can thus be expected to fight for what they are convinced is right, and perhaps more significantly, against that which they are convinced is wrong' (1979, p. 16). This leads to the possibility of thinking about organizational politics as a way in which the plurality of values, aspirations, desires and needs of organizational members can be expressed. It is through political engagement that different voices can be brought into the mainstream of organizational discourse. Interestingly, by suggesting that sometimes people engage in political activity to put forward their views of what is 'wrong', Mangham hints at a link between acting politically and acting ethically.

Another way of thinking of the purpose that organizational politics serve is by considering how limited resources are distributed through an organization. No organization works with unlimited resources. Even those that are cash rich will still have to fight for the best people and the time to accomplish goals. Although elaborate planning processes exist by which resources are allocated, rationality can only go so far in prioritizing among competing demands. Every decision will be based on certain assumptions and the basis for those assumptions will often be grounded in history, powerful people's habits of interpretation and uncertain projections into the future. Subjective judgements always come into play about what is more important, who is more likely to succeed at what they want to do or which market might be most promising. Accordingly, the question of how resources are allocated is often a function of how vying parties position their own view. Such positioning is at the heart of political behaviour.

How people exert influence as they manoeuvre politically can be done from different motivational positions. Some people can exert influence towards ends that are solely self-serving. They want more of the resource in order to build their own empire or to gain more power in the organization. Such self-centred political positioning is often associated with unethical political practices. However, along with a small band of others (Baddeley and James, 1987; Ellen et al., 2013), I am suggesting the possibility of political manoeuvring undertaken for the good of the organization or a larger stakeholder group. A model developed by the British psychologists Simon Baddeley and Kim James is offered as way of understanding how that might be possible.

Owl, fox, donkey or sheep: the possibility of behaviour that is both politically and ethically astute

As a result of research undertaken with local government authorities in the UK, Simon Baddeley and Kim James developed a framework for conceptualizing different kinds of political behaviours within groups or organizations. At the heart of their framework are two behaviours that operate along different continua. The first is called 'reading'. This capacity is similar to the ability to exercise moral perception discussed in Chapter 4 and involves being alert to both the 'visible' and 'invisible' aspects of organizations. For instance, if you are skilled at reading the organization politically, you will not only recognize its formal structure and reporting lines but you will also be aware of the informal ways that work gets accomplished. You will be alert to the networks of relationships and allegiances which mean, for instance, that although one senior manager may have the sign-off authority for budgetary items, it is that manager's personal assistant who really has the power in terms of what gets brought to the budget-holder's attention. Often in organizations those in seemingly 'lowly' positions play gatekeeper roles, which means that certain information is passed on to higher levels of the hierarchy and other information is not. Recognizing the way in which work is actually accomplished is key to reading the political landscape of the organization in which you work.

You can either be very adept at reading these invisible and largely informal aspects or you can be very poor at it. You may even ignore these aspects altogether because of a belief that even to pay attention to them is to 'play politics'. Baddeley and James suggest that being aware of the political landscape you work in is important and that it is the *intention* you hold in reading political territory that differentiates (or can differentiate) between ethical and unethical behaviour.

This dimension of intentionality is picked up in their second continuum: 'carrying'. 'Carrying' refers to the predisposition we carry into specific situations from various self or other orientations. For instance, we can carry the intention to work for the greater good, that is, for the organization at large; or we can carry into the situation the desire to serve our own individualistic purposes. This is not to say that serving the organization can't also serve oneself – in fact these motivations often overlap – however, their continuum suggests that most people will have an overriding intention to be self- or other-serving in a specific situation. If we are primarily concerned about getting ahead ourselves without recourse to the organization's needs, this orientation fosters the kind of self-serving behaviour often associated with political games playing. If, on the other hand, one is using their knowledge

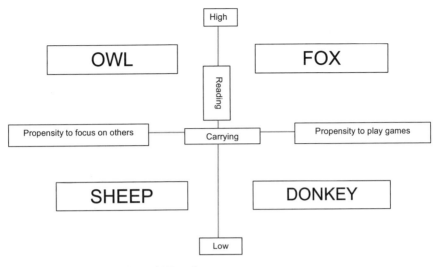

Source: Adapted from Baddeley and James (1987, p. 11).

Figure 8.1 Owl, donkey, fox, sheep modes of political behaviour

of 'the way the organization works' to benefit the organization more broadly, Baddeley and James suggest that this can result in 'wise' political behaviour, which can be aligned with ethical behaviour.

Baddeley and James intersect these two continua to create a two-by-two matrix, in which four different kinds of behaviour are identified. Each of these behavioural quadrants is described in a bit more detail below and shown in Figure 8.1.

In the lower-left quadrant is what they consider to be 'innocent' political behaviour (associated with the animal image of the sheep). This is behaviour that arises from not reading the organization's politics very well, largely due to holding the view that even to read the political landscape is to engage in (bad!) political behaviour. This orientation is underpinned by the desire to do good for the organization and the refusal to engage politically is often grounded in deep-seated ethical values. What is interesting about this position is that, contrary to its intentions, it can result in behaviour that can be dangerous for the individual undertaking it, as well as others reliant on their judgement. Indeed, holding a great deal of positional power within an organization while exercising 'innocent' political behaviour can result in unwitting damage. Birgitte Nyborg, the heroine of the Danish political thriller *Borgen* could be seen to be operating from this position in her early days as prime minister. Not taking the time to read the international political landscape she is operating within causes her to lose credibility with her party, for instance, as she negotiates Denmark's response to the USA's desire to use Danish airspace to transport political prisoners. As we have seen in the previous chapter, not perceiving what is going on or turning a blind eye to things you would rather not see can make you just as ethically culpable as actually committing an act with ill intent (especially if you are in a position of power).

The second way of not reading the organization's political landscape well but carrying into it a predisposition or intention to be self-serving results in 'inept' (or 'donkey-like') political behaviour. This is the kind of behaviour associated with being a bull in a China shop and results from wanting to have one's way but treading on many toes on the way to getting it. Generally those who engage in 'inept' political behaviour do not advance as far as they would like in organizations because they do not have the 'reading' skills that would enable them to do so. They can also be used as organizational 'fall guys', taking the blame for others' bad judgements.

The kind of behaviour most frequently associated with political behaviour is that which comes at the intersection of the ability to read the situation well and using that astuteness to further one's own ends. Baddeley and James label this behaviour as 'clever', which in British terminology has the sense of being smart but perhaps a little *too* smart (the fox). Those who engage in 'clever' political behaviour also often master the capacity to move on to a new position before any catastrophes created in their wake can be attributed to them.

The final intersection, that of high 'reading' skills and the predisposition to work for the benefit of the organization results in what Baddeley and James label 'wise' political behaviour (the owl). Such a way of operating can be aligned with ethical behaviour. Here the person is able to read the organization's formal and informal systems well, and brings a predisposition to work for the greater good (whether conceived as the greater good for the organization or the larger community). 'Wise' political behaviour can often be novel and occasionally unorthodox, and can prompt solutions that fall 'outside the box' of conventional responses. The actions taken by New York Mayor Michael Bloomberg in response to protesters at the Republican National Convention in 2004 could be interpreted as 'wise', for example. In alliance with retailers and public attractions in the city, Bloomberg initiated discounts for 'peaceful protestors' in a range of New York's museums, hotels and restaurants. Rather than focussing predominantly on controlling and restraining the 200 000+ people expected to protest during the convention, Bloomberg's action recognized that the incomers would need food and accommodation. Welcoming them, rather than resisting them, could be a positive move for both the protesters and the city at large.

Of course, not everyone interpreted Bloomberg's solution as 'wise' and many commentators noted its economic focus. Protestors themselves were reported to be rather confused and bemused by the move and the issue of how to really distinguish 'peaceful' protestors from inflammatory ones was never entirely resolved. Indeed, there was still a high degree of protesting activity, with thousands arrested (although 90 per cent of those arrested were quickly released). Tear gas was deployed against crowds in at least one instance. Still, it is interesting that Bloomberg tried something different in this event, which might have been interpreted as 'wise', 'innocent' or 'inept', depending on where his behaviour is seen to lie on the 'reading' and 'carrying' continua.

A few things to note

Throughout the description of the model above the word 'behaviour' has been used in relation to these different modes of operating. It is important to notice that the model was never intended to be used as a way of labelling people. Instead, it is a framework for understanding different ways of acting from a political perspective. It recognizes that in different situations, we can all exercise any of the four different types of behaviour. For instance, within my organizational setting I might have the very best interests of those I work with at heart and consciously try to carry that motivation into my dealings with others. In my family situation, however, long-established feuds and smouldering disagreements between family members (think of the Ewing family in *Dallas*!) may mean that I operate from a much more self-centred place.

Similarly, once you have worked in an organization for a significant amount of time, you may be aware of its political territory almost unconsciously. Moving to a different organization requires you to be open to different assumptions and ways of operating that may be so far outside your 'frame' for how organizations work you may not even see what is going on. The awareness that reading a new organization is important may be obvious, but you may not be able to do so for a while.

Now carry out the activity in Box 8.4, paying attention to political behaviours in light of the model described above.

BOX 8.4

ACTIVITY: POLITICAL BEHAVIOUR IN FILMS

Choose one of the following films to watch:

Margin Call
The Wolf of Wall Street
Hotel Rwanda
Erin Brockovich
Enron: The Smartest Guys in the Room
Thirteen Days

Or any other film that you know that has political operating at its core.
As you watch the film, be particularly attentive to the differing political behaviours characters demonstrate.

 QUESTIONS TO CONSIDER

1 Can you see how sometimes characters switch from what could be described as politically 'innocent' behaviour to politically 'inept' or even 'clever' behaviour?
2 What does it take for characters to be able to enact politically 'wise' behaviour?
3 What happens that enables them to do so?
4 What do you learn from watching how these different behaviours emerge?

As some of the characters in these different films show, it *is* possible to combine political astuteness with ethical action. In fact, political astuteness and ethical behaviour share the common need for sophisticated understanding of the system in which one is located and the intentions, desires and proclivities of others within it. The difference between ethical and shrewd behaviour is where the locus of attention is in terms of the desired outcome. This is not to say that any other-oriented action will not also benefit the individual. Behaviours can be beneficial for the common good and also advantageous to the individual. However, the difference is that the common good is foregrounded in ethically sound political behaviour.

As has been noted earlier, acting wisely often involves innovative and unexpected behaviours. We will examine these kinds of behaviours more closely in Chapter 10. To complete this chapter a strategy developed by the American organizational theorist Debra Meyerson is offered as a practical means of intersecting politically wise and ethically astute ways of operating. Meyerson coined the term 'tempered radicals' to describe those people who strive to discover ways of expressing their value-based individuality within organizations.

Tempered radicals

Intrigued by how individuals in organizations find ways of balancing their values with those of the organizations in which they work, Debra Meyerson of Simmons College in the United States conducted research into what she subsequently called 'tempered radicals' (Meyerson, 2001). Such individuals remain attached to an organization while simultaneously exerting influence on it in an effort either to express their authenticity or change the way it operates. It is a way of being both 'radical' and taking account of the 'norms' of organizational life while trying to change them.

Meyerson offers four types of behaviours indicative of acting as a tempered radical. She suggests that they are progressively more difficult and demanding, developing along a continuum from behaviours which are more 'personally oriented' to those more public and apparent to others.

The first involves what she calls 'disruptive self-expression'. This is a way of being in the world that disrupts others' expectations about how the individual should present themselves within the organizational space. She cites a number of examples of senior women executives who through their choice of clothing or personal appearance exhibit their femininity in traditionally male contexts. One of my favourite examples is of a woman surgeon who chose to wear socks trimmed with frills in the operating theatre as a way of expressing her femininity in that very male-dominated space. Others express their ethnicity through their clothing or hairstyles. Although these gestures in themselves may not change a culture, Meyerson argues that they can disrupt and enlarge it by providing evidence that there are different ways of being or acting within a seemingly prescribed organizational space.

The next strategy Meyerson labels 'verbal *jujitsu*'. She purposely conjures up the martial arts' image of using an opponent's strength against themselves with her choice of the word '*jujitsu*'. When others make demeaning or inappropriate comments, the tempered radical finds ways of turning this inappropriate energy back on the person making such comments. She provides an example of a gay man being insulted by a pre-meeting conversation denigrating a Gay Rights parade. Instead of ignoring the insulting comments, the tempered radical in this case pointed out in a humorous way how much he felt affronted by the photos of their wives many of his heterosexual colleagues kept on their desks. He made the point, without being overly aggressive or shaming. One of the skills central to exercising 'verbal *jujitsu*' is speaking directly from one's own experience rather than blaming or pointing out another's behaviour to be 'wrong'. In owning his own discomfort at a similar display of sexual attraction as his colleague had been dismissing about gay men, this particular tempered radical owed his own experience of a similar phenomenon that heterosexual people assume to be 'normal'.

The third strategy is called 'variable-term opportunism'. This involves being very awake and open to taking opportunities to make small changes when and where they crop up. Meyerson relates the story of a manager becoming aware of the large amount of waste in his company's canteen created by boxing sandwiches in styrofoam containers that were almost immediately discarded. He suggested to the head of the kitchen staff that perhaps the sandwiches could only be boxed when staff requested them to be, thereby saving money and creating less waste. This small change was easily introduced into the canteen's way of operating, with a resulting reduction in rubbish destined for landfill. Key in operating this strategy is the ability to be attentive to the opportunity for these small changes. Additionally, Meyerson points out the importance of tackling 'low-hanging fruit', that is, changes that are easily accomplished and provide quick win/win outcomes.

The final, and most public of Meyerson's strategies she calls 'strategic alliance building'. In identifying this strategy, Meyerson recognizes that significant change in organizations often occurs only through the concerted efforts of disparate groups of people working together. In order to build strategic alliances, individuals must be on the lookout for others who might share similar views to their own. Importantly, this requires identifying those closest to home, in one's own department or part of the organization but, more importantly, outside of one's own familiar territory in other parts of the organization. Strong strategic alliances are those that bring together the interests of people from throughout the organization. Central to building such alliances is to approach others openly without holding past prejudices and by using inquiry to explore how people view the organization's policies and practices.

Meyerson's work is directed at those attempting to alter organizations in ways that make them more humane places. In particular, tempered radicals offer a means by which the organization is called to appreciate the diversity of views and perspectives within it. Tempered radicals are motivated by the desire to make organizations better places to work by initiating change 'from the inside'. I suggest that the strategies Meyerson offers are practical guides for how ethical goals can be pursued and achieved in the rough and tumble world of organizations (Box 8.5).

BOX 8.5

ACTIVITY: EXPERIMENTING WITH 'TEMPERED RADICAL' STRATEGIES

Select one of Meyerson's tempered radical tactics to experiment with in your own life. For instance, you may choose to build your strategic alliances by getting in touch with people who work in departments other than your own or you may experiment with 'disruptive self-expression' by wearing something to work that expresses a part of yourself you normally 'leave at home'. Take an action aligned with the tactic you choose.

 QUESTIONS TO CONSIDER

1 Why have you chosen that action? What is your aspiration for choosing that practice?
2 What is the outcome of the action you take?
3 What do you learn about yourself through taking this action?
4 What do you learn about others and about your organization?
5 How will you take this learning forward?

Write your observations down in your learning journal, and if you are working with a group, spend some time discussing what you have learned from doing this activity.

This chapter has examined the role that an organization's culture, structure and performance management systems play in its members' ability to both perceive and act on ethically salient situations. One of the key learning points I hope you have gleaned is that as an individual you can be completely committed to acting ethically at work but still find yourself compromised due to the very nature of your organization. By being alert to the ways in which seemingly neutral aspects of organizational life impact on your ability to act on your own ethical values, you can be better prepared to navigate wisely through this territory.

The next chapter draws the circle of ethical awareness that much bigger, by considering issues at stake when attempting to work ethically beyond the bounds of your own organization.

NOTE

1 See http://retailindustry.about.com/od/retailbestpractices/ig/Company-Mission-Statements/Amazon-com-Mission-Statement.htm; accessed 10 February 2014.

9

Ethics beyond the organization: stakeholders and intercultural contexts

The previous chapters have focused on developing ethical astuteness from within organizational boundaries. It is clear, however, that organizations create impacts beyond their bounds and therefore have ethical responsibilities beyond them too. Organizations and their activities affect the communities they operate within on many levels: they play a role in how social relationships within communities develop; they affect local, national and international economies and their use of raw materials and ways of disposing waste make significant impacts on the environment. Not only do their actions have consequences in the present time but organizations' activities will also touch future generations. This chapter addresses how you might bring ethical astuteness to your engagement with this range of external stakeholders. Most importantly, it prompts you to think beyond your organization's shareholders in terms of those who also deserve moral consideration.

Examples of the situations central to the concerns of this chapter include the following:

- General Motors' decision to close the bulk of its factory lines in the 1990s, a decision documented in Michael Moore's film *Roger & Me*. Not only did the closure affect those who lost their jobs but it has also been implicated in the decline of socioeconomic prosperity in Flint, Michigan.
- BP's negligence, which resulted in the *Deepwater Horizon* oil spill in April 2010. The spill dumped more than 200 million gallons of oil into the Gulf of Mexico, killing 11 employees living on the rig and causing untold environmental damage to the Gulf and its flora and fauna.
- The financial crisis of 2008, largely the consequence of bad banking decisions, which resulted in the collapse of hundreds of small businesses and the livelihoods of those dependent upon them throughout the USA and Europe in particular (with knock-on effects felt throughout the world).

- The way in which Western-based supermarkets are implicated in slavery within Thailand's fishing industry, particularly in relation to the catching and processing of prawns.

Each of these examples illustrates how the actions of an organization can result in damage far outside its boundaries. Hundreds and thousands of innocent people as well as creatures have been badly affected by the kind of ethical malfeasance evident from these cases. How might organizations begin to think about those who will be affected by their activities? Stakeholder theory, introduced below, provides one starting point.

Stakeholder theory

The USA-based strategy theorist R. Edward Freeman is credited for bringing the notion of stakeholder theory into popular usage. Although the term first appeared in the 1960s, his book, *Strategic Management: A Stakeholder Approach* (Freeman, 1984), is credited with bringing the concept into broad awareness within organizational thinking. He defines a stakeholder as: 'any group or individual who can affect or is affected by the achievement of the organization's objectives' (ibid., p. 46).

Although stakeholder theory is often assumed to be connected with how a firm acts from an ethical perspective, there is no intrinsic link between ethics and stakeholder theory. The roots of stakeholder theory are situated squarely within the field of strategic management rather than business ethics. Following from this, the theory is not primarily concerned with ethical relations among stakeholders. From a cynical point of view it can be viewed as a means by which firms identify factions that could stop them from doing business, ethical or not, and this is the primary purpose of stakeholder 'mapping'.

Kenneth Goodpaster (1991) elaborates on this idea when he suggests that there are two distinct ways in which stakeholder theory can be used. First, and most commonly, it can be used as a tool for stakeholder analysis. This involves merely identifying a firm's stakeholders and imagining the positive or negative impacts each of those stakeholders could exert on the firm. Ideally it would also include the positive and negative ways in which the firm's actions can impact on the stakeholders. Goodpaster claims such stakeholder identification and 'mapping' to be 'ethically neutral' (although in a footnote he does highlight the fact that 'the very process of *identifying* affected parties involves imagination in a way that can lead to a natural empathetic or caring response' (ibid., note 4, p. 70; original emphasis).

Goodpaster labels the second use of stakeholder theory 'stakeholder synthesis'. This involves prioritizing different stakeholders' views (it is virtually impossible for a firm to please *all* of its stakeholders simultaneously!). This leads to choices being made about how stakeholders' perspectives will be considered, what actions will be aligned with those choices and, finally, the learning that comes as a consequence of these actions and their subsequent impacts and responses.

A key question Goodpaster's article poses is: 'When does the substance of stakeholder theory become ethical?' (1991, p. 57). In raising this question he notes that stakeholders are often regarded instrumentally and reflects that stakeholder analysis is frequently used as a means of minimizing damage to the organization itself, rather than to identify the harm the organization could cause others. In this way Goodpaster raises the issue of power and the idea that sometimes less powerful voices can be ignored during the stakeholder synthesis part of the process.

Goodpaster highlights two points that are of particular importance in relation to ethics. First he notes that government and regulators are often seen as responsible for taking care of those without a voice (thus reducing a firm's responsibility to do so). However, he goes on to point out that whereas previously governments in the USA may have seen looking after less powerful stakeholders as key to their roles, more recently governments seem to act in favour of big business. He also asserts that, generally speaking, the impact of any action on a firm's shareholders is most commonly used as the 'normative touchstone' around which all other decisions are made. This in itself can compromise ethical intent because when differing interests need to be prioritized, more often than not shareholder views will trump those of less powerful voices. The following activity in Box 9.1 aims to indicate how difficult prioritizing stakeholders' viewpoints can be.

👥 BOX 9.1

ACTIVITY: STAKEHOLDER MAPPING

This activity aims to evoke a sense of the complexities involved with judging priorities between competing stakeholder needs. Think of an organization that you currently work for or have worked for in the past or an organization that you know quite well. It could, for instance, be the university you are enrolled in, your church or any community organization you are familiar with:

➡

- Identify the stakeholders who are most central to the organization's ways of operating.
- Identify other stakeholders who operate at the boundaries of the organization.
- Now stretch your imagination to think of different groups of people who may be affected by the organization's actions but who are not directly connected to the organization. For instance, this might include those living in the community where the organization operates and not just those who are alive now but also future generations. Consider those who are affected by the CO_2 emissions produced through the organization's processes that live many miles away. Call to mind those who will be affected by the organization's waste products.
- Working with this list of different stakeholders, some more directly affected by the organization's operations than others, list two or three key concerns they will have in relation to the organization's operations.
- As you review this list of concerns, can you identify any that are diametrically opposed? For instance, a key concern of those employed by the organization may be to stay in work, which may translate into selling more products (which necessarily creates more CO_2), whereas a key concern of another stakeholder may be to avoid rising CO_2 levels in the atmosphere in order to avert climate change.
- How do you prioritize these competing perspectives and desires? If you are working in a learning team, have different people in the team represent different viewpoints and discuss their perspectives.

Reflect on what you learn by undertaking this activity.

Goodpaster suggests that the ethical solution is for every stakeholder to be given equal moral consideration in cases where perspectives and desires of stakeholders differ. However, this way of thinking results in what he calls the 'stakeholder paradox', which arises from the logical view that the duties a firm has to its shareholders are qualitatively different from those the firm has to its stakeholders. The way through this paradox is by suggesting that organizations owe the same duty of ethical care to others outside the organization as does any individual. He explains this, writing: 'the way out of the stakeholder paradox lies in understanding that the conscience of the corporation is a logical and moral extension of the consciences of its principals' (ibid., p. 68).

In other words, organizations must accept their moral obligations as members of communities and should 'not injure, lie to or cheat these stakeholders *quite apart* from whether it is in the stockholders' interests' (ibid., pp. 69–70; original emphasis). Goodpaster does not make any explicit recommendations about how this can be accomplished. As the activity above highlighted, there are other issues besides 'injuring, lying and cheating' that can still have dire consequences for stakeholders not central to an organization's operations.

Assessing an organization's responsibilities to those external to it is a key challenge for ethical mastery.

One means by which organizations have attempted to take up such responsibility towards their communities and wider stakeholder groups is through corporate social responsibility programmes. The next section of the chapter describes corporate social responsibility and how organizations are using it to meet their ethical aspirations.

Corporate social responsibility (CSR)

The concept that corporations should be in some way answerable to stakeholders beyond their owners can be identified as long ago as 1946, when the then Dean of Harvard Business School, Donald David, told the graduating class that future business executives needed to 'take heed of the responsibilities that had come to rest on their shoulders' (quoted from Carroll and Shabana, 2010, p. 86). Indeed, although we may think of corporate social responsibility (CSR) as a relatively new idea within management circles, the assumption that organizations in general, and corporations in particular, have responsibilities to those other than just their shareholders is as old as the Industrial Revolution itself. It was really only with Milton Friedman's admonishment that 'management has one responsibility – to maximize the profits of its owners or shareholders' (1970, p. 33) that management's responsibility was distilled to this sole focus.

In their excellent review of the history of CSR Archie Carroll and Kareem Shabana (2010) chart how although the concept has been around since before World War II, its emphasis has changed through the decades. For instance, during the 1960s it was linked to larger social movements concerned with civil liberties and the rights of women, whereas in the 1980s it became much more closely associated with business ethics and corporate performance. More recently it evokes the idea of 'global corporate citizenship', as the ways in which organizations' operations impact beyond national boundaries, draw on the world's resources and contribute to climate change and environmental degradation have come more sharply into focus.

Earlier, Carroll, who has become one of the USA's leading scholars researching CSR, offered a definition highlighting the scope of CSR activities: 'the social responsibility of business encompasses the economic, legal, ethical and discretionary/philanthropic expectations that society has of organizations at a given point in time' (Carroll, 1991, p. 41). In a later article, he and Shabana make the point that the economic and legal responsibilities are 'required', the ethical responsibilities are 'expected', and the discretionary/philanthropic activities are 'desired' (Carroll and Shabana, 2010, p. 90).

The key question becomes, how do organizations actually enact CSR-based activities? One common tactic has been through using a 'triple bottom line' approach, in which organizations consider the impact of their activities in three different arenas: the economic, the social and the ecological (Elkington, 1999). The notion is that to operate well and responsibly, an organization must make trade-offs between these, rather than focus, for instance, entirely on maximizing profits to the exclusion of social and ecological considerations.

Organizations take up their corporate social responsibility in many different ways. Some of the most popular include:

- volunteer schemes whereby organizational members are given time off to work with the local community or sometimes the not-so-local community when people are seconded to foreign developing countries;
- raising money for local concerns;
- taking part in beach cleans or other environmental activities relevant to the local community in which the organization is situated;
- sponsoring local sports clubs or after-school activity clubs for children, teenagers or other members of the local community;
- linking with communities in developing countries to provide consulting services or other knowledge exchange programmes (Grayson and Exter, 2012).

There is a good deal of criticism of corporate social responsibility initiatives from both popular and scholarly accounts (see Fleming, Roberts and Garsten, 2013). These include:

- the concern that CSR activities are more accurately described as public relations activities than as means for providing lasting value to the community as a whole;
- that such activities are used to cover up a multitude of offences and it would be better for organizations to address those rather than obscure them with activities that do not address the harm their activities cause;
- that rather than being of lasting environmental value, many of the activities undertaken by corporates constitute nothing more than 'greenwash' intended to have marketing benefits.

These concerns raise questions about the ways in which organizations make decisions about the kinds of CSR activities they undertake. How do organizations make sure that the actions they initiate create the impact they intend to have? The following activity in Box 9.2 invites you to consider a real case of CSR activity and its intended benefits.

 BOX 9.2

ACTIVITY: EXPLORING CSR

Identify an organization you would like to know more about in terms of its CSR activities. Search for as much information you can about how this organization approaches CSR. You can find this information through visiting its corporate website, through reading its annual report or media reports.

 QUESTIONS TO CONSIDER

1 What does this organization actually do by way of CSR-focused activities?
2 How do the initiatives occur? Who decides what is to be done? Do companies decide what they will do in conjunction with the stakeholders they hope to benefit?
3 What percentage of the firm's time/budget is allocated to this work?
4 Is there any monitoring in place to determine the outcomes of the actions taken? How does the firm assess what it is doing? If there is monitoring, is this done in a participatory way?
5 Are there actions the organization could take that would be more beneficial to the intended recipients of the action?
6 Are there actions the organization should STOP doing that would have a greater impact from a CSR point of view than the things the organization is *trying* to do?
7 Are there conflicting accounts about what the organization claims it is doing and what the media reports claim? How do you account for this discrepancy?

Discuss what you have found with your learning buddy or in your learning group. What have you noticed about the way organizations approach CSR from this activity?

Are CSR-based activities always ethical?

There is an underlying assumption that CSR activities are by their nature, ethical. However, as this book has already demonstrated, deciding about whether an activity is ethical or not, and in relation to which stakeholder group, is not always completely straightforward. This can be particularly apparent in relation to the CSR-based initiatives undertaken by organizations. Case Study 9.1, based on research conducted by Rajiv Maher while he was undertaking his UK-based PhD demonstrates this point.

CASE STUDY 9.1

Mining in the Huasco Valley, Chile

The Huasco Valley is a corridor of fertile land amidst one of the world's most arid deserts in Northern Chile. For generations it has been farmed by the Diaguita people, an indigenous community who earn their livelihood by farming. Growing food there relies heavily on the clean water that flows in rivers originating in the glaciers in the mountains that surround the valley.

In the 1980s, the Canadian company Barrick Gold gained rights to begin mining gold in the Huasco Valley. Their work would involve destroying the glaciers surrounding the valley. Barrick Gold only began exercising the rights 20 years later at the turn of the twenty-first century. When the work began, protests from the local community resulted in the decision to 'move', rather than 'destroy', the glaciers. This was still not seen to be an acceptable solution to the local people. Protests against the mines and various types of sabotage have delayed the mining project, which if left unabated, would be the second largest gold mining operation in Latin America. The following sets out the differing positions of the community members and Barrick Gold as revealed by Maher's 18-month-long, in-depth ethnographic study (Maher, 2014). It then goes on to describe the CSR activities Barrick Gold has attempted to implement in order to appease the community.

The community

The community largely comprises indigenous farmers (the Diaguita people) who have worked the land for generations. Grapes are their major cash-earning crop and their growth is dependent on access to the clean water of the Huasco River. Maher's study indicates that for the most part, the people are contented with their way of life and do not want the trappings of 'development'. In their view, 'development' is not necessarily a good thing, or something they aspire towards. They want to remain on the land they have inhabited for generations, doing the farming that they do and enjoying their local environment, or '*pachamama*' as they call it.

Their main argument against the mine concerns the fear that the removal of the glacier will dry up the local River Huasco, their main source of water, and that the tailing (mining waste) works will pollute the river that is essential to the growing of their crops. Additionally, community members fear the social impact of the influx of miners and the drunken and aggressive behaviour associated with those who travel to work in small communities and have little to do in their free time.

Barrick Gold

A Canadian-based multinational mining company, Barrick Gold is in the business of discovering and extracting mineral resources that are increasingly in demand throughout the world.

CASE STUDY 9.1 *(continued)*

Barrick Gold is extracting minerals to fulfil the needs of the likes of you and me, who require the minerals for the many forms of technology we use, as well as for displays of wealth (in the case of gold mining). In other words, the mining is being done to fulfil the needs of much that we consider a normal part of living in the developed world.

From Barrick Gold's point of view, its work is helpful in that it provides minerals demanded by both developed and developing nations. Additionally, it generates wealth to the host nation and community through paying for mining rights and by bringing employment to the communities proximate to their activities. In these ways, the development it initiates is seen as contributing to human welfare.

CSR activities

Upon meeting the opposition of the community, Barrick Gold instigated a vigorous CSR campaign in order to win the support of the community. This largely focused on helping the Diaguita people to gain recognition from the Chilean government as a bona fide indigenous group. They engaged anthropologists and social scientists to work with the Diaguita people to unearth their history and to complete the documentation required to achieve indigenous status.

What is interesting about this approach is that it could have worked against Barrick Gold's interests because with a heightened sense of their own heritage and legal status it could be anticipated that the Diaguita people would be a more formidable force against the company. A number of community members question the extent to which Barrick Gold's ways of going about helping them were truly generous, however. The timing of the granting of indigenous status occurred after the mining rights were given, thus lessening the impact of this status (had the Diaguita been given this status prior to the mining grants, they would have had more power in halting the mining programme). Additionally, in the anthropologists' account of the Diaguita history, their engagement with small-scale mining, rather than farming, was empha-sized. This was seen as a way to make the case that the mining that Barrick Gold was going to do was in keeping with the Diaguita's cultural history.

Other CSR-based initiatives started by Barrick Gold included courses on cake baking and doll making, which, from the company's point of view, were a means of providing additional skills to the local people. From the community's point of view, these initiatives were interpreted as demeaning and patronizing. If Barrick Gold really wanted to help them, the company would provide more money for education or health facilities, was the commonly held view among community members.

Take a look at some questions for discussion in Box 9.3.

BOX 9.3

ACTIVITY: DISCUSS WHAT YOU LEARN FROM THE HUASCO VALLEY CASE STUDY

? QUESTIONS TO CONSIDER

1 Describe the different positions taken by the Diaguita community and Barrick Gold. Can you identify each player's schemas? What are the assumptions underpinning each view?
2 What do you think about the CSR initiatives taken by the company in terms of its ethics?
3 How do you see issues of power impinging on the case?
4 What does the case tell you about the nature of CSR activities?

The case begins to demonstrate some of the difficulties that arise from an ethical perspective when working interculturally. Given the different values held by those of different world views, how is it possible to discover which is 'right' when they come into conflict? This is an especially important question to ask when the parties involved are working from vastly different power bases. Western-based corporations increasingly have the support of hosting governments, as these governments see the wealth generated through mining activity as beneficial for their people. However, as is clear in the case of the Huasco Valley mining project, such activities can have unwanted and sometimes disastrous consequences for those who live proximate to the mining project.

Indeed, whether you assume 'development' itself to be a 'good' or 'questionable' activity depends on your own schema and the culture that informs your thinking. The next part of the chapter takes a closer look at the impact of national culture on how such contested issues can be interpreted from an ethical point of view.

Ethics in an international context

If ethics are a way of regulating social relations, the taken-for-granted assumptions about what is a 'correct' way of regulating those relations differ from culture to culture. Difficulties can arise when cultures with very different assumptions about 'what is correct' begin to interact. Questions such interactions raise include the following:

- Is it right to abide by the adage 'when in Rome, do as the Romans do?'
- How ethical is it to force one culture's ethical standards on another?
- Is there an ethical standard that trumps others, for instance are there 'human rights' issues that are superordinate to individual national standards of behaviour?
- How does the individual manager cope with being 'caught between cultures'?

Let's refer to the fictional story of Help-Others to illustrate some of the issues at stake:

> Simon Hill works for an American-based international charity, Help-Others, which operates in some of the most poverty-stricken areas of the world. Help-Others is determined to act ethically wherever it operates and offers very clear guidelines as to how its members should interact with people and communities it is trying to assist. One of the lynchpins of its ethical policy is that members of the charity should not accept any gifts from community members.
>
> In a number of the countries within which Help-Others works however, gift-giving is a central way in which relationships are formed. Gift-giving is a means by which newcomers are welcomed into the community and it facilitates social relations by embodying the give and take of societal reciprocity. In his first overseas environment, Simon is placed in a Ghanaian community where gift-giving is part of the culture. He soon discovers that Help-Others completely ignores head office's edicts prohibiting the acceptance of gifts and finds that staff members often receive eggs, chickens, artwork and sometimes alcohol and other luxury items from those they are working with. When he asks his boss about the practice, he is told that 'head office doesn't understand the nature of the work that is being done "on the ground"'. If he and his staff do not accept the gifts, the community will feel unable to accept their help. It is a means of normalizing relations between Help-Others and the community so that they are seen to be working in partnership rather than Help-Others providing 'charity'.
>
> Simon feels very uncomfortable with the practice, even though he does understand the rationale behind his boss's thinking. Additionally, this is his first placement and he doesn't want to upset a way of working that seems long established. His conscience tells him he should report what is happening back to head office but another part of him wonders what purpose that would serve.

What should Simon do? The activity in Box 9.4 helps you explore this question.

👥 BOX 9.4

ACTIVITY: DISCUSS SIMON'S OPTIONS

If you are working in a learning group, discuss what you see as Simon's options with other members of your group. What assumptions underpin the different options you discuss?

This story reveals the difficulties that can arise when an individual wants to adhere to the ethical code of their organization but finds the code at odds with the national culture in which their work is situated. How does the individual make sense of the circumstances and move forward in a way that appeases their own ethical sense while at the same time respecting that sometimes ethical values differ?

In order to begin to address these questions, the next part of the chapter covers the following territory:

- What ethical differences exist between different cultures?
- What are some of the aspects that make working ethically across culture so difficult?
- What models exist for making sense of different ethical orientations?
- What practical steps can an individual take when faced with these types of issues?

Ethical differences between cultures: what is the cause?

As mentioned earlier in this chapter, embedded within national cultures are different understandings of the optimal way of regulating social relations. For example, in the Arab world the concept of 'wasta' operates, which involves 'a social network of interpersonal connections rooted in family and kinship ties' (Hutchings and Weir, 2006, p. 278). In practice this translates into the expectation that if you have done well in the world, you will help those closest to you by finding them jobs or giving them favours. This way of helping family members (though it is, of course, also done in the West) is not accepted or expected in the same way and can be labelled 'nepotism'. In many European countries business is regularly conducted within social worlds: in Finland business people take saunas together, in Italy dining together is an essential part of building trusting business relations. This expectation is not quite so marked in the USA where, although there can be overlap between business and social events (for instance, on the golf course), the 'correctness' of a gap between the two is seen as normal.

The American business ethicists Wines and Napier (1992) identify three ways in which national culture can affect how ethics are viewed and acted upon in different national cultures:

Where the national culture is in terms of its developmental/temporal scale.

This idea arises from the hypothesis that ethics develop according to how 'advanced' a culture is. Similar to Kohlberg's (1984) notion of individual moral development (see the Glossary for a summary of this theory) national cultures are seen to be located on a continuum from the less ethically sophisticated to the more ethically sophisticated. This idea can be seen to play out historically, for instance, in a practice such as slavery. In the eighteenth and nineteenth centuries in Europe and the United States, it was considered by some that enslaving Africans was ethically permissible. (It must be noted that not all of those within the USA felt this to be morally acceptable. Significant elements of the population found slavery to be morally abhorrent but the dominant political culture allowed it to exist until the time of the Civil War.) This ethical wrong was dismantled after the Civil War but continues to exist in some countries in the world today.

This argument is based on the view that there are some ethical rights that are more advanced, or superior, to others. Certainly, this would seem to be the case in an issue such as female genital mutilation (FMG), which may be seen to be ethically acceptable in some countries but which is seen as abhorrent and in breach of basic human rights in others. Although perhaps intuitively satisfying in some ways, there are also difficulties associated with this idea of development, however. Who gets to decide what is 'ethical' or not when working across cultures is often a function of which nation has the greater political clout (see Michaelson, 2010 for a critique of the notion that more developed countries exhibit more developed ethics, for instance). The ethics of the 'developed world' may be seen to be superior to 'less developed' nations; however, we have already seen in the case of mining in the Huasco Valley that dismissing the views of indigenous peoples can lead to questionable ethical decisions.

The weight accorded different or competing values

Different national cultures rate some values as more important than others. For instance, in the culture where Simon worked, gift-giving was part of the nature of communal reciprocity. It is based on an understanding of the way human relationships work and how gift-giving builds relationships. In such cultures gift-giving is associated with affluence and the person who gives the larger gift is seen as most important. Such reciprocity and the way it cements trusting relationships is more important than the avoidance of favourable consideration. Help-Others, however is governed by a different national culture, and one in which the giving of gifts is associated with bribery, rather than with the give and take of relational ways of operating.

Of course these differences can also be apparent within the same national culture. For instance, in the USA both the sanctity of life and the rights of the individual to exercise free choice are upheld. These values come into conflict when the question of the acceptability of abortion is raised: pro-lifers argue that the sanctity of life should trump individual freedom, whereas others support the right of the mother to make her own choice. When two different values collide, which should take precedence?

The question of *how* to take such a decision is also fraught. Is it more appropriate to incorporate rationally based analytic ways of reaching decisions or is it more important to respond emotionally in a way that accounts for relational ties? Is it better to use formalized systems or more informal 'intuitive' ways of making these kinds of judgements? Rather than even attempting to resolve these questions here I am suggesting that being aware of them is a first step in addressing them. From there, applying the foundational skills of moral perception, imagination and inquiry provides a means by which resolution can emerge.

The manner in which the society applies the abstract value

Although many national cultures may share a belief in the appropriateness of abstract terms such as 'justice', 'fairness' or even 'compassion', those cultures may have very different ways of putting those concepts into practice. For instance, 'justice' is a concept upheld in both UK- and USA-based judicial systems. However, in some states within the USA, capital punishment is seen as an acceptable way of enacting justice in the case of capital crimes, whereas in the UK justice is seen to be done in such cases through the application of life sentences.

Wines and Napier provide the example of past cultures that had an abstract ethical value about revering their dead. In the Andean culture this sense of reverence was enacted by relatives eating their dead family members, whereas in Hindu culture the dead were cremated (Wines and Napier, 1992, p. 833).

Dimensions of culture

Another way of thinking about the difference between national cultures is through the generalized ways in which those within a culture typically respond according to different parameters. For instance, those from the United States generally have a more 'individualistic' orientation, whereas the Chinese are recognized to have a more 'collectivist' culture. In other words, within the USA, the rights of the individual are more often seen to carry greater weight than the rights of the collective, whereas the rights of the collective are generally thought to be more important than those of the individual in China. There are two well-known frameworks for considering such cultural dimensions, that developed by the Dutch social-psychologist Geert Hofstede (Hofstede, 1980) and a later one developed by the English sociologist Charles Hamden-Turner and his Dutch colleague Alfons Trompenaars (Hampden-Turner and Trompenaars, 1993). These two frameworks can be combined to suggest nine different 'cultural dimensions' along which a national culture can be described. These dimensions are outlined in Table 9.1.

Table 9.1 Dimensions of culture

Dimension	Description
Individualism/collectivism	Individualist cultures prioritize the interest of the individual over the collective, whereas collectivist cultures prioritize the interests of the collective over those of the individual
Power distance	In those cultures exhibiting high-power distance there is an acceptance that individuals of higher status have certain privileges that those of lower status do not, whereas in low-power distance cultures democratic participation is favoured
Uncertainty avoidance	Within high-uncertainty-avoidance cultures written rules and procedures are preferred, with little tolerance for deviance from these, whereas low-uncertainty-avoidance cultures rely less on formal procedures
Masculine/feminine	Masculine cultures prioritize achievement and material success whereas feminine cultures prioritize quality of life and relational aspects
Universalism/particularism	More universalist cultures look to act on generalizable principles, whereas more particularistic cultures tend to consider individual cases
Achievement/ascription	Achievement-oriented cultures base status on what has been accomplished by the individual, whereas ascription-oriented cultures base status on inborn characteristics, such as gender or social class or on those that naturally accrue, such as age

Table 9.1 Dimensions of culture

Dimension	Description
Analysis/integration	High-analysis cultures tend to consider factors within a particular domain, whereas high-integration cultures tend to look beyond the domain to consider more holistic and global factors that may impact on a situation
Orientation to the environment	This refers to the extent to which the external environment is accounted for in how choices are made. Those cultures with an external focus consider the ways in which the external environment impacts on choices available, whereas those with a more internal focus believe it is possible to control one's life circumstances and try to control the external environment
Orientation towards time	Those cultures with a longer-term time horizon consider the way in which actions taken today will impact on the future, whereas those with a shorter time horizon disconnect the present from the future

Source: Derived from Thorne and Saunders (2002).

 BOX 9.5

ACTIVITY: CONVERSE WITH SOMEONE FROM A DIFFERENT NATIONAL CULTURE

Identify an individual from a national culture different from your own. Choose three of the dimensions listed in Table 9.1 and have a conversation with them about how they see their national culture operating in relation to yours.

 QUESTIONS TO CONSIDER

1 What are the ethical implications for the differing ways you see each other's cultures? For instance, if one of you assumes you come from an economically wealthier culture, what are the implications for how you relate together?
2 What does the person you've been speaking with find most difficult to understand about your culture?
3 What do you find most difficult to understand about their culture?
4 Can either of you identify ways in which your values clash that you believe are based in your national cultures?

Reflect on your conversation and jot down in your learning journal any insights that arise from it. In particular, note any responses from the person you spoke with that you found particularly surprising.

As I hope the activity in Box 9.5 might have revealed, understanding something about the differing dimensions along which national cultures prioritize their social relations can provide insight into why those from particular cultures read and act on ethical dilemmas in the way they do. However, knowing these dimensions doesn't tell you how to resolve these differences when you are faced with them. For example, Simon may now understand that the culture he is working in might be more 'feminine' in its orientation than the organization he works for (Help-Others). Knowing that, however, doesn't help him decide whether or not he should inform Head Office that the branch he works for is ignoring its policy about the exchange of gifts. It may be helpful to suggest a few guidelines for using these dimensions within real-life situations:

- First, it is important to remember that even though the cultural dimensions provide some insight into the kinds of positions that might be taken by those of particular cultures, even within cultures there are subgroups of people who will hold different views. This is also apparent when you are looking at the different view of indigenous peoples, who may reside within a particular national culture but who may have very entrenched and strong perspectives of their own. The learning point here is that these dimensions serve only as a guide and a point of reference for thinking about the assumptions underpinning different position-taking across cultures.
- The end point of what is ethical to do in any situation very much depends on the assumptions you are holding as you encounter the situation. This point has been made previously in the book but never is this clearer than in the arena of cross-cultural assumptions about what desired outcomes should be prioritized when engaging with one another ethically.
- In such situations there is no 'right' answer that will suddenly make itself known, no matter how much you analyse the situation. What *is* important from an ethical perspective is the *process* used for coming to a decision. Within that process it is important to recognize the role power dynamics play and how they influence the process undertaken to achieve resolution. Otherwise, it is all too likely that those with the greatest power are the ones who have their ethical assumptions taken as the way forward. Is it ethical that in the end those in power are the ones who have their ethics come to the fore? If those in power are the ones whose voice overrides those without power, is there mitigating action that is right for the powerful party to take? For instance, should indigenous people such as the Diaguita be compensated 'over the odds' in order to be recompensed in some way for the fact that their voices have been overruled?

Before moving forward, it may be useful to take a moment and reflect on these guidelines, either on your own or with your learning team. (1) What further issues do these suggestions raise for you? (2) Are there additional guidelines you would offer based on your own experience of working in this territory?

This section of the chapter has revealed some of the complexity involved in engaging in ethical terrain across different cultural boundaries. The next part of the chapter introduces specific aspects of organizational operations that particularly lend themselves to ethical issues arising beyond the organization's bounds.

Supply chain issues

In 1991 the international sporting goods company Nike came into disrepute when newspaper stories emerged about the conditions under which its products were being manufactured. The bad press focused particularly on Nike's factories in Indonesia where workers suffered in very poor conditions and were being paid 'slave wages'. Executives from the company were, on the surface anyway, surprised to learn of the conditions. Allegedly, they had not visited the manufacturing facilities once this work had been outsourced and were shocked at the conditions they found once they did so. After seven years of increasing public outcry the then CEO, Phil Knight, announced that 'Nike products had become synonymous with slave labour, forced overtime and arbitrary abuse' and that he 'truly believed American consumers did not want to buy products made in abusive conditions'.[1] A series of processes were put into place to halt abusive practices within factories outsourced to create Nike products. These culminated in Nike being the first major retailer to produce a list of all of its factories throughout the world, making them open for scrutiny in a way previously unheard of.

More recently, supermarkets within the UK have come under pressure to be aware of the inhumane conditions suffered by workers in their supply chains in order to harvest seafood such as prawns and tuna. In particular, the brutal conditions present in Thailand, including the re-emergence of slavery and the trafficking of people into the trade has come to the public's attention (Hodal et al., 2014). It will be interesting to see if public pressure once again asserts itself in forcing supermarkets to reassess their ethical stance and reconsider how they procure seafood products.

Understanding the conditions in which subcomponents of their products are produced is a major challenge for organizations dependent on global networks of suppliers. Given that the decision to off-shore manufacturing or service aspects of work is often made on the basis of lower labour costs it is reasonable to expect that such lower costs can go hand in hand with lower levels of care for workers. This, of course, has ethical implications, as Nike discovered.

There are, however, also questions about conditions that are considered unacceptable in some Western countries but may not be considered so abhorrent in other countries. For instance, although in most Western countries child labour is seen to be an unquestioned evil, in some poorer countries, the ability of children to work is a vital resource for a family's economy. Is it correct to place restrictions on children's ability to work when doing so creates greater hardships for families and their communities? On the other hand, does 'going along with' such practices prevent them from changing?

From an ethical perspective, internationally based supply chains then raise questions such as:

- How far does a parent company's responsibility extend in policing the activities of firms within its supply chain?
- What kinds of standards should be applied to supply chain companies? Is it correct to apply the same standards in very different nations?
- What about pay? Is it right to pay workers more or less than they would earn if they were working in a different country? What about comparable pay? Is it right to pay workers more than is traditional for their area but more aligned with the parent company's policies even if this drives up costs for the overall community?

Unfortunately, I am not suggesting there are easy answers to these questions! I hope the book has indicated that there are rarely generalizable answers that will be correct for every context. What is vital is that these and other questions like them need to be raised and considered in relation to the context within which an organization operates. Otherwise, as Nike and numerous other multinational firms have discovered, public displeasure may force such questions to be addressed.

The ethics of selling – *who* do you sell *what* to?

A second key area of ethical concern when working cross-culturally questions the appropriateness of selling certain products into markets that may have lower levels of regulation than the market in which the product is manufactured or developed. For instance, what are the ethics of tobacco companies targeting customers in Africa, Greece and other countries where regulators do not restrict the kind of packaging that can be used on tobacco products as they are regulated in the USA, the UK or much of Europe?

The Swiss food company Nestlé faced negative public pressure in relation to its marketing of baby-milk products in countries such as Mozambique where clean water supplies for mixing the milk could not be guaranteed. Certainly consumers around the world who have boycotted Nestlé's products in response to its selling techniques (which included having sales staff dressed in nurses' uniforms to enhance their credibility when selling the product) believe such practices to be unethical.

Similarly, what are the ethics of selling weapons and war machinery to 'rogue nations' who have been implicated in the killing of ethnic groups within their own populations? What about selling arms to poor nations whose citizens are starving? Is it only ethically correct to sell weapons to the 'good guys'? How do you know who they are?

Bribery

Probably the intercultural ethics issue most readily discussed and the focal point of much debate in the arena of intercultural ethical practices concerns the question of bribery (Martin et al., 2007; McKinney and Moore, 2007). Many Western-based organizations have formal statements prohibiting the paying of bribes. Whether or not such codes exist, executives can find themselves at one time or another being faced with the choice of being able to facilitate business quickly through paying a bribe or not.

Anecdotally, a number of junior managers I have worked with over the years report being told to 'get the job done, no matter what it costs', from senior managers. Such a nudge-and-a-wink approach to condoning the paying of bribes can leave the individual manager very exposed.

Here, as with the previous two specific aspects of cross-cultural ethics, it is vital to be alert to the nuances of context in play. Additionally, understanding your organization's approach to bribery and how it may or may not be explicitly articulated in a code of practice is vital in helping you navigate this difficult ethical territory.

Conclusion

This chapter has focused on one of the most difficult aspects of ethical mastery in organizations – that of how and to what extent organizations and individuals within them are morally responsible for the ripple effects of their activities. This is being written shortly after the US Attorney General's conclusion that BP as an organization, and the two senior supervisors aboard the *Deepwater Horizon* oil rig as individuals, are responsible for 14 criminal offences including 11 counts of manslaughter in relation to the explosion and subsequent oil spill that occurred on that rig in April 2010.[2] BP has accepted its guilt and will pay £4 billion in fines and penalties associated with that disaster. It is expected that BP executives will go to prison for their negligence in relation to this case.

The *Deepwater Horizon* case presents a dramatic demonstration of the way in which the effects of an organization's activities extend well beyond the boardroom, the canteen, or even the physical plant associated with it. In our ever more connected world, organizations' activities affect all of us. Having the moral perception and imagination to apprehend possible ethical consequences will be an increasingly vital area of managerial expertise as we move through the twenty-first century. The next and final chapter of the book summarizes the path we have travelled so far in preparing you for that challenge.

NOTES

1 See http://www.businessinsider.com/how-nike-solved-its-sweatshop-problem-2013-5 for more information about this case; accessed 13 June 2014.

2 See http://www.theguardian.com/environment/2014/jun/05/bp-deepwater-horizon-spill-report-failures-risks; accessed 9 June 2014.

10

Continuing the journey towards ethical mastery

> [The master at ethics] does not act out of ethics, but embodies it like any expert embodies his know-how; the wise man is ethical, or more explicitly, his actions arise from inclinations that his disposition produces in a response to specific situations.
>
> (Varela, 1992, p. 30)

This book has offered an approach towards ethics that, if practised, can lead to a more sophisticated level of ethical astuteness, regardless of your starting point. This final chapter summarizes key points that have been offered, along with providing pointers for continuing your journey towards ethical mastery. It does this by focusing on four specific areas:

- the nature of practice itself, and what you need to do in order to practise well;
- key practices for ethical development;
- holistic ethical exemplars as captured in the terms 'phronesis' and 'crazy wisdom';
- suggesting practical ways in which you can keep the learning process of mastering ethical astuteness alive.

Practise, practise, practise

As was suggested in the introductory chapter of the book, the key to becoming good at anything is the commitment to practising. In truth, we are always practising something. With every action we take (or don't take) we are rehearsing a way of being in the world. Those behaviours that we perform by rote, like brushing our teeth, eating with chopsticks or knives and forks or even engaging in chitchat with colleagues or friends, were at some point behaviours we had to learn. Some behaviours seem to 'come naturally' but that's because we have done them so often they have become a habit.

There are important differences between repeating the same actions or behaviours over and over again from a sense of habit and practising in a way that leads to improvement. The kind of practice that leads to ethical mastery (or indeed mastery of any kind) requires a particular kind of attention and commitment. Three characteristics of this kind of practice are discussed in more detail below:

Set time aside

As has also been mentioned throughout the text, situations rarely appear labelled as 'ethical dilemmas'. Instead, the realization that the issue you are working with has an ethical component generally emerges as the situation unfolds. In this way, practising the behaviours that lead to ethical mastery is different from becoming a master of piano playing through setting aside an hour a day to rehearse scales. Seemingly it is more difficult to set aside an hour a day to 'practise being more ethical'.

However, this book has introduced a number of 'practices' that are part of developing ethical mastery, like active listening, asking questions or making a conscious effort to 'notice what you are noticing'. Although you may not be able to set aside an hour a day to 'practise being ethical', it *is* possible to set aside time to rehearse one of these constitutive practices. Better still, you can work these practices into your normal life as you engage with other people, either in organizational settings, like meetings, or just in day-to-day conversations. For instance, you can commit to practising your active listening skills when you attend a departmental meeting, and refrain from jumping in and asserting your point of view, as may be natural to you. If your proclivity is to hang back and just listen and not say anything at such events, you could commit to practising the habit of asking good questions.

In everyday interactions it is possible to practise 'noticing what you are noticing'. In fact, unless you begin to practise this capacity within everyday situations, you will not benefit from this capability. 'Noticing what you are noticing' begins to be beneficial when you are able to do so within the rigmarole of daily life. Before you have developed this habit, however, committing to 'noticing what you are noticing' within specific situations, or at particular times of the day, can help to make this kind of awareness second nature. Some people set their watch to beep every hour to remind them to take a moment to consciously 'notice what they are noticing' at that particular instant of the day. In such ways it is possible to ring-fence particular meetings or events to make them occasions to practise focusing your attention and taking time to notice.

Be specific in reflecting

Repeating something over and over again does not necessarily result in expertise. You need to bring a particular *kind* of engagement to the practice arena to benefit from it. That is, you need to attend to what you are doing and be as specific as possible in discerning what causes lead to what effects. If you are playing football/soccer and persistently lose the ball when tackled on the left side, you have to understand what you are doing on that left side to perpetuate that cycle. Similarly, if you find yourself continually flying off the handle in situations where you would like to be calm, and you know better outcomes would result if you were more considered about how you approach them, then you need to dissect what is occurring *before* you fly off the handle so that you can understand something of your 'trigger points'. You need to be sleuth-like in understanding what has happened to lay the ground for your undesirable behaviour. Once you have identified the prompts that set your reaction in motion, you can create strategies for recognizing and dealing with them differently in the future.

One of the key jobs for music teachers is to help students to reflect constructively on what they are doing as they play and how they can alter it to produce more pleasing results. The teacher can be particularly helpful in enabling the aspiring musician to notice what it is they are doing that is holding them back from being able to progress. The more specific the feedback is, the better chance the student has of being able to alter the particular way of playing that is inhibiting them.

Similarly with learning ethical astuteness, what is critical is to be able to identify the precise actions or behaviours that hinder your ability to work well from an ethical perspective. It is important to question whether the difficulty you have in acting ethically arises because you repeatedly do not notice the ethical component of a situation before it is too late. Or instead, does your failure arise from not mustering the courage to speak when you notice an ethical issue that is not being attended to by anyone else? Both of these shortcomings inhibit your ethical response but each requires a different 'remedy' to become more ethically masterful.

This kind of self-reflection can be difficult. Even in the example of learning to play an instrument, the importance of having a teacher is clear. Teachers can see you and the way you are playing the piano (or acting in social situations) in a way that is difficult, if not impossible, for you to see yourself. Within this textbook you have been encouraged to discuss your thoughts about different cases or activities with a 'learning group'. Such a group provides a useful mirror to the blindspots and ways of doing things that may be inhibiting your own ethical development. In life more broadly it can be difficult to involve such a group of people to turn to on an ongoing basis. If such a group is impossible for you to organize, there are two other avenues you might explore. (1) Engage the help and support of another individual to talk with about these ideas. This can be someone within your organization or it can be a friend or a coach external to your organization. Issues to discuss and your behaviours in relation to them don't have to be framed as 'ethical', they can be of any content. (2) Keep a learning journal like the one you have been using through this textbook. The process of writing something down can itself bring new insight into the situation. Furthermore, having something written down means you can refer to it, reflect on it and see what you are saying in a different light from when it just whirls around in your mind.

Be specific about experimenting with new actions

As well as the need to be specific about the behaviours you aim to practice, it is crucial to be specific about the ways in which you will experiment with new behaviours. For instance, if you commit to becoming a better listener, what precise behaviour associated with listening do you want to practise? Do you want to practise the skill of really paying attention to what the other person is saying, without forming your retort as they speak? Do you want to practise the skill of summarizing what you are hearing and checking whether or not you have heard it correctly before responding? Do you want to practise asking good questions as a result of what you are hearing, rather than just barging in with your opinion about what you *think* the other person has said? These are all different aspects of active listening, which together create the capability of being an effective listener. In order to practise active listening, in the first instance you may want to concentrate on just one of these components.

The critical point is you need to reflect on what has happened and what you will do differently. There is a lovely poem by Portia Nelson that summarizes the journey of practising and improving very well:

I walk down the street.
There is a deep hole in the sidewalk.
I fall in.
I am lost . . . I am helpless.
It isn't my fault.
It takes forever to find a way out.

I walk down the same street.
There is a deep hole in the sidewalk.
I pretend I don't see it.
I fall in again.
I can't believe I am in the same place.
But, it isn't my fault.
It still takes me a long time to get out.

I walk down the same street.
There is a deep hole in the sidewalk.
I see it is there.
I still fall in. It's a habit.
My eyes are open.
I know where I am.
It is my fault. I get out immediately.

I walk down the same street.
There is a deep hole in the sidewalk.
I walk around it.

I walk down another street.
(Nelson, 2012, p. 3)

In other words, Portia Nelson's poem is suggesting that through practising noticing, reflecting and experimenting, it is possible to learn to walk around the 'holes' that plague one's life!

Practise *what*? The P-A-I-R model

Generally speaking, this textbook has refrained from offering prescriptive models about how to achieve ethical mastery. *However*, I also recognize the value of a mnemonic that could help you to easily recall some of the key learning points that have been offered. The PAIR mnemonic is therefore introduced as a way of remembering four behavioural practices that are core to developing ethical mastery. They can be used as 'memory touchstones', with the added suggestion that you can choose to focus on one a day or even one a week, in order to develop each skill.

Pause: practise negative capability

As I hope has been highlighted throughout the book, the ability to 'pause' is critical to attaining ethical mastery. It is aligned with the notion of 'negative capability', which was introduced in Chapter 6. It is the capacity to dwell with difficult situations rather than immediately reacting in a knee-jerk fashion. This can be difficult when emotions run high or when you are feeling under pressure. However, pausing can enable you to reflect momentarily on the action you are about to take and consider its longer-term consequences.

The 'pause' is also useful, in that it can provide a space for deeper intuitive knowing of what might be 'right or wrong' in a given situation to arise. If you immediately act, there is a good chance you will be acting from ingrained emotional patterns (until you actually reach a point of ethical mastery!). If you can't take a full-blown stop, just practising a fleeting pause can be beneficial. Before barging into someone's office to tell them what you think of what they are doing – *pause. Breathe.* Now think again about what you are doing. Is there a more constructive or appropriate way of moving forward?

Attend: notice what you are noticing

In recent years there has been growing interest in the notion of 'mindfulness' and how it can be of use within the managerial arena. Mindfulness is a practice of noticing what the mind is noticing.[1] At a simplistic level it involves attending to the way thoughts arise and then dissolve within our attentional awareness. A key route into mindfulness is through the practice of following one's breath. Just notice the breath and where it is in the body. Noticing thoughts, rather than judging them, and watching as they rise and dissolve can tune you into your inner arc of awareness and how it creates helpful *and* unhelpful interpretations. Becoming stuck on a particular way of interpreting events can limit the capacity to see a situation from a broader perspective. Becoming aware of how the story you are telling yourself colours your perceptions can be a first step in inviting moral imagination in – how might this situation look from the other person's point of view?

One of the very best examples of how the mind tells stories that can lead to action with disastrous ethical consequences is that of Othello. In Shakespeare's play, Othello comes under the influence of his second in command, Iago, who, unbeknownst to Othello, hates him and wants to damage him. He plants seeds of distrust in Othello's mind about his wife Desdemona's fidelity. From mere scraps of data, such as Desdemona's handkerchief being in Iago's possession, an entire (erroneous!) story of infidelity is created, which results in Othello murdering Desdemona. This outcome has been manufactured merely through the internal story that Othello tells himself, which is fed by Iago's innuendos and false statements.

How often do we ourselves find ourselves acting in ways we regret because of 'stories' we have told ourselves? The practice of mindfulness – 'noticing what one is noticing' and noticing the story one is telling oneself about circumstances and how they fit together – is vital to being able to stop our internal monologue from creating fabrications that can lead to unfortunate action.

Inquire: practise asking artful questions

Chapter 3 introduced the foundational practice of inquiring. Like 'paying attention', inquiring is such an important practice it is vital to reiterate it here. Following from the suggestions concerning mindfulness, one of the key actions you can take to discover the veracity of the stories you are telling yourself is through being inquiring of those you are making the stories about. What are their motives? What is their perception of the way things are? It is also important to be inquiring about your own behaviour. 'What is motivating me in this situation?' is almost always a good question to ask. Answering this question may provide information about what you are 'carrying' into the mix (to refer back to Baddeley and James' notion of the 'carrying' component of organizational politics in Chapter 8). Being able to ask questions that evoke the other person's reality is vital and having the openness of mind to believe what is being said is also essential if an ethical response is to be discovered.

Chapter 3 noted the preference for asking questions that are open rather than closed, such as:

● How do you see this situation?
● What is behind what is going on here?
● What is the goal you are after?
● Is there something you are trying to avoid here?
● Where is the pressure coming from in terms of the decision-making process?

One of the key aspects of artful inquiry is being alert to who you are asking. Asking those you suspect will have a different point of view from your own is vital to unearthing new information. Seek out perceptions from throughout the organization, as well as within the parts of the organization you are familiar with. This suggestion aligns with Debra Meyerson's fourth tenet of being a tempered radical offered in Chapter 8, that of 'strategic alliance building'. One of the best ways of building such alliances is proactively seeking out others to discover how they view situations and why. Generally speaking, people love being asked about their viewpoints, so garnering this kind of information is usually not very difficult!

Having said this, the manner in which you ask questions will influence the quality of response you get. Be aware of the power dynamics that are inevitably at play. It is perhaps more common to reflect on how they work if you are the one with more power than the person you are asking (e.g., how can you create more of a chance that you will be eliciting a truthful account and not just what the other person thinks you want to hear?). However, power dynamics will also affect the conversation if you are talking with someone of a higher status position than yourself (e.g., how can you ask question in a way that allows them to save face?). The art of asking good questions then, is not just in framing questions well, but in the very way you comport yourself as you ask them.

Reflect: practise reflectiveness

As has been highlighted in the opening section of this chapter, in order to gain from practice you need to reflect on what you have done, the effect it has had and what specific actions you might take should you want to make a change in outcome. Making time to reflect on a regular basis is essential to mastering any capability. A way to integrate spaces for reflection into your day-to-day routine will increase the chances of it becoming a beneficial habit. For instance, taking 15 minutes prior to a meeting to reflect on its purpose, what you want to notice during it, and how you want to contribute to it, can become part of your routine relatively easily. Scheduling an extra ten minutes after meetings to reflect on them and what you have learned from them can similarly be a way of interweaving reflection time into your daily habits.

Being self-critical in a constructive manner is vitally important. Remember, as Robert Quinn demonstrates in his book *Change the World: How Ordinary People can Accomplish Extraordinary Results* (Quinn, 2000) you and your actions are the one thing you have any control of in trying to change any system. Quinn highlights the importance of being 'other focused' but 'self-directed' in initiating change. In other words, it is important to notice how others are and how they react to situations and circumstances. However, in trying to create change, the only person you can actually change is yourself. Especially if you are a person with power in the system, any behavioural change you make will reverberate through the larger group or organization.

These four meta-practices for achieving ethical mastery are represented in Figure 10.1.

$$P_{ause} \Longrightarrow A_{ttend} \Longrightarrow I_{nquire} \Longrightarrow R_{eflect}$$

Figure 10.1 PAIR mnemonic

Holistic approaches to ethical mastery – from '*phronesis*' to 'crazy wisdom'

I'd like to end the book by introducing two approaches that represent holistic accounts of ethical mastery. The first comes from the Greek tradition and is associated with Aristotle. This is the idea of '*phronesis*'. The second was hinted at in Chapter 7 and is the concept of 'crazy wisdom'. Let's begin by examining the concept of *phronesis*.

Phronesis

In popular terms, *phronesis* has come to mean 'practical wisdom'. It is the kind of wisdom that enables one to deal with the everyday ethical issues they face in a competent way. To understand the full potential of *phronesis*, however, it may be helpful to return to its Greek roots. *Phronesis* is one of the virtues that Aristotle introduces, alongside other virtues such as *techne* (craftsmanship) *sophia* (wisdom) and *logia* (knowledge gained through calculation). In his categorization of virtues, Aristotle divides virtues into two types, 'intellectual' virtues, excellences of 'mind', which can be developed through rational attention, and 'ethical virtues', or virtues of 'character', which are described as being more holistic, embodied and integrated into the way one 'is' in the world.

Within Aristotle's system, *phronesis* is unique in that it is categorized both as an intellectual and as an ethical virtue (Eikeland, 2008). In other words, *phronesis* combines both a capacity to engage intellectually well and to work from an excellence of character in meeting the demands of living in community. The notion of community as being the arena in which *phronesis* is exercised is critical and perhaps why *phronesis* is referred to as 'practical wisdom'. It is what enables you to negotiate the competing demands arising from working and living with others and deciding whose best interests to serve. As such it is a vital virtue for anyone hoping to work ethically within organizations to develop.

How is it possible to develop *phronesis*? Aristotle is clear about this: *phronesis* can only be developed in community with wise others; by watching them operate and, if possible, through discussion with them. Deliberating is crucial because, according to Aristotle, *phronesis* is not about complying to externally developed rules or 'codes of conduct' but requires attention to the particularities of the given situation. Moreover, he argues that it is impossible to know all of the details of a situation oneself and that for achieving a broader perspective, one must rely on talking with others. In this way, the means by which an action is determined are always the point of ethical deliberation. How one 'gets to' a resolution is as important, if not more important, than the resolution itself, which may inevitably be shown to be more or less 'ethical' in the future. Before moving on to consider the notion of 'crazy wisdom', let's ground the concept of *phronesis* by populating your own 'phronetic' community in Box 10.1.

 BOX 10.1

ACTIVITY: BUILDING YOUR COMMUNITY OF *PHRONESIS*

This activity is designed to help you create your own community of *phronesis* – wise others you can deliberate with when you face tricky ethical dilemmas.

- Identify people you know who you would wish to be part of your own phronetic community. This might include people you currently work with or attend university with, it may include members of your family, it may include friends. Make a list of these people and for each one note why you would want them to be in your community. What virtues do they embody for you? Can you think of a situation you have seen them handle that you have particularly admired? In what ways would you like to be like them?
- Now think of church, political, community or other leaders or people of note still living that you would like to include in your community. Make a list of them, and similar to what you have done in the first part of this activity, note why you hold them in such esteem and what it is about each of them that you value enough to be included.
- Now think of historic figures who you admire and would like to include in your community of *phronesis*. Add them to your list and, once again, note the reasons why you would like to include them.
- Finally, think of mythological or fictional characters you would like to include. Again, after listing them be sure to note why you would like to include them. What particular aspects of ethical dilemmas do you believe they would be able to help you with?
- Now that you have assembled your community of *phronesis*, choose one person, either living, deceased or even fictional, to write a letter to. In this letter, tell the person why you are including them in your community, and what you hope they will be able to help you with in particular, as you practise the skills of developing ethical mastery.
- If the person is living, you may consider sending your letter to them. If they are not alive, it may be useful to read the letter to someone you trust and to explore their response.

One of the important aspects of this activity is for you to learn that there is a range of people you can call on for their views when you face difficult ethical territory. Becoming a master is never something you do on your own!

Crazy wisdom

The final concept to introduce to you as you embark on your journey towards ethical mastery is 'crazy wisdom'. Crazy wisdom is an orientation that enables you to act in ways that may seem strange, and sometimes even unethical but that often reveal a critical dynamic or truth about the situation at hand. It is often expressed through paradoxical behaviour akin to the kind of 'wise political' behaviour introduced in Chapter 8. The most important characteristic of crazy wisdom is that it cannot be logically determined in the way often suggested by frameworks promoting ethical decision-making. It emerges from a wellspring of experience and reflection and involves being able to see beyond the illusions of situations as they present themselves, to more basic and underlying dynamics.

In Chapter 8, the example of Mayor Michael Bloomberg welcoming protestors to New York City during the 2008 Republican Convention was offered as indicative of 'wise' political behaviour. I think it might also be considered as a piece of 'crazy wisdom'. Rather than building up the police presence and fostering the atmosphere of conflict, welcoming protestors was apparently a 'crazy' move. We can never know whether it diffused the level of possible violence that might have ensued during that weekend, but we can see that it recognized a different way of dealing with the potential problem.

On a similar note, the incoming CEO of Hydro Aluminium Corporation in Norway, Johnny Undeli, took a very different approach when faced with the likely fall of the company into bankruptcy in the late 1990s. He painted the entire factory white. Instead of insisting everyone undertook 'change management' courses this slightly crazy move had the effect of reinvigorating factory workers until it became one of Norway's top performing companies in the aluminium extrusion field (see Barry and Meisiek, 2010, for the full story). By painting the factory white, Undeli tackled the issue with an aesthetic solution, rather than a rationally derived one, and his staff responded in a similarly holistic, embodied way.

Another example of a person who could be seen to enact 'crazy wisdom' is the Nobel Peace Prize winner Wangari Maathai. A Kenyan environmentalist, Maathai led the Green Belt Movement in Kenya, most famously planting trees within a part of the Karura Forest in Nairobi designated to be transformed into a golf course. Maathai and many of her followers were arrested when they came into conflict with construction engineers and workers ready to begin their assault on the area. However, the distribution of a film of that event caused worldwide uproar and led the Kenyan officials to release those held in prison. Her work has made an impact on the environmental movement throughout the world, starting with her stubborn insistence that planting trees could make a difference.

When I have asked colleagues and friends for instances of 'crazy wisdom' in their experience, examples have been few and far between. For all of its rarity, however, 'crazy wisdom' may be a worthy aspiration, especially for its capacity to shake up preconceptions and ways of seeing the world that keep us treading unquestioned pathways. Box 10.2 invites you to consider your experience of crazy wisdom.

 BOX 10.2

ACTIVITY: IDENTIFYING ACTIONS INDICATIVE OF CRAZY WISDOM

Have you experienced someone acting in response to an ethical dilemma or, in fact, any kind of challenging situation with the kind of 'crazy wisdom' introduced here? Describe the situation and the person's response.

 QUESTIONS TO CONSIDER

1 Why do you think it is indicative of 'crazy wisdom'?
2 How did their action enable you to see the situation differently?
3 Have you ever responded to a situation yourself with an approach akin to 'crazy wisdom'?
4 Where did your idea for your response come from?
5 What do you learn by considering 'crazy wisdom' as an apt response to ethical dilemmas?

Keeping the quest for ethical mastery alive

In coming to the end of this particular part of your journey towards ethical mastery, let's return to the story of Parsifal introduced in Chapter 3. As you will recall, in this story Parsifal set off, leaving his mother and his home, to undertake a quest. When he lumbered away on his old horse with his sack of belongings slung over his shoulder, he didn't quite know where he was going or indeed, why. He just knew he had to go. Previously when we examined this story, we focused primarily on why Parsifal failed to ask the King what was wrong in the Kingdom when they first met. In revisiting the legend, I'd like to dwell with three other aspects of Parsifal's quest and how they are analogous to the journey towards ethical mastery.

Intrinsic vs extrinsic motivation

Thinking back to the legend, you will remember that Parsifal set off on his quest because of an internally directed need to do so. There was no externally driven reason for him to leave his mother and the safety of their home together. In fact, some would say that there were compelling and even 'ethical' arguments for him staying to care for her. After all, she was ageing and he was her only son. However, Parsifal experienced an inner yearning to go out into the world and to learn what it was like for himself. This intrinsic motivation for growth carried him through the difficult times ahead. It was as if he knew that in order to grow up and become a man, he needed to leave home and discover who he was away from the safety and comforts he had known all of his life.

Similarly, the journey towards ethical mastery relies heavily on the intrinsic motivation to become more ethically astute. As has been shown throughout the text, organizational dynamics can often work *against* ethical engagement and action, rather than nudging you towards them. There is much that will call you back to the comfort of conforming, remaining silent rather than asking difficult questions, remaining within your own silo of acquaintances rather than reaching out to others across the organization, trying to avoid, rather than trying to engage with, those stakeholders whose lives your decisions will affect. Often, like Parsifal setting off on his quest, you will not know exactly where you are going or even why. The important thing is to remain alert to the context, accept help from wise others and learn from mistakes you make along the way. For certainly, as was the case in Parsifal's story, you will make mistakes!

The learning that comes from mistakes

In the very brief summary of the Parsifal legend given in Chapter 3, very little detail was given about the number and type of adventures Parsifal had along his journey of self-discovery. But there were many: he trusted the wrong people, his small bundle of belongings was stolen, he lost his horse, from time to time he fell into bad company. He did some fairly stupid things to draw the attention of a damsel he wished to woo. Like the person continually falling into the hole in Portia Nelson's poem, he didn't always get out the first time round. However, through engaging with the world around him and reflecting on the quality of that engagement, Parsifal does eventually learn. This is evidenced by the fact that on his second visit to the dying Kingdom, he asks what is wrong. He has learned the power of asking such questions and has also developed the courage to ask them.

Similarly, as you try out the foundational practices of paying attention and asking questions, you may initially become frustrated at your inability to pay attention or to come up with a question you feel is worth asking. You may get to the point where you know a great question to ask but you are too fearful of the consequences of asking it. It is important in such circumstances to reflect on what has happened and then develop a plan for how you will respond differently next time. (There will *always* be a 'next time'.) Rather than remaining silent, for instance, you may promise yourself you will at least ask, 'Could you explain a bit more about why this is being done this way?' You may plan to talk with people before an important meeting where decisions are being made to understand more of the political undercurrents in operation. You might think of ways of reframing the situation and your role within it. Probably most importantly, you could speak with someone else about it and together develop a plan for how you might engage differently should a similar situation arise in the future.

The wisdom gained from those you meet along the way

Throughout his quest, Parsifal continually encounters others: sometimes creatures or other humans who readily offer him help or encouragement, and sometimes bandits who cause him trouble but in retrospect turn out to be his most valuable teachers. Parsifal eventually learns that everyone he meets along the way is potentially a teacher. Guides in legends like Parsifal often fall into one of three categories and I suspect these might also turn up on the ethical journey:

Creatures

These are often animals or trolls, who have intuitive powers of and other than rational ways of knowing. Their presence echoes John Dewey's suggestion ([1934] 2009) that in order to really be present in the moment and learn to trust our intuitive, embodied apprehensions, we should watch animals. They are naturally attuned to the present moment and also sense things that human beings readily dismiss. This is certainly true in the legend of Parsifal where his horse provides a constant source of intuitive knowing for him. Where/who are your creaturely sources of intuitive knowing?

Bandits and other bringers of misfortune

These are the robbers who explicitly steal all of your worldly goods as well as the snake-oil sellers who tempt you into doing things you know you shouldn't. Often by losing their material goods travellers on their hero or heroine's quest discover internal resources that may have been buried before misfortune draws them forth. By continually falling under the spell of seduction travellers have the opportunity to face temptation and choose differently. Who have been the bringers of misfortune in your life? In retrospect have they also brought you awareness or insight you would otherwise have missed?

Witches and wizards and those with supernatural powers to do good (or evil!)

A bit like bandits, witches and wizards are not always what they seem along the heroic quest. The gifts and powers that such characters can bestow often have some kind of 'hook' attached. Midas discovered this after a genie granted his wish for the power to transform everything he touched into gold. Be careful when witches or wizards suggest they can grant your wishes! However, witches and wizards don't only grant wishes, they can be the source of wisdom and guidance and can be important members of your community of *phronesis*. Referring back to the film *The Scent of a Woman* which we explored in Chapter 7, the blind ex-commander, Frank, proved to be an important wizard in Charlie's life. Who are the witches and wizards in your life? How can you partake of their knowledge and experience?

Finally . . .

If you pick up any newspaper in the world and study the items considered newsworthy, you will notice how questions of ethics play a central role in our human preoccupations. There are reports about companies dodging tax and CEOs who have been economical with the truth, there are stories about people overstepping limits and all manner of violent engagements around the world. There are questions that fall into ethically 'grey' areas – what is the balance between a government's desire to keep its citizens safe and surveillance that intrudes on privacy? There are also stories of courageous women and men who have put their own needs, and sometimes well-being, aside to come to the aid of others. Questions of ethics are at the core of much that we find interesting as human beings; they are central to the legends that have been passed down through history, they are at the nub of popular films ranging from *Harry Potter* to *12 Years a Slave*.

This textbook aspires to help you identify this core aspect at the heart of human relations, whether it arrives packaged as an 'ethical issue' or not. Through paying attention, asking good questions and being willing to step into the emotional world of 'the other', you will progress some way towards developing the kind of astuteness necessary to navigate organizational micro-worlds often at odds with your own ethical intent. However, as you will be aware by now, to those who are masters, the journey is never over. You can always improve your capacity to see, feel and act from an ethical perspective. In this way the quest towards ethical mastery is an ongoing commitment. You will, however, be able to note your progress as you begin to act with greater awareness, see the ethical component of situations as salient, and increase your capacity to stop, pause, inquire and be reflective about what you might do next. More importantly, this book offers you the challenge to continually ask yourself, 'Who do I want to be?' as you engage with organizational contexts, as well as the larger community and world which we share.

NOTE

1 For more information about mindfulness as a practice see Thich Nhat Hanh's book *The Miracle of Mindfulness* (1991) or Jon Kabat-Zinn's book *Wherever You Go There You Are: Mindfulness Meditation in Everyday Life* (1994).

References

Addams, J. (2002), *Democracy and Social Ethics*, Urbana, IL: University of Illinois Press.

Albert, S. and G.G. Bell (2002), 'Timing and music', *Academy of Management Review*, **27**(4), 574–93.

Allison, G. (1969), 'Conceptual models and the Cuban missile crisis', *The American Political Science Review*, **63**(3), 689–718.

Anderson, M.L. (2003), 'Embodied cognition: A field guide', *Artificial Intelligence*, **149**(1), 91–130.

Angwin, R. (1994), *Riding the Dragon: Myth and the Inner Journey*, Shaftesbury, UK: Element Books.

Arendt, H. (1971), in M. McCarthy (ed.), *The Life of the Mind*, New York: Harcourt.

Aristotle (2009), *The Nicomachean Ethics* (D. Ross, trans.), Oxford: Oxford University Press.

Baddeley, S. and K. James (1987), 'Owl, fox, donkey or sheep: Political skills for managers', *Management Learning*, **18**(1), 3–19.

Barry, D. and S. Meisiek (2010), 'The art of leadership and its fine art shadow', *Leadership*, **6**(3), 331–49.

Barsalou, L.W. (2008), 'Grounded cognition', *Annual Review of Psychology*, **59**(1), 617–45.

Bartunek, J.M. (1984), 'Changing interpretive schemes and organizational restructuring: The example of a religious order', *Administrative Science Quarterly*, **29**(3), 355–72.

Bartunek, J.M. and R.A. Necochea (2000), 'Old insights and new times: Kairos, Inca cosmology, and their contributions to contemporary management inquiry', *Journal of Management Inquiry*, **9**(2), 103–13.

Benedikt, A.F. (2002), 'On doing the right thing at the right time', in P. Sipiora and J.S. Baumlin (eds), *Rhetoric and Kairos: Essays in History, Theory, and Praxis*, Albany, NY: State University of New York Press, pp. 226–35.

Blum, L.A. (1994), *Moral Perception and Particularity*, Cambridge, UK: Cambridge University Press.

Brown, M.E. and L.K. Treviño (2006), 'Ethical leadership: A review and future directions', *Leadership Quarterly*, **17**(6), 595–616.

Caldwell, D.F. and D. Moberg (2007), 'An exploratory investigation of the effect of ethical culture in activating moral imagination', *Journal of Business Ethics*, **73**(2), 193–204.

Callahan, D. (2004), *The Cheating Culture: Why More Americans are Doing Wrong to Get Ahead*, Eugene, OR: Harvest Books.

Callicott, J.B. (1996), *Earth Insights: A Multi-cultural Survey of Ecological Ethics from the Mediterranean Basin to the Australian Outback*, Berkeley, CA: University of California Press.

Carroll, A.B. (1991), 'Pyramid of corporate social responsibility: Toward the moral management of organizational stakeholders', *Business Horizons*, **34**(4), 39–48.

Carroll, A.B. and K.M. Shabana (2010), 'The business case for corporate social responsibility: A review of concepts, research and practice', *International Journal of Management Reviews*, **12**(1), 85–105.

Cheffers, M. and M. Pakaluk (2005), *A New Approach to Understanding Accounting Ethics*, Manchaug, MA: Allen David Press.

Cheney, J. and A. Weston (1999), 'Environmental ethics as environmental etiquette: Toward an ethics-based epistemology', *Environmental Ethics*, **21**(2), 115–34.

Christensen, D., J. Barnes and D. Rees (2007), 'Developing resolve to have moral courage: A field comparison of teaching methods', *Journal of Business Ethics Education*, **4**, 79–96.

Clement, G. (1996), *Care, Autonomy and Justice: Feminism and the Ethic of Care*, Boulder, CO: Westview.

Cohan, J.A. (2002), '"I didn't know" and "I was only doing my job": Has corporate governance careened out of control ? A case study of Enron's information myopia', *Journal of Business Ethics*, **40**(3), 275–99.

Cooperrider, D.L. and S. Srivastva (1987), 'Appreciative inquiry in organizational life', in R. Woodman and W. Pasmore (eds), *Research in Organizational Change and Development, Vol. 1*, Greenwich, CT: JAI Press, pp. 129–69.

Darley, J.M. and B. Latane (1968), 'Bystander interventions in emergencies', *Journal of Personality and Social Psychology*, **8**(4), 377–83.

Dewey, J. ([1934] 2009), *Art as Experience*, New York: Perigee Books.

Dillard, J.F. and K. Yuthas (2002), 'Ethical audit decisions: A structuration perspective', *Journal of Business Ethics*, **36**(1–2), 49–64.

Drumwright, M.E. and P.E. Murphy (2004), 'How advertising practitioners view ethics: Moral muteness, moral myopia, and moral imagination', *Journal of Advertising*, **33**(2), 7–24.

Easwaran, E. (2007), *The Bhagavad Gita*, Tomales, CA: Nilgiri Press.

Eikeland, O. (2008), *The Ways of Aristotle: Aristotelian Phronesis, Aristotelian Philosophy of Dialogue, and Action Research*, Bern: Peter Lang.

Elkington, J. (1999), *Cannibals with Forks: The Triple Bottom Line of 21st Century Businesses*, Oxford: Capstone.

Ellen, B.P., C. Douglas, G.R. Ferris and P. Perrewe (2013), 'Authentic and political leadership: Opposite ends of the same continuum?', in D. Ladkin and C. Spiller (eds), *Authentic Leadership: Clashes, Convergences and Coalescences*, Cheltenham, UK and Northampton, MA, USA: Edward Elgar Publishing, pp. 231–36.

Eterovich, F.H. (1966), 'Classical and medieval intellectualist thought: Plato, Aristotle, Aquinas', in J.A. Mann and G.F. Kreyche (eds), *Approaches to Morality: Readings in Ethics from Classical Philosophy to Existentialisam*, New York: Harcourt, Brace & World, Inc, pp. 26–60.

Fleming, P., J. Roberts and C. Garsten (2013), 'In search of corporate social responsibility: Introduction to special issue', *Organization*, **20**(3), 337–48.

Freeman, R.E. (1984), *Strategic Management: A Stakeholder Approach*, Boston, MA: Pitman.

Friedman, M. (1970), 'The social responsibility of business is to increase its profit', *New York Times Magazine*, 32–9.

Gaarder, J. (1997), *Hello? Is Anybody There?*, London: Orion.

Garcia, S.M., K. Weaver, G.B. Moskowitz and J.M. Darley (2002), 'Crowded minds: The implicit bystander effect', *Journal of Personality and Social Psychology*, **83**(4), 843–53.

Gilligan, C. (1982), *In a Different Voice: Psychological Theory and Women's Development*, Cambridge, MA: Harvard University Press.

Gioia, D.A. (1992), 'Pinto fires and personal ethics: a script analysis of missed opportunities', *Journal of Business Ethics*, **11**(5), 379–89.

Gladwell, M. (2009), *Outliers: The Story of Success*, New York: Penguin.

Goodpaster, K.E. (1991), 'Business ethics and stakeholder analysis', *Business Ethics Quarterly*, **1**(1), 53–72.

Grayson, D. and N. Exter (2012), *Cranfield on Corporate Sustainability*, Sheffield, UK: Greenleaf.

Guttieri, K., M.D. Wallace and P. Suedfeld (1995), 'The integrative complexity of American decision makers in the Cuban missile crisis', *Journal of Conflict Resolution*, **39**(4), 595–621.

Hamington, M. (2004), *Embodied Care: Jane Addams, Maurice Merleau-Ponty and Feminist Ethics*, Chicago, IL: University of Illinois Press.

Hampden-Turner, C. and A. Trompenaars (1993), *The Seven Cultures of Capitalism*, New York: Doubleday.

Hanh, T.N. (1991), *The Miracle of Mindfulness*, London: Rider.

Hartman, E.M. (2006), 'Can we teach character? An Aristotelian answer', *Academy of Management Learning & Education*, **5**(1), 68–81.

Heidegger, M. (1971), 'On the essence of truth', in D. Krell (ed.), *Basic Writings: Martin Heidegger* (6th ed.), London: Routledge, pp. 111–38.

Heugens, P., M. Kaptein and J. (Hans) Van Oosterhout (2008), 'Contracts to communities: A processual model of organizational virtue', *Journal of Management Studies*, **45**(1), 100–121.

Hodal, K., C. Kelly and F. Lawrence (2014), 'Revealed: Asian slave labour producing prawns for supermarkets in US, UK', *The Guardian*, 10 June, accessed 20 November 2014 at http://www.theguardian.com/global-development/2014/jun/10/supermarket-prawns-thailand-produced-slave-labour.

Hofstede, C. (1980), *Culture's Consequences: International Differences in Work-related Values*, Beverley Hills, CA: Sage.

Hoskin, K. (2004), 'Spacing, timing and the invention of management', *Organization*, **11**(6), 743–57.

Hume, D. (1751), *An Enquiry Concerning the Principles of Morals*, London: A. Millar.

Hutchings, K. and D. Weir (2006), 'Understanding networking in China and the Arab world', *Journal of European Industrial Training*, **30**(4), 272–90.

Hutter, A.D. (1982), 'Poetry in psycho-analysis: Hopkins, Rossetti, Winnicott', *International Review of Psychoanalysis*, **9**, 303–16.

Jackall, R. ([1988] 2010), *Moral Mazes: The World of Corporate Managers*, New York: Oxford University Press.

James, H.S. (2000), 'Reinforcing ethical decision making through organizational structure', *Journal of Business Ethics*, **28**(1), 43–58.

Jansen, E. and M.A. Von Glinow (1985), 'Ethical ambivalence and organizational reward systems', *The Academy of Management Review*, **10**(4), 814–22.

Johnson, M. (1993), *Moral Imagination: Implications of Cognitive Science for Ethics*, Chicago, IL: University of Chicago Press.

Jones, C. (2003), 'As if business ethics were possible, "within such limits"...', *Organization*, **10**(2), 223–48.

Jones, T.M. (1991), 'Ethical decision making by individuals in organizations: an issue-contingent model', *The Academy of Management Review*, **16**(2), 366–95.

Jones, T.M. and L.V. Ryan (1998), 'The effect of organizational forces on individual morality', *Business Ethics Quarterly*, **8**(3), 431–45.

Kabat-Zinn, J. (1994), *Wherever You Go There You Are: Mindfulness Meditation in Everyday Life*, New York: Hyperion.

Kant, I. ([1785] 1938), in O. Manthey-Zorn (ed. and trans.), *The Fundamental Principles of the Metaphysic of Ethics*, New York: Appleton-Century-Crofts Inc.

Keats, J. (1970), in R. Gittings (ed.), *The Letters of John Keats: A Selection*, Oxford: Oxford University Press.

Kohlberg, L.A. (1984), *Essays on Moral Development: Vol 2. The Psychology of Moral Development: The Nature and Validity of Moral Stages*, San Francisco, CA: Harper & Row.

Ladkin, D. and K. Turnbull-James (2009), 'The making of moral myopia: The case of British Members of Parliament and their expenses claims', 8th International Studying Leadership Conference, Birmingham, UK.

Lovelock, J. (2009), *The Vanishing Face of Gaia*, London: Penguin.
MacIntyre, A. (1985), *After Virtue* (2nd ed.), London: Duckworth.
Maher, R. (2014), 'What influences community positions towards nearby mining projects: Eight cases from Brazil and Chile', unpublished PhD thesis, Cranfield School of Management, Cranfield, UK.
Mangham, I. (1979), *The Politics of Organizational Change*, Westport, CT: Greenwood Press.
Marshall, J. (1999), 'Living life as inquiry', *Systemic Practice and Action Research*, **12**(2), 155–71.
Martin, K.D., J.B. Cullen, J.L. Johnson and K.P. Parboteeah (2007), 'Deciding to bribe: a cross-level analysis of firm and home country influences on bribery activity', *Academy of Management Journal*, **50**(6), 1401–22.
May, D.R. and K.P. Pauli (2002), 'The role of moral intensity in ethical decision making', *Business and Society*, **41**(1), 84–117.
McKinney, J.A. and C.W. Moore (2007), 'International bribery: does a written code of ethics make a difference in perceptions of business professionals', *Journal of Business Ethics*, **79**(1–2), 103–11.
McVea, J.F. and R.E. Freeman (2005), 'A names-and-faces approach to stakeholder management: how focusing on stakeholders as individuals can bring ethics and entrepreneurial strategy together', *Journal of Management Inquiry*, **14**(1), 57–69.
Merleau-Ponty, M. (1962), *Phenomenology of Perception* (C. Smith, trans.), London: Routledge.
Metzger, M., D.R. Dalton and J.W. Hill (1993), 'The organization of ethics and the ethics of organizations: The case for expanded organizational ethics audits', *Business Ethics Quarterly*, **3**(1), 27–44.
Meyerson, D.E. (2001), *Tempered Radicals: How People Use Difference to Inspire Change at Work*, Boston, MA: Harvard Business School Press.
Michaelson, C. (2010), 'Revisiting the global business ethics question', *Business Ethics Quarterly*, **20**(2), 237–51.
Midgley, M. (2000), 'Biotechnology and monstrosity', *Hastings Center Report*, **30**(5), 7–15.
Midgley, M. (2003), *The Myths We Live By*, London: Routledge.
Mill, J.S. ([1863] 2002), *Utilitarianism* (2nd ed.), London: Hackett Publishing.
Mintzberg, H. (1983), *Power in and Around Organizations*, Englewood Cliffs, NJ: Prentice Hall.
Moberg, D. and M. Seabright (2000), 'The development of moral imagination', *Business Ethics Quarterly* ,**10**(4), 845-884.
Morgan, G. (1986), *Images of Organizations*, Newbury Park, CA: Sage.
Needleman, J. (1990), *Lost Christianity: A Journey of Rediscovery to the Centre of Christian Experience*, Shaftesbury, UK: Element Books.
Nelson, P. (2012), *There's a Hole in My Sidewalk*, New York: Beyond Words.
Neubert, M.J., D.S. Carlson, K.M. Kacmar, J.A. Roberts and L.B. Chonko (2009), 'The virtuous influence of ethical leadership behavior: Evidence from the field', *Journal of Business Ethics*, **90**(2), 157–70.
Noddings, N. (1984), *Caring: A Feminine Approach to Ethics and Moral Education*, Berkeley, CA: University of California Press.
O'Reilly, C.A., J. Chatman and D.F. Caldwell (1991), 'People and organizational culture: A profile comparison approach to assessing person–organization fit', *Academy of Management Journal*, **34**(3), 487–516.
Orlikowski, W.J. (2006), 'Material knowing: The scaffolding of human knowledgeability', *European Journal of Information Systems*, **15**(5), 460–66.
Orlikowski, W.J. (2007), 'Sociomaterial practices: Exploring technology at work', *Organization Studies*, **28**(9), 1435–48.

Palmer, D.E. (2009), 'Business leadership: Three levels of ethical analysis', *Journal of Business Ethics*, **88**(3), 525–36.

Quinn, R.E. (2000), *Change the World: How Ordinary People Can Accomplish Extraordinary Results*, San Francisco, CA: Jossey-Bass.

Rest, J. (1986), *Moral Development: Advances in Research and Theory*, New York: Praeger.

Revans, R. (2011), *ABC of Action Learning*, Farnham, UK: Gower.

Rokeach, M. (1968), *Beliefs, Attitudes and Values: A Theory of Organization and Change*, San Francisco, CA: Jossey-Bass.

Schein, E.H. (1992), *Organizational Culture and Leadership* (2nd ed.), San Francisco, CA: Jossey-Bass.

Schon, D. (1984), *The Reflective Practitioner: How Professionals Think in Action*, New York: Basic Books.

Scott-Villiers, P. (2009), 'A question of understanding: Hermeneutics and the play of history, distance and dialogue in development practice in East Africa', PhD thesis, University of Bath, UK.

Simpson, P.F., R. French and C.E. Harvey (2002), 'Leadership and negative capability', *Human Relations*, **55**(10), 1209–26.

Singer, P. (1995), *Animal Liberation* (2nd ed.), London: Pimlico.

Sison, A.J. (2003), *The Moral Capital of Leaders: Why Virtue Matters*, Cheltenham, UK and Northampton, MA, USA: Edward Elgar Publishing.

Smith, A. ([1776] 1863), *The Wealth of Nations: An Inquiry into the Nature and Causes of the Wealth of a Nation*, Edinburgh: Blacks.

Smith, A. ([1759] 1982), *The Theory of Moral Sentiments*, Indianapolis, IN: Liberty Classics.

Taylor, S.S. (2011), *Leadership Craft, Leadership Art*, New York: Palgrave Macmillan.

Taylor, S.S. (2012), 'Little beauties: aesthetics, craft skill, and the experience of beautiful action', *Journal of Management Inquiry*, **22**(1), 69–81.

Ten Bos, R. (2003), 'Business ethics, accounting and the fear of melancholy', *Organization*, **10**(2), 267–85.

Tenbrunsel, A.E. and D.M. Messick (1999), 'Sanctioning systems, decision frames, and cooperation', *Administration & Society*, **44**(2), 684–707.

Thorne, L. and S.B. Saunders (2002), 'The socio-cultural embeddedness of individuals' ethical reasoning in organizations (cross-cultural ethics)', *Journal of Business Ethics*, **35**(1), 1–14.

Treviño, L.K. and K. Nelson (1995), *Managing Business Ethics: Straight Talk about How to do it Right*, New York: John Wiley.

Untersteiner, M. (1954), in K. Freeman (ed.), *The Sophists*, Oxford: Blackwell.

VanSandt, C.V., J.M. Shepard and S.M. Zappe (2006), 'An examination of the relationship between ethical work climate and moral awareness', *Journal of Business Ethics*, **68**(4), 409–32.

Varela, F. (1992), *Ethical Know-how: Action, Wisdom and Cognition*, Stanford, CA: Stanford University Press.

Victor, B. and J.B. Cullen (1987), 'A theory and measure of ethical climate on organizations', in W.C. Frederick (ed.), *Research in Corporate Social Performance and Policy*, Greenwich, CT: JAI Press, pp. 51–71.

Watley, L.D. and D.R. May (2004), 'Enhancing moral intensity: The roles of personal and consequential information in ethical decision-making', *Journal of Business Ethics*, **50**(2), 105–26.

Werhane, P.H. (2002), 'Moral imagination and systems thinking', *Journal of Business*, **38**(1/2), 33–42.

Whetstone, J.T. (2001), 'How virtue fits within business ethics', *Journal of Business Ethics*, **33**(2), 101–14.

Wines, W.A. and N.K. Napier (1992), 'Toward an understanding of cross-cultural ethics: A tentative model', *Journal of Business*, **11**(11), 831–41.

Yunus, M. (1998), *Banker to the Poor: The Story of the Grameen Bank*, London: Aurum Press.

Zhong, C.B. (2011), 'The ethical dangers of deliberative decision making', *Administrative Science Quarterly*, **56**(1), 1–25.

Glossary

Akrasia: moral laziness. This results from knowing what one should do from an ethical perspective but not being disciplined or courageous enough to do it.

Appreciative inquiry: An approach to engaging with others, organizations, or systems that starts by inquiring into what is already going well for that person, organization or system. Used as an approach to consulting, embedded within it is an understanding of the power of asking questions and how questions direct energy. Its primary premise is that by focusing on aspects that are already working well, those aspects can be enhanced. Those aspects that aren't working so well can then diminish through lack of attention.

Categorical imperative: A directive concerning something that should be done from the perspective of reason alone. The term is most frequently used in relation to Kant's notion that what is ethical is that which can be said to be ethical for all people, in all circumstances, at all times. It is the basis of his deontological approach to ethics.

Crazy wisdom: The ability to respond to situations in a way that may seem unorthodox, unusual, and indeed even 'unethical', but that speaks to a deeper understanding of the dynamics of the situation. The biblical story of the judge who suggests cutting a baby in two so that each of the women contesting its ownership can have half is an example of such insight (the real mother, not wanting the baby to be killed says she would rather the other woman have her child than allow the child to die).

Deontological: An approach to ethics based in the notion that there are generalizable ethical rules that should be obeyed. These include maxims such as 'do not kill other people' or 'do not steal from others'. A deontological understanding of ethics is the basis of many organizational 'codes of practice'.

Ethics: A branch of philosophy concerned with the study of morality, that is, the assumptions of how we should relate to one another and the bounds of acceptable behaviour.

Ethics of care: An approach to ethics that places relationships at its centre. Rather than considering objective 'rules' this approach suggests one needs to consider the particular people involved, their relations, and the context within which they are operating in order to come to a correct ethical relationship.

Inner arc of awareness: Attentional awareness that focuses on the inner stream of thoughts, images and perceptions. Akin to 'stream of consciousness', our inner arc of awareness works in dynamic interrelation with our 'outer arc of awareness', described below.

Kairos: An approach to time that recognizes the importance of 'timing', that is, the subjectively experienced unfolding of events. Key to the notion is taking action at the 'right moment', rather than acting because it is the correct 'chronological' time. From a kairotic perspective one may eat when one is hungry, whereas from a chronological perspective, one eats dinner at 6pm because it's 6pm.

Kohlberg's theory of moral development: This theory is based on Lawrence Kohlberg's experiments with youngsters in which he tried to discern if and how our moral sense is developed over time. Analysis of his data suggested three different phases of moral development: (1) pre-conventional, in which judgements are made based on the physical consequences of carrying out certain acts; (2) conventional, in which judgements are made through internalizing the moral standards of adults or others in authority; (3) post-conventional, in which judgements are made based on self-chosen principles. The epitome of post-conventional ethical behaviour according to Kohlberg is reliance on rationally derived universal principles in decision-making. The theory has been critiqued on many counts, including its research design. Feminist ethicists such as Carol Gilligan (who in fact worked with Kohlberg in the original development of the theory) particularly question its recognition of rationality as the most highly developed arbiter of ethical judgement.

Micro-world: The interrelated aspects of context that situate us in a particular frame of reference and thus determine 'correct' action. For instance, when in class, the micro-world is where sitting at desks and listening to someone talk is an acceptable way of being, whereas attending a football match creates a different micro-world context in which other behaviours are expected.

Moral imagination: The capacity to imaginatively extend our understanding of how a certain situation or decision might affect another being, whether in the present or indeed in the future.

Moral intensity: The way in which certain situations carry more weight with us because of the way we identify with them. For instance, being a refugee oneself can prompt a greater appreciation for other refugees or displaced people.

Moral myopia: Not being able to perceive the moral or ethical component of a situation. Moral myopia can range from being completely blind to any moral aspect, to being rather 'short-sighted' and not taking into account the full moral consequences of one's behaviour or the situation one finds oneself in.

Moral perception: The ability to recognize the moral aspect of a situation. For moral perception to occur one must both be able to comprehend a constellation of occurrences as a 'situation', and then to be able to perceive its moral component(s).

Moral resolve: The intention to act with courage when faced with an ethically challenging situation. Studies have shown that moral resolve can be heightened, especially through reference to stories about others who have exercised moral courage.

Morals: The way in which we navigate social relations in a way that takes into account the needs, wants and desires of those involved in any situation. Morals are often normatively prescribed, and are evident in the formal and informal codes of behaviour that infuse human cultures.

Negative capability: The capacity to contain one's fear and anxiety when faced with a challenging situation and not spontaneously respond with a knee-jerk reaction. Rather than 'doing nothing' negative capability is the capacity to wait, observe and inquire into a situation as it unfolds in order to discover an optimal way forward.

Outer arc of awareness: The field of attention that we observe existing outside of ourselves. The 'awareness' refers to the fact that although at any moment we are bombarded by a myriad of different perceptions, we will only be consciously aware of certain ones. There is a dynamic relationship between the 'inner arc of awareness' described earlier and one's 'outer arc of awareness'.

Phronesis: Often defined as 'practical wisdom', *phronesis* is one of the virtues that Aristotle describes in his *Nicomachean Ethics*. Both an intellectual virtue and a virtue of character, *phronesis* enables people to come to the best ethical decision within a particular context. Importantly, *phronesis* is developed by living in community with wise others.

Salience: That which has most relevance and attention in a given situation. Those aspects that are salient are those that you take as being of most importance within the broad perceptual view under consideration.

Schema: The internal framework that organizes how we think about things. Largely unconscious, schemas enable us to make sense of situations rapidly, but they can also hinder us from recognizing components that are not readily sorted by current schemas. Organizations often operate within schemas concerning financial viability, for instance, which can block people from seeing actions that can have ethically questionable consequences.

Tempered radical: Those who find ways of bringing their values or important aspects of their identity into the workplace. The phrase was coined by Debra Meyerson (2001) in her study of executives who aimed to change the organizational systems they worked in from within. Meyerson identified four key strategies used by tempered radicals: disruptive self-expression; verbal *jujitsu*; variable-term opportunism; strategic alliance building.

Utilitarianism: An approach to resolving ethical dilemmas based on the idea of causing the least harm to the fewest people or the greatest happiness to the most people. In other words, what is 'good' is determined by the consequences of an act. Associated with philosophers such as Jeremy Bentham and John Stewart Mill, it can also be called 'consequentialism'.

Virtue ethics: An approach to ethics grounded in the belief that what is ethical is that which is 'virtuous'. Being ethical is dependent on building 'character', something that can only be done through living in a community with 'wise' or 'virtuous' others. Based in Aristotle's notion of virtue, virtue ethics has been updated by Alistair MacIntyre in his book *After Virtue* (1985).

Index